Education Is Upside-Down

Education Is Upside-Down

Reframing Reform to Focus on the Right Problems

Eric Kalenze

ROWMAN & LITTLEFIELD
Lanham • Boulder • New York • London

Published by Rowman & Littlefield
A wholly owned subsidiary of The Rowman & Littlefield Publishing Group, Inc.
4501 Forbes Boulevard, Suite 200, Lanham, Maryland 20706
www.rowman.com

Unit A, Whitacre Mews, 26-34 Stannery Street, London SE11 4AB

British Library Cataloguing in Publication Information Available

Library of Congress Cataloging-in-Publication Data

Kalenze, Eric, 1971–
Education is upside-down : reframing reform to focus on the right problems / Eric Kalenze.
pages cm
Includes bibliographical references.
ISBN 978-1-4758-0993-0 (cloth : alk. paper) — ISBN 978-1-4758-0994-7 (pbk. : alk. paper) —
ISBN 978-1-4758-0995-4 (electronic)
1. School improvement programs. I. Title.
LB2822.8.K35 2014
371.2'07—dc23
2014022947

∞™ The paper used in this publication meets the minimum requirements of American National Standard for Information Sciences Permanence of Paper for Printed Library Materials, ANSI/NISO Z39.48-1992.

Printed in the United States of America

Contents

Preface

The first thing you need to know is that I never intended to write a book.

All I really wanted to do was make better sense of my work in and with schools. I wanted to temper my frustration and bring my confusion down a few notches, simply by becoming better informed about all of the issues in play. When I started this project, I was only a handful of years into what is now an almost-twenty-year career in education. But even then, I was sure something was deeply, fundamentally wrong with the whole operation. And as far as I could tell, there were only three possibilities: I was incapable of grasping something incredibly important about how public schooling works, I was old-fashioned beyond my years, or I was outright crazy.

The feeling that something was off began back in my teacher-training program, where what I was being taught about "ideal" teaching and learning often clashed with my own beliefs about why schools existed and how to draw the best out of children. Overall, the program didn't pay much attention to the knowledge and skills students would need to become disciplined learners and succeed in the world that awaited them after graduation. The coursework was far more concerned with how to *engage* students by making learning more *active* and *inquiry-based*; how to account for and appeal to each student's innate preferences, sensitivities, and abilities; how to create individually appropriate assessments of students' learning; and so on.

Rather than accept all of these lessons at face value, I spent most of the program thinking about what turned out to be fundamental questions: Do schools and teachers actually look like this? Could they? *Should* they? And if they do, are their graduates more successful? With teachers doing all this work to keep students comfortable and happy during their learning, when are kids expected to rise to a challenge? Was school even supposed to be *hard* anymore? Am I allowed to teach anything in particular? Or will the act of choosing certain subject matter over other topics be too invasive and demotivating?

Thankfully, the combative positions I took in class and the soapboxing papers I wrote did not get me kicked out of the program. Eventually I emerged with the proper credentials, along with many more questions than answers about the craft of teaching, the mission of schooling, and how I was going to manage it all in the real world.

A few months later, after taking a job teaching high school English, I considered myself lucky because my students were no problem. I loved working with them, and they seemed to enjoy themselves without needing to throw me under the bus to do so. (Most of the time, anyway.) The vast majority of my students, many of whom had arrived in my class with little previous success in English literature and very little love for the typical classroom tasks, earned passing grades. Fairly early into my tenure I earned a reputation as a teacher who could get a lot out of "difficult" kids, a fact I still take tremendous pride in.

But the philosophical tension persisted. Something was wrong with the whole endeavor, even if I couldn't put my finger on exactly what it was. And no matter where I looked, whether within my own school's faculty or to outside education experts, it was exceedingly difficult to find fellow professionals who agreed with my instructional and classroom management practices, let alone the underlying philosophy. These practices were working well for me and for my students, and I was building a favorable reputation. Still, what I was doing and what I believed always seemed to look vastly different from everyone else's ideas of "best practices."

So what of this mysterious Something Wrong? How, exactly, did my practice and philosophies differ from those of my colleagues and from those promoted in my training program? Did I believe in corporal punishment? Public shaming? Worksheets filled with drill after drill? Lockstep compliance?

No. Far from it. Anyone who observed my classes would say they were fairly high-paced and fun, with lots of discussion and activity. (They bordered on being too loud, actually.) The big difference was that I didn't run a particularly "child-centered" classroom as defined by the best-practice playbooks of my training program, my mandatory ongoing professional development, and most of my colleagues.

Let me give you a few examples. When teaching literary concepts, I didn't go out of my way to account for students' various learning styles—meaning I did not assign art projects, say, about the concepts at hand to make sure my visual-spatial or kinesthetic learners would best be able to understand them. When working on essays, I didn't design alternative assessments for students who didn't consider themselves strong writers. I always made my students *read* difficult texts (using reasonable ways to hold them accountable if necessary) instead of watching the movie version in class. I resisted teaching works with little time-tested value or critically affirmed artistic merit. I, and no one else, set the classroom rules.

Why did I stick with this traditional approach? Because when I deviated from these methods in favor of so-called "best practices," I was never quite sure what students were taking away. Did that cooperative poster-making activity really help students understand all Fitzgerald was communicating with his use of color in *Gatsby*, or did it just help them understand how to make a cool poster? I figured that if I didn't know the answer, I probably wasn't doing my students any favors by plowing ahead with them.

As I designed learning activities according to the state academic standards–aligned curriculum's content and skill requirements and then adapted these activities to the realities of what my students needed, I always made sure to ask this guiding question:

How can I teach this in a way that aligns with the expectations students will face outside of school?

You could say I always thought of my students first. Yet I was not, by definition, a *student-centered* designer of instruction. I rarely made a point of fulfilling each student's personal preference, comfort, learning style, or ability level when setting performance-level bars of activities and assessments. Though I certainly cared about those things (especially in how I supported struggling students toward achieving competency), I considered them less important than students' ultimate ability to function and succeed in the world outside of school. Truthfully, I believed this was my primary duty as a teacher.

In short, I was less interested in teaching the whole child and more interested in teaching the child's whole life. When students would complain about what I was asking of them (usually by drawing comparisons to what neighboring teachers were asking of their students), I'd remind them that life would regularly ask them to work hard and perform proficiently with little regard for their level of interest. (And growing up in northern Minnesota as the son of a concrete worker and a secretary, I was intimately familiar with this dynamic.) What we are doing here, I would explain, is simulating that reality while gaining valuable knowledge and skills. That's what school *is*. And if you learn how to succeed within this environment, I would tell them, what you learn will work *for you* in many different future settings—college, a job, home ownership, the economy, personal relationships, and on and on.

And guess what? They bought into it. Once they understood the reason why we were learning this way, kids rarely had problems with my "non-student-centered" approach. They rose to the challenge. And we liked each other, to boot.

Radical, I know.

Nevertheless, my beliefs and practices often isolated me from my colleagues and left me sneering through professional development workshops. The longer I stayed in teaching, the bigger the disconnect became between what I kept hearing were best practices and what I found to actually work.

My frustration reached a peak during the early 2000s, when the results-focused No Child Left Behind (NCLB) act spurred schools to become more effective as evidence-based instructional planners. This mindset gave rapid rise to constructed teacher-collaboration models like Professional Learning Communities (PLCs), where co-planning and common assessments became more or less mandatory. Which meant my days of silently disagreeing with my colleagues and doing things my own way were numbered. More and more, I was called to defend my positions in collaborative settings (or risk having to remake my practices altogether). It was around this time that I intensified my search for educational viewpoints that aligned with mine.

Surprisingly, I learned I was not crazy. The questions I had about the purpose of schooling and the evidence for educational best practices weren't all that obscure. They weren't the purview solely of babbling hermits and wild-eyed recluses. *Lots* of people felt the way I did throughout the history of American education, up to and including today. In fact, some of the people who came up with the concepts I was rejecting eventually circled back to criticize the educational establishment for misunderstanding and misapplying their philosophies! My compatriots were legion, but they were largely disregarded by best-practices-determining and -broadcasting entities like ed schools.

As I learned more about the history of these buried thoughts and decades' worth of insights and evidence, I knew I couldn't stay quiet. It was too important for other education practitioners and leaders to learn everything I was learning.

Right about this time, I thought, "Maybe I could write a book."

Before I wrote the first paragraph of my great educational tract from the trenches, however, American education underwent a defining transformation. While my independent research had me hoping for reforms that would address persistent achievement gaps with sound cognitive science and greater institutional alignment, a set of very different reforms came sweeping across the country.

Born of the same test-and-punish DNA as NCLB, these reforms went far beyond getting schools to organize practitioners into data-driven PLCs. Indeed, it was almost as if each reform was just one small part of a larger strategy to "private-sectorize" education entirely. Union busters spurred teachers into higher performance by making them question their job security. Charter-school legislation encouraged more competitors to join the education marketplace. The federal government started handing out cash to states that promised to install data systems that would better measure the bottom line. And thoroughly revised professional evaluation processes put still more pressure on teachers.

Something really big was happening. America (or certain constituents who now had outsize influence) was fed up with the national education system, and they were taking action.

As these reforms gathered steam from 2010 onward, however, I was struck by how few of them dealt directly with improving instructional practice. For the most part, all I could see in the new reforms were lots of big sticks (and spreadsheets) swinging around. But sticks only work when the mule is lazy, which wasn't the main issue with American education. No, the educational enterprise's biggest problem was *blindness*. It couldn't see where it was going. Even if it knew it was headed in the wrong direction, it couldn't find the right one. Accordingly, all the sticks in the world wouldn't help. So while these reformers had intended to improve education, all my research showed that what they were doing was still wrong.

I left teaching, but I still followed the debate from my new professional vantage point in private-sector program development and later in public school administration. My research continued. I hadn't given up trying to figure out what exactly was going on. And eventually I realized that this book had been writing itself all along. So I saw it through for the same reason I started asking questions in the first place: to make better sense of American education, both for myself and for others.

Whether you work in education, have kids in the U.S. education system, or are a taxpayer who wants to learn more about Common Core standards, NCLB, Race to the Top, social-emotional learning, public education in Finland, or many other topics, this book is for you. It will put these and other issues into a larger context, so you can see how (and why) we got here. It will explain the basics and some of the nuances, too, showing how these factors affect one another and how they prepare children for the post-K–12 world.

This book shows one way forward. It builds a case for actions American education should pursue immediately, as well as the ones it should stop, and why. And ultimately, this book takes a rather unique tack in today's highly contentious and politically polarized environment; it resists the practitioners-vs.-reformers blame game by pointing out how we're *all* wrong.

Finally, and as I will point out over and over again in the coming pages, if we seek to change American education, we're going to have to dig all the way down to its foundation. This book reframes educational reform, and my pie-in-the-sky hope is that it will help you turn your attention to the real problems we face in American education and do your part to make change happen. If we can do that, the positive impact on our kids and our society will be immeasurable.

Acknowledgments

To start, thanks to Rowman & Littlefield for making this dream come true. I'm particularly grateful for Tom Koerner, Christine Fahey, Patricia Stevenson, and Caitlin Crawford. All were reliably wise, patient, and responsive, no matter how goofy my novice-level question.

Next, thanks to those who helped shape this book and who, though they did not sign up to do so, continue teaching me about the importance of asking for help. Specifically, thanks to Justin Ley and Gerry Zelenak, who read sections along the way and offered insights.

To my editor and friend Lars Ostrom, as much as you brought to this project, it seems insufficient to thank you for "editing" alone. I appreciate your help, humor, and skill more than I know how to show. While I figure that out, count on me to pick up tabs for lunches and drinks.

This book could never have happened without those I've worked alongside in education. Particularly huge forces along this journey include Dr. Bob Perdaems, Kelly Skare-Klecker, Eric Ruska, Jackie Trzynka, Steve Smarjesse, Terry Westermann, Todd Bloom, Sue Berg, Deb Appleman, Joe Nathan, Steve Flisk, and my school-improving teammates at Minneapolis Public Schools. Thanks, all of you, for pushing me to think harder about each student, effective practices, and leadership. Similarly, thanks to the MPS principals and teachers who have taught me so much about our enterprise's complexity. And to Chris Wills from Student Paths: thanks for getting me to make the first step toward a project like this. I wouldn't trade all I've learned for anything.

Finally, thanks to my wonderful family. To my parents, Les and Ruth, and my brother Ethan: thanks for instilling, from the start, a deep appreciation for education. And to Susie, Lydia, and Ava (and, of course, Louis the

Puggle): your unfailing patience and support helped fill these pages, and every moment we have together fills me. With all my love, thank you.

Chapter One

Of Mismatches and Missions

> The world we see that seems so insane is the result of a belief system that is not working. To perceive the world differently, we must be willing to change our belief system, let the past slip away, expand our sense of now, and dissolve the fear in our minds.
>
> —William James (1842–1910), American philosopher and psychologist

Clearly, things are not working very well in American public education. We're told it all the time and in every way imaginable.

Without fail, reports about education share frustrating news. Student bullying up, student test results down. Teacher quality poor, strict new evaluations on the—wait, scratch that: *principal* quality poor, strict new evaluations on the way. More taxpayer money needed to enable smaller class sizes. Less progress made to eliminate yawning racial achievement gaps. In a suburban school, a teenage shooter leaves several dead, while in another a teenager commits suicide, both tragedies apparently spurred by social media–driven taunts. Still more test results, plummeting this time, thanks to revised academic standards that caught school districts—entire states, even—flat-footed. And on and on.

The education beat's bad news is such a common touchstone in the United States that nearly all education-related titles on sellers' bookshelves open with paragraphs just like those above. Indeed, in the first pages of books about educational practice, policy, and reform, it seems more or less understood that any game-changing arguments within must be prefaced by the customary resigned sigh.

The collective resigned and somewhat bewildered spirit is coming at the end of what has been a brutal three decades to work in education. Over that span—roughly since the 1983 publication of *A Nation at Risk*, a government-commissioned report on public education—observations, critique, and statistics related to education starkly point out, over and over and over, that the potential of America's education system is not being realized.

Regular check-ins on U.S. students' performance in regard to national and international standards (as with National Assessment of Educational Progress [NAEP], Trends in International Mathematics and Science Study [TIMSS], the Programme for International Student Assessment [PISA], and others) commonly describe American students as lagging behind students from other industrialized nations, suggesting large practical holes.

Some suggest that alarm over American children's results on such assessments is unnecessary, maintaining that reported results are either not as bad as they look on their faces or altogether invalid.[1]

Reviewing a number of internal indicators, however, suggests that alarm is most certainly warranted. No matter how comparison studies over time or across nations may show reasons why we shouldn't panic about the state of American education, considerable evidence exists that K–12 paths are unreliable. They send far too many students into post-secondary study and employment unprepared and, even more disturbingly, unaware of their poor preparation. So set up to fail, too many young Americans are left to head into deep spirals of debt and, with or without post-secondary credentials, early-adulthood instability.

At a spring 2010 hearing with Capitol Hill lawmakers, American College Testing (ACT) chief operating officer Cynthia Schmeiser explained that, out of the 1.5 million high school graduates who took the ACT during the academic year 2008–2009, shockingly high numbers were not considered college- or career-ready. (Readiness in this context means "not needing to take remedial courses in post-secondary education or training programs.") Among this group, she reported that

- 33 percent were not ready for college-level English,
- 47 percent were not ready for college social science,
- 58 percent were not ready for college algebra,
- 72 percent were not ready for college biology, and
- only 23 percent were ready to enter college-level courses without remediation in any of the four subject areas.[2]

Very similar results showed up among takers of the SAT, another widely used standardized test of academic aptitude. The College Board's 2013 "SAT Report of College and Career Readiness" showed that, for the fifth year running, less than half of 1.66 million SAT-takers performed at levels considered college ready.[3]

Many within education considered these results overblown; they neither provided a full picture of education's effectiveness nor communicated how substantially matters have improved over recent decades. Still, questionable data continues to pop up.

Case in point: "Pathways to Prosperity," a 2011 study from the Harvard Graduate School of Education, showed that nearly half of all U.S. students entering college drop out before earning diplomas. When asked why they dropped out, study participants gave reasons like "not being prepared for the rigors of academic work,"[4] a charge that should be difficult for K–12 educators to swallow.

Couple Harvard's study with longitudinal research published in 1999 (and followed up in 2006) by the National Center for Education Statistics (NCES) of American students' ultimate college degree completion (and the factors impacting and predicting it[5]), and it should become more than clear: whatever American K–12 education is doing, it is not aligned with the academic expectations that come after American K–12 education. Ultimately, it doesn't matter how our students compare to those in other countries. To American educators, it only matters that ours can't cut it academically, before and after graduation.

Another troubling situation lies beneath the surface of these statistics: how well different demographic groups perform within each category, on average. Dig a bit further into any of the data points above and it's nearly guaranteed that students within racially nonwhite and low-income subgroups will come up short more often than their white, financially stable counterparts. Though the depth of this gap varies across the United States, its consistency and stubbornness remain great concerns for educators everywhere.

To sum up, for all that American education has done to create more college-ready students, it appears that it has really only created more college-*admissible* students. And if, after all that preparation, only one out of every two students admitted to college actually has the stuff to earn a degree, the entire educational enterprise is doing all degree-aspiring students a grave disservice. When you consider that this already poor ratio becomes even more lopsided for students belonging to race and income identifications on the wrong side of the achievement gap, it starts to look a lot like outright failure.

On the other hand, not everyone needs a college degree to succeed in the world beyond senior year. So perhaps the apparent mismatch between K–12 education and post-secondary education isn't actually such a big problem. Maybe the problem more worthy of attention is our institutional overemphasis on the necessity of college completion.

This argument is currently gathering steam in many educational circles, likely in response to the growing numbers of K–12 graduates bouncing degreeless from colleges and universities.

Though we've pushed kids so hard toward completing four-year degrees, the apologists say, perhaps the statistics mentioned above (the low levels of college readiness, the close to half of all college-admitted students dropping out before completing degrees, etc.) are not actually indicators of poor-quality schooling. Rather, they insist, those statistics are just a natural consequence of our own obsession with the four-year degree.

These ideas are definitely worth considering, especially as the "college for all" movement has always been based more on workforce forecasts and industry leaders' warnings than it has been on empirically confirmed truths. As much as we may want to rely on this kind of future-projection and use it to set our goals for students, our technologically nimble age has a way of creating new career opportunities faster than we can track them; as today's young people grow up so technologically aware, maybe the specialization acquired at the collegiate level won't be as necessary as many in industry seem to think. Maybe, then, we should all back off the idea of college for all. Fewer kids will get set up to fail, statistics will come around to reflect as much, and the panic we all work ourselves into can die down.

In addition, those who maintain that the necessity of post-secondary education is only manufactured argue that many fabulous career opportunities have always existed and will always exist that do not require bachelor's degrees. Many of these opportunities—if graduates are patient, hungry, and willing to work their way up ladders from entry levels—require no post-secondary study at all.

In defense of the education enterprise (and likely to relieve the results-based pressures bearing down on it by various reformers and assessments), education historian and advocate Diane Ravitch recently joined the fray to cast some doubt on the necessity of a college education for a person to become a productive and fulfilled member of American society. Ravitch's work refers to forecasts by the Bureau of Labor Statistics that are apparently intended to set collective minds at ease: namely, that despite policymakers' predictions of doom for young people without bachelor's degrees, millions of jobs will be available in arenas like customer service, fast food, retail, and construction through 2018.[6]

As much as educators must appreciate Ravitch's efforts to deflect criticism, it would be hard to find many educators who are bending over backward to help students find work at the local Subway or TJ Maxx. The intent here is not to offend these businesses or their employees. Very simply, however, when hard-working teachers stay late grading papers, designing lessons, or giving additional help, they do not envision their students spending a lifetime slinging sandwiches and folding T-shirts for meager paychecks and nominal (if any) health coverage.

As long as we're on the subject of jobs students can win if they choose to bypass college out of high school, let's take a closer look at the hiring preferences of organizations that do not require post-secondary study for entry-level positions. Will they really be more forgiving of the education that students do or do not receive in American schools?

As it turns out, professionals in hiring—even for jobs that will not require employees to read and perform math directly in routine tasks—do, in fact, prefer levels of reading and mathematical proficiency similar to those demonstrated by college-ready students on standardized measurements.[7] So while it may be true that these proficiencies are not universal prerequisites to employment, not having them will make it harder to get in the door.

Having established the above, let's build onto the K–12 and post-secondary misalignment: the college-readiness that students believe they're entering college with (and that almost one in every two later realizes they don't actually have) is also a *career*-readiness students don't actually possess when they apply for jobs—even jobs many would consider "low-skill."

And none of this looks much better when comparing ourselves to populations outside the United States. Regardless of the skills American workers may or may not need to secure gainful employment or how these skills may translate into productive careers, workforce analysts have detected a growing "skills gap" between our country and other nations. Identified and studied exhaustively in recent years via results on multinational, wide-age-range assessments of literacy, math, and IT-enabled problem-solving skills, the skills gap shows the United States workforce trailing well behind a number of its global competitors—a troubling consideration in our ever flatter, more connected world.

Recent reports have even shown the United States falling behind *itself* over time: in the Organization for Economic Cooperation and Development (OECD)'s 2013 "Skills Outlook," literacy skills of thirty-year-old Americans assessed were actually lower than those recorded by thirty-year-old Americans in 1994.[8]

College and career success aside, one goal of American education has always been (and always should be) to equip U.S. citizens with enough functional ability in reading, mathematics, and civic awareness to participate fully in society, make reasonable and nation-improving democratic decisions, avoid being taken advantage of, and contribute positively to both the lives of their neighbors and the health of their communities.

In America, after all, schooling has never been intended solely as job training. Indeed, schooling is an institution that should give graduates the tools they need to independently, actively, discerningly, and productively interact with the world they are joining, like it or not.

Within the deepest, eighteenth-century origins of American public schooling, advocates of free public education for all—like Thomas Jefferson—imagined an experience that was essential to maintaining the young nation's democratic ideals. They envisioned a common experience that would braid America's plurality into a single, uniquely diverse society by installing the necessary knowledge, abilities, and values. In effect, public schools were viewed, commissioned, and operated as places where the American *pluribus* would be made *unum*.

If, however, recent American history is any indication of just how united the United States is—and how well we are living up to our democratic ideals—now appears to be a good time to reexamine how we are preparing citizens to participate in mainstream institutions. Because no matter who it is that's getting it wrong, the Common Good is showing signs of ill health.

Democratically, voters act more from their guts and less according to objective information, turning elections into popularity contests featuring sound bites, image presentation, and issue distraction calibrated to lowest common denominators. The resulting lawmaking bodies, continually strategizing toward future elections and/or to serve the lobbies funding election campaigns, carry out agendas that don't pay much mind to the best interests of their constituencies. U.S. voters, meanwhile, report one set of interests in opinion polls before turning around to vote for candidates who actively oppose such interests.

Also, looking through an ethical scope, similar me-first, win/get-revenge/save-face-at-all-costs attitudes drive countless scandals and tragedies. From the far-too-common response of bullied students packing weapons to shoot offending peers at the school level to nationally reaching financial, athletic, and academic cheating scandals, to the outright shameful distribution of national wealth, our age regularly displays worrying lacks of tolerance, sacrifice, self-control, grace, and teamwork.

In the first decade of the twenty-first century, a number of cultural critics and scholars picked up on this intellectual, democratic, and ethical institutional dip—enough so, anyway, as to indicate that something bigger was going on than just a hot publishing angle.

No doubt dispirited by recent, particularly frustrating democratic and economic decisions by the American people, multiple thinkers suddenly took a particular interest in exploring the nation's historic, maddening turn for the stupid. Sometimes darkly funny (Charles P. Pierce's *Idiot America: How Stupidity Became a Virtue in the Land of the Free*) and other times just dark (Chris Hedges's *Empire of Illusion: The End of Literacy and the Triumph of Spectacle*), such works examine, over and over, the New Irrationality's depth, breadth, origins, and future impacts.

The most thorough of such titles, Susan Jacoby's *The Age of American Unreason*, pans across American history to show how the United States' current mass irrationality is actually somewhat predictable in light of the nation's long-existing, pronounced streak of anti-intellectualism.

However Jacoby may acknowledge this predictability, she argues that the intellectual tendencies of the American public should raise concern about its long-term health. One such tendency would be how Americans assign as much rational credibility to mass-popular-culture-peddled "junk thought" as they do to scientifically verified facts and/or opinions of demonstrated experts. As she shows alternatives to the "gutter" of mass popular culture shrinking to nearly nothing in contemporary America, Jacoby offers little optimism that such trends will reverse.[9]

Where Jacoby leads her reader through a measured, incisive tour of yesterday's and today's Americas toward her conclusions, Rick Shenkman comes at readers like a flat-footed brawler in his *Just How Stupid Are We? Facing the Truth about the American Voter.*[10]

Largely eschewing the wide historical angle preferred by Jacoby, with evidence and illustrations drawn chiefly from the 2000 and 2004 presidential elections, post-9/11 policy and paradigm, and politics from the Nixon era on, Shenkman still has no shortage of raw argument-supporting material. Indeed, even limiting himself to mostly recent history, his book makes a compelling, near-depression-inducing case that today's American public is doomed to be manipulated by the politicians and corporations who depend on public support.

In Shenkman's view, two prime factors will forever put the public two steps behind all such attempts at manipulation: (1) a lack of basic knowledge about how American politics and economics work, and (2) reliance on inadequate shortcuts to compensate for gaps in knowledge.

While thinkers like Jacoby and Shenkman expressed concerns about the nation at large, a separate strain of critics seemed troubled by intellectual and dispositional patterns emerging from their younger co-citizens. For in the younger generations especially, tendencies were detected that seemed to point to more and greater cultural division moving into the future.

Mark Bauerlein, Emory University English professor and former National Endowment of the Arts director of research and analysis, is one such example. In his book *The Dumbest Generation*, Bauerlein zooms closely in on the millennial generation (born after the year 1982) and their expectations of society and general intellectual preparation. There, he finds a problem so pronounced that he promises his supporting evidence will "dismay anyone who cares about the health of U.S. democracy and the intelligence of U.S. culture."[11]

In a chapter titled "Knowledge Deficits," Bauerlein makes good on his promise with over a dozen pages of lowlights plucked from large-scale studies of today's teens' and young adults' knowledge, skills, and intellectual habits. In exploring possible reasons for such realities, other sections of *The Dumbest Generation* examine matters from young people's online and screen-viewing patterns, growing reluctance to read, and mystifyingly ballooning self-esteem.

Jean Twenge, a psychology professor from San Diego State University, complements Bauerlein's observations, though not beginning with today's young adults' academic competence. Rather, she begins with troubling psychological generalities of the millennials and works backward to their socializing institutions.

In her book *Generation Me*, Twenge offers that though millennials have been raised more than previous generations to put personal happiness and fulfillment first, this quality has certainly not been altered or helped by the contemporary age's educational structures. On the contrary, Twenge asserts, the educational institution has taken the protection of children's self-esteem to near-damaging levels. "The first change we must make," she says,

> is to abandon our obsession with self-esteem. Instead of creating well-adjusted, happy children, the self-esteem movement has created an army of little narcissists. Schools should eliminate self-esteem programs. It does not do any good for a child to hear that he or she is "special" or to "win" a trophy just for participating. Decades of research have shown that high self-esteem does *not* cause good grades or good behavior. So the programs are not doing any good. What's more, they may actually be harming some kids by making them too self-centered. Praise based on nothing teaches only an inflated ego. The purpose of school is for children to learn, not for them to feel good about themselves all the time.
>
> Another facet of this movement says that teachers should not correct children's mistakes, lest this hurt their self-esteem. This is extremely misguided: children learn by having their mistakes corrected, and their self-esteem is hurt when they later find out that they've been doing something wrong for years and aren't prepared.[12]

Of course, laying the findings of Jacoby, Shenkman, Bauerlein, Twenge, and others all at the feet of American education would not be fair. As the one common, mandatory, intellectual, civic-preparatory, and values-shaping experience we all undergo, however, public schooling should definitely be examined for how it contributes to the overall intellectual, ethical, and civic health of the American society. When the health of a societal structure this important appears to be flagging, it only makes sense to ask ourselves what we have put it through that may have caused it to wobble, weaken, and wear out.

As the education system exerts a daily influence on the intellectual development and preferences of each successive generation, it should, as a system, assume some responsibility for societal deficiencies of intellect, foundational knowledge, curiosity, motivation, empathy, and personal responsibility that educators, researchers, and cultural critics have brought to light.

To sum up, in addition to preparing students poorly for college and careers, schools are failing to prepare students to become effective participants in mainstream American institutions like democracy, the economy, and U.S. communities. And the more time that passes, worsening effects are arising across our society at large and in the severe deficiency of more recent K–12 graduates. Put another way, public schools are not delivering on the promises their framers envisioned and their taxpayers expect in return for their continuing contributions.

Back to the beginning: American education is not working as our society and our youngest members need it to work. Although this reality may not be a dire national security threat or a harbinger of cultural apocalypse, American K–12 education is failing to meet the reasonable expectation of continually strengthening America's mainstream institutions by providing an effective path for young people into post-secondary study, careers, and meaningful institutional participation.

This isn't a new problem. But despite considerable research, adjustment, and costly reform, the issue isn't getting much better over time. In fact, looking at those who have passed through U.S. schools in the past two reform-heavy decades, indications are that these graduates are entering our society with troubling deficits—of necessary skills, dispositions, expectations, and more—that only seem to be worsening.

And what about those reforms? With so many sweeping, expensive reform efforts currently in progress throughout American education, and with results that remain consistently frustrating, it is absolutely time to ask some tough questions:

What is preventing measureable improvement?
What qualities are missing in American education?
Why is education so impervious to reform?
Are the right reforms in place? Do they even exist?
And, most important, what can we do about it?

This book aims to answer these questions, often by challenging the answers others have offered up over the last century, and particularly during the past three decades of intense but impotent reform. But here is why the conversation gets complicated so quickly: no single answer, in and of itself, is *wrong*. No single thing is to blame for the current state of American education: not No Child Left Behind, not charter schools, not ignoring students' social-emotional learning needs. Not even Facebook. In fact, the reality is quite the opposite. Namely, the fact that *so many things* are to blame is one of American education's most crucial issues.

Setting aside the rightness or wrongness of any single solution, the entire enterprise of education finds itself in a time of crisis; a time when all proposed answers are competing for time, attention, and resources. They pull against one another in ways that cause the system to perform even more poorly as a whole, ultimately generating the kinds of symptoms we all recognize as signs of disease and decay.

Over several generations, the countless technical answers practitioners and reformers have nailed onto foundational defects have resulted in a mess of possible solutions. This mess only complicates and compromises each overlapping solution's potential effectiveness. It never even seeks to understand and address the foundational defects each of its solutions professed to solve.

Accordingly, this book's arguments and evidence go back to that foundation—to the origin of American education's fundamental beliefs and mission, resisting the impulse to add to the mess by insisting that *just one more* reform effort will finally deliver the results we've all been waiting for.

Two big ideas will guide us along the way.

First, we need a new mission and guiding philosophy.

To make all of the moving parts in education work more effectively and route well-prepared students into mainstream institutions of post-secondary study, careers, and participation in the economy and community, schooling must reexamine and rework its current operating mission and guiding philosophy. These are responsible for spawning practices, procedures, structures, and reforms based in honorable philosophical ideals, but not actually supported by cognitive-scientific evidence or even by clear advances in student outcomes. In reality, these practices *prevent* students from learning to their fullest potentials. Additionally, practices that stem from this misguided mission and philosophy distort what students expect from post-secondary school and careers, further damaging their chances of future success.

Second, current reforms are trying to solve the wrong problems.

Current reformers approach education fully inspired by the private sector, emphasizing intensive study of student outcome data, increasing teacher/administrative efficacy, seeking innovative (if unproven) solutions, and making ineffective heads roll. Though all of these are important priorities, none of them has delivered (or will deliver) the "turnaround" they promise. To have a turnaround kind of impact on the broader system or locally, reformers must question and work to overturn education's current misguided mission. Without addressing the larger issue, the only thing today's reformers succeed at is getting practitioners to more forcefully and more efficiently throw flawed practices at baffled students.

Needless to say, the blame game raging among educational practitioners and reformers adds profound tension and complexity to all improvement efforts. It obstructs views of the root causes of institutional flaws and seeds mistrust that will likely grow far into the future. For those who truly care about the long-term health of American education, it's not worth taking a side in this increasingly destructive war of words whose casualties include hope, respect, and progress.

In the next two chapters, we will focus on two main ideas: the ways in which American public education's current mission and philosophy of practice are disoriented and how they got that way in the first place.

NOTES

1. Diane Ravitch, *Reign of Error: The Hoax of the Privatization Movement and the Danger to America's Public Schools* (New York: Alfred A. Knopf, 2013), chapters 5–7.
2. Valerie Strauss, "What Does Being 'College and Career Ready' Mean?" *The Answer Sheet* (blog), *Washington Post*, April 29, 2010, http://voices.washingtonpost.com/answer-sheet/no-child-left-behind/what-is-being-college-and-care.html.
3. Julia Ryan, "This Year's SAT Scores Are Out, and They're Grim," *The Atlantic*, September 26, 2013, http://www.theatlantic.com/education/archive/2013/09/this-years-sat-scores-are-out-and-theyre-grim/279999/.
4. Lou Carlozo, "Why College Students Stop Short of a Degree," Reuters, March 27, 2012, http://www.reuters.com/article/2012/03/27/us-attn-andrea-education-dropouts-idUSBRE82Q0Y120120327.
5. Clifford Adelman, *Answers in the Tool Box: Academic Intensity, Attendance Patterns, and Bachelor's Degree Attainment* (Washington, DC: U.S. Department of Education, 1999). See also Clifford Adelman, *The Toolbox Revisited: Paths to Degree Completion from High School through College* (Washington, DC: U.S. Department of Education, 2006).
6. Ravitch, *Reign of Error*, 88–89.
7. ACT, Inc., *Ready for College and Ready for Work: Same or Different?* (Iowa City: ACT, Inc., 2006), accessed October 24, 2013, http://www.act.org/research/policymakers/pdf/ReadinessBrief.pdf.
8. Eduardo Porter, "Stubborn Skills Gap in America's Work Force," *New York Times*, October 8, 2013, http://www.nytimes.com/2013/10/09/business/economy/stubborn-skills-gap-in-americas-work-force.html?_r=0.
9. Susan Jacoby, *The Age of American Unreason* (New York: Pantheon, 2008), 210–41.
10. Rick Shenkman, *Just How Stupid Are We? Facing the Truth about the American Voter* (New York: Basic Books, 2009).
11. Mark Bauerlein, *The Dumbest Generation: How the Digital Age Stupefies Young Americans and Jeopardizes Our Future, *Or, Don't Trust Anyone under 30* (New York: Jeremy P. Tarcher/Penguin, 2008), 16.
12. Jean M. Twenge, *Generation Me: Why Today's Young Americans Are More Confident, Assertive, Entitled—and More Miserable than Ever Before* (New York: Free Press, 2006), 223.

Chapter Two

How to Use a Funnel

> The qualifications for self-government in society are not innate. They are the result of habit and long training.
>
> —Thomas Jefferson (1743–1826), American president and Founding Father, to Edward Everett in 1824

Before examining how our educational priorities and practices got so turned around, we need to look at where they came from in the first place. And that means taking a closer look at our institutional mission. Or rather, our lack of one. Because, as you may have guessed, it's a vast overstatement to say that a single, clearly stated institutional mission exists to guide practices consistently across the entire enterprise of American education. This reality, it should go without saying, presents a significant problem.

Consider three other publicly funded institutions and their familiar missions:

- Police: To uphold the Constitution of the United States and maintain law and order.
- Firefighters: To preserve life and property and promote public safety.
- Military: To deter war and protect the nation's security.

In all these examples, clarity of purpose helps define which actions should be taken, how resources should be used, and how priorities should be established.

Look across Americans' beliefs about why schools exist and what their purpose might be, and you will find no such clarity or focus. Compared to those of the police, firefighters, and military, the institutional mission of American education is pulled in many directions by a vast number of competing stakeholders. With so many different groups exerting influence on what American education *should* do, the true mission can be hard to find.

One group with strong influence is the parents of American schoolchildren. This group's versions of schooling's mission vary wildly, contrasting from individual to individual within each American classroom, school, and district. To some, schools exist to provide children with the practical tools necessary to be productive and independent after high school graduation. Others believe schools exist to provide authentically rigorous academic experiences and prepare students to compete for top collegiate slots.

In terms of shaping children's behavioral habits, some parents depend on school to pick up child-rearing and disciplinary slack they cannot fully provide at home, while others will litigate the second they perceive schools have even slightly overstepped their bounds as academic-only preparers.

Public policymakers also have beliefs about why schools exist. These beliefs vary from place to place, changing with every election according to constituents' preferences. Some policymakers see schools as factories designed to prepare the next generation of American workers, while others believe schools should instead reflect the wishes and sensibilities of local communities, even wishes that run counter to federal statute.

No matter where policymakers land on the spectrum, however, their influence weighs heavily on the mission itself. Their decisions provide funds, steer public opinion, and shape the standards to which educators are held accountable. In this regard, policymakers wield unrivaled power.

Industry leaders also weigh in on this question every few years, in somewhat predictable ways. Trendy skills or qualities observed in new employees, for example, drive what industry believes about education's reason for existing. So do shifting economic factors like suddenly booming sectors, employment statistics, and GDP growth rates in other industrialized nations.

Additionally, industry leaders adjust their ideas of education's mission according to which sectors *in education itself* are either historically or suddenly rich with cash, whether subsidized by the government or philanthropic benevolence. If the Department of Education begins awarding large amounts of money to schools to fund STEM (science, technology, engineering, and mathematics) programs, for instance, industry leaders—especially those whose companies may be able to assist with expensive technology to help guide such work—tend to become vocally supportive of education's latest commitment.

In short, industry's stake in education is nearly always based on the bottom line. To serve profitability by reducing employee training costs or winning grant-funded contracts, industry will believe and broadcast . . . well, pretty much whatever they think financial decision makers want to hear about the mission of education. And in the event they don't feel these decision makers are interested enough in the priorities they'd like education to exhibit (i.e., the ones that will fatten their bottom line the most), many in industry will steer decision makers and policy with campaign donations and teams of lobbyists.[1]

Somewhere among the parental, policymaking, and industry groups, a nuance-resistant mass media tends to repeat each party's ideas at face value. While headlines like "Some say schools need to make Chinese language classes mandatory. Local leaders agree" or "Parents outraged by amount & rationale of local schools' testing loads" hit at least part of the mark on education's large issues, they more often only add to the noise. By reporting these kinds of conflict-heavy, often sensationalized items about education's mission-related controversies and clashes, mainstream media outlets keep the multiple ideas of What Education Exists to Do stirring, colliding, and negatively reacting with each other. And as a result, competing stakeholders dig in more deeply, raising their voices to even higher levels against one another in free-for-alls for airtime.

On the ground and in the schools themselves, meanwhile, American education's practitioners share very different beliefs about their mission. These beliefs often pulse with an idealism practitioners feel that outside groups—out of touch, as they are, with the daily realities of the modern classroom—cannot fully grasp.

It is here that we can find the closest thing to a unifying institutional mission for education. Though not necessarily posted on classroom walls or even mentioned in staff meetings, the priorities and practices found in public schools today do in fact share a common thread—one that can serve as a foundational guiding philosophy. And the idea that has guided American education's practical decisions and aspirations for the past century is this:

Schools exist to provide the whole development of each individual child.

Emerging practitioners' training in education schools and current practitioners' ongoing professional development often trace back to this idea. So do most policies about student behavioral expectations, curriculum design, instructional delivery, systems of academic and behavioral intervention, placement with specific teachers in specific courses, and much more. At the root of every educational intention, the complete development of each individual student is the foundational, driving ideal.

From an institutional perspective—and particularly from a publicly funded, order-establishing, and order-maintaining institutional one—this mission and its derived practices and policies are misguided. While it might be easy to just declare this situation a mess, a wreck, or an epic fail, what is most important to realize is that the mission is not simply wrong.

It is upside-down.

So how did it get this way? Let's start with one important observation. Unlike the missions of the police, firefighters, and military, the implicit mission of education bears no responsibility to a larger common entity such as "public safety," "the Constitution of the United States," or "national security." No, education's practitioners organize their priorities and actions around each individual student.[2] In light of the numerous and diverse indicators of low post-K–12 readiness in recent graduates, the lack of a common good in education's mission speaks volumes. If American education designs most of its practice and policy around the good of each individual, is it really surprising that such high numbers of graduates and dropouts struggle when they come face to face with real-world expectations? Real-world expectations, after all, don't necessarily have to relate directly to students or to individual students' personal development.

Put another way, United States schooling's emphasis and the practices/methods it activates are equipping graduates poorly for the expectations, codes, and rules of the institutions that follow the required K–12 experience. These expectations and codes are generally not prioritized around the interests, desires, and skills of each individual, making American education's institutional mission, practices, and methods upside-down in comparison.

Upside-down as the mission may be, it works surprisingly well for many, many students. (You may be one of them.) The white and the affluent, for example, do incredibly well on average compared to their nonwhite, poorer counterparts in post-K–12 paradigms. This distribution can be predicted with remarkable (and tragic) accuracy. This is just another indicator, however, of how American education's mission, practices, and methods are upside-down.

What would a right-side-up mission look like? For starters, it would bear, demand, and perfect practices and methods that guide *all* students more effectively into mainstream institutions. It would help students understand what these institutions expect and how they operate. A right-side-up mission would adjust its practices as necessary for those who enter school with further to go before they can achieve the qualities mainstream institutions require.

Our current mission doesn't do this. It does the opposite, and it has been doing so for the last century. During that period, national averages of student performance show over and over that the system really only fulfills its key promises to children lucky enough to have been raised according to the expectations and codes of mainstream American institutions. If you're of a historically privileged race, for instance, statistics show that you stand a much higher chance of success in American schools and hence afterward. From a middle-class-or-above socioeconomic background or from parents who've attained college degrees? Same thing. Though the current mission seeks to honor every student as an individual, historical data show unquestionably that schools work best for those who enter schools from points closer to America's mainstream.

If the mission remains upside-down too much longer, the United States will soon see broad negative impacts within its mainstream institutions. In fact, several recent political, economic, and social developments suggest that we are already there.

Putting aside how an upside-down mission may have allowed frightening amounts of human potential to go unrealized (as if that is a small thing!), it is time to admit that the current mission is impossible to achieve. Wholly and fully developing every last child may be an inspiring ideal, but the fact that it has as many objectives as it does students renders it both unattainable and unsustainable. Think of it this way: While the U.S. Post Office has structures and systems to deliver letters and packages to any U.S. address at rates that are accessible to all, it is not set up to offer special packaging services, a range of package insurance options, or significantly expedited delivery times, à la Federal Express or UPS, at a nation-comprehensive scale. Schools' implicit mission, however, sets the enterprise up to offer FedEx services at a U.S. Post Office scale.

Many American educators will continue to say they could accomplish this mission if they only had more resources. Frankly, it is hard to imagine just how much funding would be necessary to cover the full scope of this ambition.

For argument's sake, multiply the following: the broad range of incoming students' issues and deficiencies, the near-infinite numbers of all students' interests and passions, and the near-infinite number of possible post-secondary pathways available to each student. How many dollars per student would it take to effectively accommodate all students individually and comprehensively? Would we need twice as many professionals? Three or four times as many, maybe? Would even that be enough? Ask anyone working in a school what it takes to add even one more staff to their building and it quickly becomes obvious that a staffing explosion is at best extremely unlikely.

In lieu of this kind of staffing explosion, teachers are asked to do the next best thing: differentiate classroom instruction by individual student preference, learning style, background, strengths, weaknesses, and so on. Considering how schools are currently structured, it is completely unreasonable to expect any single teacher to individualize instruction for classes full of students according to each child's level of mastery, preferred learning style, personal interest, parents' ideas of what they should be accomplishing, and so forth, all while moving toward on-time completion of state-mandated learning standards mapped out to grade levels and academic disciplines.

There are teachers who can pull this off. In fact, they exist fairly regularly. (Again, you may be one of them.) Anyone who has encountered one of these "superteachers" knows how rare a specimen this is. The superteacher is not the kind of professional we can count on to come to the rescue.

As much as we may want to (or at least hope to) build an army of superteachers through proper professional development, try this: call a superteacher to mind. When you do, ask yourself if you believe that person's combined organization, charisma, hustle, enthusiasm, content mastery, altruism, ability to inspire, sensitivity to human nature, and ability to improvise are the result of attending just the right workshops. (If you can say unequivocally that the person you pictured was indeed built solely by great university training and/or great professional development workshops, please send the sequence and course titles to the offices of this book's publisher. Thanks in advance.)

But let's keep the thought experiment going. Let's say we could create hundreds of thousands of superteachers if they simply attended a couple dozen workshops. Is now the right time to ask Americans for the extra funding to do it? The American public is past impatient with their education system. They are constantly reminded that results are not good, have not been good for some time, and that the whole operation seems immune to intense, if largely nonsensical (more on that later), reform efforts. At the current moment, it's plainly hard to envision that the public will put even more trust in the education enterprise, especially if that trust must take the form of significantly higher or wildly restructured taxes.

Even if American education could deliver on each child's complete development of self and on-time accomplishment of mandated academic standards if it were funded at levels commensurate to these goals, the money it would take to do this would easily eclipse what we spend on our entire military. This isn't going to happen. Fixing the mission means staying in the real world.

You may say that a properly prioritized nation would make the switch in a heartbeat, and the old joke about bake sales for bombers would come true. Or maybe we could fix education more easily if we first decided to end poverty. Maybe so. But educational practitioners have no direct control over those realities. What we do have control over is our classrooms. And in our classrooms, people—even those beginning far from America's mainstream—can become better prepared to face and succeed within the world after school. The thing is, to achieve our ideals around the nation's priorities, we're going to have to be a lot more than just idealistic.

It is absolutely true that education does not receive the kind of funding it deserves for its crucial charge and its myriad issues. It is also absolutely true that the effects of poverty are far more damning to students' chances of academic success than any instruction-level variables, and that addressing this is an urgent need for America's long-term health. Plainly and sadly, however, there is little reason to hope that this will occur, at least in the foreseeable future.

For professionals currently within American education, the choice is simple: make the best of a bad situation, or leave education to join the protesters and activists on the capitol steps. Before continuing you should know that this book, authored by an individual who passionately believes our enterprise possesses the greatest power to ultimately correct society's largest issues, will operate according to the former of these two choices. Rather than blame the state of American education on America's woeful distribution of wealth, for example, this book will present what American education needs to do to level playing fields and ultimately *change* the woeful distribution of wealth—all realistically (and, frankly, resignedly) within the parameters we have been granted.

To design the best system possible within the parameters we have been granted, it is crucial to better understand our current upside-down position and turn it right-side-up. To do that, we will use research that has emerged in the last three decades about human learning and habits necessary for post-secondary success.

When right-side-up, American education's institutional mission—and all its attendant practices and policies—will be less focused on every individual child and more focused on schooling's larger responsibility to society. Less an attempt to *teach the whole child*, then, and more one to *teach the child's whole life*. When right-side-up, American education's institutional mission reads as follows:

To prepare young citizens for meaningful participation in mainstream institutions.

Why upside-down? Why not sideways, or backwards, or plain old screwed up? Because institutions, in a general sociological sense (i.e., as rule-structures guiding human interactions and cooperation[3]), are essentially *funnels*.

Just as a funnel's design allows it to harness gravity and influence the direction of material from its source downward and inward into a receiving vessel, institutions use laws, habits, and customs to guide individuals into effective, meaningful participation in specific communities.

Funnels are meant to appreciate the value of the material passing through them. They are engineered to convert materials in inert, potential states to applied, useful states in the most efficient manner possible. (No wasted drops of gasoline from gas can to gas tank, for example.) In the same way, institutions appreciate individuals' potential worth, providing guides and expectations (toward social-group membership) that help define individuals' personal roles, orders, and purposes.

And just as funnels help channel large amounts of material into receiving vessels with narrow openings, so too are the controlled states of the institutions defined by their own "narrow openings." For one to achieve effective institutional participation, one must be and act according to the specific, explicitly and implicitly shared conditions of the institution. (Not everyone gets to be a neurosurgeon just because they really, really want to be one, for example.)

The institution of American education is the funnel between the diversity of America's youth and the institutions students will join after the required K–12 experience. The institutions that education transfers young people into, of course, are not static receptacles, but are also funnels themselves, channeling citizens into even more specialized environments through domain-specific expectations and codes: from college to medical school to a neurosurgery residency to the operating room; from high school to vocational school to automotive dealership to the mechanic's bay; from living in one's parents' home to the college dormitory to a rented apartment to full homeownership, and so on.

In short, positioned where it is and taking in, as it does, large and diverse numbers of young people, the K–12 education should provide a largely standardized, fundamental, first-level funneling of our nation's raw material into the first stage of refinement—into generally applicable foundational knowledge, generally moldable practical skills, and generally employable dispositions and habits.

Seems simple enough, right? That education systematically brings the diverse abilities and backgrounds of its youngest members downward and inward into society's institutions? That, after having passed through the educational funnel, society could count on, at minimum, the following from young adults: they would understand, accept, and practice the implicit and explicit conditions of our democracy and economy, and they would possess the skills, habits, and knowledge necessary to participate in these endeavors successfully?

These aims were precisely what the founders of America's free public education system had in mind when they determined the system's necessity and designed its structures. The founders saw American public schooling as the funnel through which all citizens would pass in order to function effectively in the receiving vessel of society.

Whenever institutionally focused policies and practices are promoted over individual-child ones, many educators resist them out of hand. But public education's founders were not interested in creating a system that mechanized the control and homogenization of American minds and behavior, subjecting them to perpetually subordinate lives. Much to the contrary, the founders sought a system of education capable of creating a society that was to be the first of its kind in world history: uniquely diverse and democratically governed, offering unprecedented freedoms of expression, life, and economic opportunity, plus sufficiently driven, skilled, organized, and collaborative to lead the world economically, intellectually, and morally.

Horace Mann, an early champion of the common schools that would eventually become the American public school system, never envisioned a system of schooling that churned out automatons for serving the wealthy. Writing in the mid-nineteenth century, he saw a hearty public education system as one way to help erase class conflict. To Mann, public education had the potential, if done right, to be "the great equalizer of the conditions of men—the balance-wheel of the social machinery . . . and, if this education should be universal and complete, it would do more than all things else to obliterate distinctions in society."[4]

In his book *The Making of Americans*, E. D. Hirsch, educational theorist and founder of the Core Knowledge Foundation, discusses key points around which founders like Mann planned this system. To be the universal and complete education Mann envisioned, the system would have to prepare students for both the public and the private spheres.

"Fundamental to this founding concept is the distinction between the public and private spheres of life," Hirsch writes.

> [T]his distinction was meant to apply very broadly in the American system. We operate whenever we vote, serve in the military, transact business, become a member of a jury or a defendant at the jury's mercy, write for a big, unseen audience, or encounter any situation where we wish to be understood by strangers. This public sphere is the melting pot, where common laws, a common language, and shared unspoken knowledge and values are needed to make the uttered language comprehensible.[5]

The proof offered until now (which, relative to the loads of ink that have been spent over the past few decades about the condition of American education, is but a small amount) illustrates how Mann's expectations are most certainly not being met. The educational funnel itself, upside-down for a century and not positioned over any particular vessel, is the main reason we're seeing the results we have for so long. Its upside-down orientation is also why, despite all of the reforms that have been attempted, substantial improvement has never been achieved.

Very plainly, the funnel between America's youth and its mainstream institutions is upside-down. Its narrow end, usually directed downward into a specific vessel, now faces upward to receive the wide stream of raw material rich with potential. Though the intent of education is to honor, appreciate, and grow each student individually, the actual practices and policies designed to do this are having opposite effects.

Much of the raw material being "poured" into the funnel from multiple sources (representing the range of schoolchildren's backgrounds and abilities) is spilling down the sides instead of going where it's supposed to go. Students are not succeeding in school and struggling to enter mainstream institutions, or the "public sphere" of American life, where their gifts and talents can be applied and they can achieve a sense of belonging to something larger.

Of all the students poured toward the opening of the upside-down funnel, statistics report predictable patterns of who will pass cleanly through into mainstream institutions. For students lucky enough to have been born into families positioned more fortunately in relationship to these institutions, the fact that the funnel is upside-down makes no difference. Because their families readily observe, abide by, pass on, and reinforce the conditions and expectations of the American mainstream, these students are more likely to fit through the "narrow opening" and pass through into rewarding careers and civic responsibilities quite easily.

For students not so fortunate, the situation is much different. For those not from mainstream-aligned families (e.g., those whose families are poorer, recently immigrated, non-English-speaking, historically oppressed on the basis of race, religion, gender, or other factors), the funnel is simply not positioned in a way that will channel them into the mainstream without a great deal of compensatory work and dedication.

Imagine fluid poured from several containers through the same funnel simultaneously. When the funnel is right-side-up, this can be done fairly easily; when it's upside-down, more will be spilled than successfully transferred. This is precisely what is happening in American schooling. Spilled down the outside of the funnel instead of pulled inward and downward, students must summon the will to either somehow make the funnel work for them, find their own ways into the receiving vessel, or fall to the floor for others to mop up.

Though student-centered educators strived to create a system that would equalize U.S. society, honoring the intrinsic desires of every student and carefully guiding them to activate authentic learning experiences, the designs have had the opposite effect. Student-first educational ideals and methods have caused too many students to spill down the sides.

Though reformers are hard at work to improve American education's systems and operations, their work is yielding very little because none of these reforms is concerned with turning the funnel right-side-up. They are all working very hard, but not on solving the true problems.

To understand this in detail, let's keep the analogy going.

Reformers do things like measure funnel inputs and outputs more accurately, all to better help the funnel improve its volume-in/volume-out/volume-spilled ratios. In addition to using ratio study as bases for improvement coaching, reformers use the information to motivate professionals into better performance through incentivizing or, more often, bald-faced shaming.

But the funnel is still upside-down.

Another school of reformers works tirelessly on innovative funnel designs, engineering improved funnels out of recently discovered materials and compounds—ones they promise will make traditional funnels obsolete. These promises often go unfulfilled, however. They, too, place their space-age-polymer funnels upside-down. The material keeps spilling down the sides, only faster.

In the next few chapters, we will look at the funnel in more concrete, practical terms. We will explore examples of what upside-down instructional philosophies and practices look like in action, how they fail to align with post-K–12 expectations and paradigms, and how schools should envision their responsibility in order to better position all their participants for success.

Then we will take a look at the reformers, seeing how and why wave after wave of standardized testing, tighter professional accountability, increased school choice, and all the rest have not, at this time of writing, delivered the improvements they're working so hard to make. Unless the funnel is flipped back over, all the measurement, private-sector-inspired incentives (and disincentives), and innovative instructional models and modes will only make things worse, causing even more spillage and institutional emptiness.

To begin this discussion, however, we first need to look at how the funnel of American education came to its upside-down position in the first place. This will shed some light on why turning the funnel right-side-up will require a total, slash-and-burn, comprehensive reconsideration of our mission, purposes, and practices.

NOTES

1. Michelle R. Davis, "Ed. Companies Exert Public-Policy Influence: Some Observers Are Alarmed at What They See as Increasingly Aggressive Moves by Companies," *Education Week*, April 24, 2013, http://www.edweek.org/ew/articles/2013/04/24/29ii-politicalpower.h32.html?tkn=SMZFnrqOI%2BEeHnBpv0iXitdqj8R7P1Y%2B1c7w&cmp=SOC-EDIT-LI&intc=EW-II413-LI.

2. And though this backwardly derived mission could certainly be challenged, skeptical readers are encouraged to randomly sample, via a basic Google search, some school-level mission statements and gauge those schools' individual commitments to the worlds outside their doors. If following such a recommendation, note how often such statements focus on the school environment/climate being aspired to (e.g., "child-centered," "positive and nurturing," etc.), and general qualities they hope to build in their students (e.g., "critical thinking" and "love for learning"). Though occasional nods are made toward students' eventual interaction with the worlds beyond school, such mission statements rarely go beyond widely generalized aspirations to create "twenty-first-century citizens" or "students prepared for global citizenship."

3. Though this broad definition of *institution* will guide the arguments made in this book, multiple schools of thought exist around the concept. As political scientist Hugh Heclo writes regarding a unified definition, "[I]t matters much more whether it is a lawyer, sociologist, economist, political scientist, or psychologist who is doing the talking" (Hugh Heclo, *On Thinking Institutionally* [Boulder, CO: Paradigm, 2008], 56).

4. Lawrence A. Cremin, *American Education: The Colonial Experience, 1607–1783* (New York: Harper and Row, 1970), 181.

5. E. D. Hirsch, *The Making of Americans: Democracy and Our Schools* (New Haven, CT: Yale University Press, 2009), 23.

Chapter Three

The Funnel Tips: A Brief Annotated History

> But what is equally important, and sobering, is how often we fool ourselves. And we fool ourselves not only individually but en masse. The tendency of a group of human beings to quickly come to believe something that its individual members will later see as obviously false is truly amazing. Some of the worst tragedies of the last century happened because well-meaning people fell for easy solutions proposed by bad leaders.
>
> —Lee Smolin, theoretical physicist, in *The Trouble with Physics*

The funnel of American education has not always been upside-down. Those who first advocated for free public education in the United States—including Founding Fathers like Thomas Jefferson—envisioned an institution designed specifically to strengthen and perpetually replenish national institutions like the economy, democracy, and local community by preparing all U.S. citizens to participate fully in a common, public sphere.

The practices the framers preferred matched up well with this mission, particularly in terms of curricular and classroom-cultural expectations. The initial objectives and attendant practices provided key levers for unifying America's diverse masses and interests over much of the nineteenth century—hardly a mean feat, especially considering the nation's explosive, comprehensive expansion over that period.

In the late nineteenth and early twentieth centuries, however, a number of forces converged to override this original impulse. The first wave of reformers saw the framers' traditional objectives and pedagogies as out of step with the needs of the growing nation as well as with then-recent findings from studies of child development and general naturalistic laws. Driven by idealism, these first reformers used their preferences to permanently reframe the national debate over American curriculum, the structure of schooling, models of practice, overarching goals and missions, and teacher-preparation requirements.

Though schools now may not look much like the schools that existed during this transitional period, the mission and practices the first reformers ultimately achieved are the same ones we recognize today—the ones that are so badly out of alignment with mainstream institutions. These ideals have so shaped pedagogy and professional preparation in the past century that the vast majority of educational professionals accept them as gospel. They are simply the correct, ideal methods, and always have been. (But as we'll see, that's not actually the case.)

One likely reason late nineteenth- and early twentieth-century efforts to "flip the funnel" of American education worked so well was because the educational philosophies and pedagogies operating at that time were indeed far from polished or equitable. Many students passed through their schooling experiences disaffected, and many others left before achieving diplomas. A look back at the history of this dissonant transformative period, though, shows that the framers' philosophies weren't given much chance to improve or adapt before being overwhelmed and ultimately reversed by those who opposed them.

In this chapter we will look more closely at the salient moments, figures, and ideas of this critical transformational period. But this will be a brief history, for two reasons: first, the intent is to provide context for upcoming discussions of practice and reform—not to offer a comprehensive standalone lesson; second, so many excellent histories already exist about this period that any effort to tell the same story here would be at best incomplete. (For further and more complete study of this period, please consult any of the sources listed in the chapter notes.[1])

When "new education" principles began to pop up more frequently during the last decades of the nineteenth century, they reflected, in the words of education historian William J. Reese, "a nation continually revitalized by waves of religious revivalism and utopian experiments during the antebellum period."[2] The new educational reformers, envisioning a more just world based on Enlightenment-inspired, universal, humanitarian, and naturalistic laws, sought to do away with the forced curricular and discipline standards of traditional educators, standards they believed would only taint or pollute the perfect, innocent spirit of the child.

These ideas most likely originated in eighteenth- and early-nineteenth-century Europe, where reformers like Switzerland's Johann Heinrich Pestalozzi, Germany's Friedrich Froebel, and Britain's Herbert Spencer spent a great deal of time hammering away at education's long-accepted, etched-in-stone truths.

Historians of education often identify these pedagogues' reforms as practical outgrowths of eighteenth- and nineteenth-century European romanticism. Where philosophers like Jean-Jacques Rousseau and poets like William Blake and William Wordsworth reimagined and redefined childhood's possibilities and fragilities for all of European society, educators like Pestalozzi, Froebel, and Spencer worked in their wakes to create educational institutions and philosophies that better met the newly reunderstood needs of children.[3]

In his famous *How Gertrude Teaches Her Children* (1801), for example, Pestalozzi urged that young children should be taught by "*things* more than by *words*," beginning a definite turn away from the dull, useless activity of book learning. His "object teaching" method provided a vehicle for driving instruction-creation away from textbooks and toward familiar, everyday objects. According to Pestalozzi, ideas in books were abstractions with no intrinsic meaning for children, and the knowledge textbooks offered was artificial; the object teaching method, on the other hand, with its reliance on familiar objects as teaching tools, offered a way of creating *real* knowledge in students.[4]

Froebel, who worked alongside Pestalozzi from 1808 to 1810, before moving on to become the father of kindergarten, picked up the basic ideas of object teaching and ran with them all the way into a far more metaphysical neighborhood. Though he agreed with and preserved Pestalozzi's belief in everyday objects as ideal instructional tools for young children, he sought to use these objects for more than teaching color, shape, motion, arithmetic, and other simple concepts. In Froebel's view, these everyday items, if strategically organized, could actually increase students' sense of social order and their individual places within it. "In the first plays with the ball the life of the child makes itself known," Froebel wrote, "and the outer world makes itself known to the child in unity."[5]

While Pestalozzi and Froebel applied romanticist-inspired philosophies and ideals to the practice of education, the work of Britain's Herbert Spencer (brought to education in the second half of the nineteenth century) distinguished itself by being based in *serious science*. As influential as Spencer's ideas were in Europe, their scientific bent validated and legitimized them in ways that fit well with nineteenth-century America's reason-hungry worldview and made them particularly attractive to America's emerging legions of professional educators.

In several ways, Spencer's recommendations about an effective education echoed those of thinkers like Pestalozzi and Froebel. Spencer's main departure, however, was in that he presented scientifically based theories, not simply insights and subsequent philosophical truths around which to build practice. Spencer's recommendations of practice, featuring a uniquely scientific backbone, went beyond a matter of *preference*. As far as the development of children was concerned, Spencer's ideas were viewed as undeniably, self-evidently *correct*.

Despite its self-professed scientific validity, the science underpinning Spencer's educational principles was at best loose. By most standards, Spencer's ideas wouldn't even be considered *science* as they did not rise from any kind of empirical study or verification. As the recommendations Spencer made about education were generally not validated by objective, controlled experiments, in other words, implementing his recommendations would not reliably produce any set of predicted outcomes. Rather, because his recommendations were based upon accepted truths about other observable natural phenomena, Spencer declared them to be scientific and good chunks of his public agreed.

The scientific engines driving Spencer's work were parallels he drew between the sequential development of, well, *everything* (e.g., matter, societies, organisms, the cosmos, etc.) and the development of young humans. According to educational philosopher Kieran Egan, Spencer's main aim was to show "how learning and development, and the daily activities of the classroom, were parts of the same laws that shaped the stars above and the earth below."[6] (Talk about a grand unified field theory.) Beatrice Webb, the renowned twentieth-century sociologist and economist, knew Spencer through her parents and often discussed his work with him. She was so unimpressed with Spencer's ideas of "science" that she described him as "the most gullible of mortals" and as having been "engaged in the art of casuistry."[7] Put another way, Spencer was about as scientific as an astrology columnist.

Here's what he came up with: Noting how all things invariably developed from simple states to more complex ones, Spencer devised a number of educational ideals to help educators capitalize on each developmental stage. In his 1860 *Education: Intellectual, Moral, and Physical*, Spencer heavily critiqued the methods of traditional education, charging that their barbarous forcing of irrelevant information into the minds of its pupils rendered them completely out of phase with his universally observed stages of natural development. Though teaching of a nation's history, for example, was commonplace in traditional schools' early grades, younger students' development—innately geared toward exploration and play—made them unready for and uninterested in such subject matter, making history teaching ineffective, inappropriate, *bad* educational practice.

To make the educational process efficient and pleasant for the child, Spencer argued, the child's own developing needs and expanding activities should be central to all curricular design and teachers' methods of delivery.[8] These ideas are now well over a century old, but should be intimately familiar to any teacher who has had to sit through a professional development workshop on using play-like activities to engage students in academic tasks.

Driven by "scientific" certainty, Spencer introduced seven principles of intellectual education, principles that effectively formed the heart of the Progressive Education movement (more on this shortly) in America and turn the instructional, philosophical funnel of American education upside-down. Combined below (and compressed for brevity's sake) are three major concepts from Spencer's seven principles that helped shape pedagogical practice, preparation, and policy well into the twenty-first century:

1. *Education should be directly experiential*: To meet students' relative developmental stages and the consistent progressions through which all systems develop, all new knowledge and skill should be introduced to students through experiences resembling the phenomena of the world directly around or accessible to them.
2. *Education should be inquiry-based*: Believing that "[c]hildren should be led to make their own investigations, and to draw their own inferences. They should be *told* as little as possible, and induced to *discover* as much as possible,"[9] Spencer recommended that teachers switch their focus from transmitting information to facilitating active learning.
3. *Education should be pleasurable and exciting*: Considering "a child's intellectual instincts . . . more trustworthy than our reasonings,"[10] Spencer urged that the engagement of the child should be placed above any particular subject matter in making curricular decisions.

With students' natural interest-states now a top priority—and with scientifically based justifications and methods as proof points—the ideas and methods of traditional education and the academic curriculum soon found themselves under heavy pressure. The funnel-turners were at their marks, getting set to lift in frightening unison.

Before moving into how education reformers applied ideals from Pestalozzi, Froebel, and Spencer to the ultimate detriment of U.S. education, let's take a moment to consider how the funnel was doing when it was in its original position. With so many thinkers rallying against its dullness, its useless content, and its barbaric lack of choice and enjoyment, the average American school must have been a pretty awful place back then . . . right?

From this far away, of course, it can be difficult to assess exactly what such schools were like. Though plenty of historical evidence exists about conditions and expectations at schools of the period, it's hard to divorce the accounts we have from the institutional expectations and mindsets of their participants (which are also difficult to ascertain), ultimately making them tricky to process.

Based on still other points of objective historical evidence, though, traditional education methods and objectives seem far from inhumane or child-damaging, especially in light of some of their outcomes. Have no doubt, framers of early public education did envision their enterprise as responsible for doing a fair amount of person-shaping. Plenty of evidence suggests, however, that we should not assume (as reformers of the time seemed to) that the resulting educational experience was a creativity-killing, mind-numbing, soul-sucking one.

Children educated under such "barbaric" expectations and conditions, after all, did ultimately possess the mental and disciplinary tools to drive an era of explosive economic and innovative growth—explosive enough to make the United States an international superpower in less than two hundred (intensely tumultuous) years of existence. Also, early American public educators were often working with huge waves of recently immigrated student populations, a reality that would have required extraordinary amounts of instructional agility and balance, cultural appreciation and understanding, and differentiation if the enterprise was to achieve the unifying potential of schooling they envisioned.

William T. Harris, an early educational leader, is just such an example. He created model environments following fairly traditional standards of student order, discipline, effort, and work. Serving as St. Louis schools' superintendent from 1868 to 1880 (during which enrollment more than *quadrupled*), Harris gained considerable renown for expanding citizens' access to education and all the attendant opportunities for unprecedented personal growth and academic enrichment.

Harris was a champion of coeducation, racial integration, and removing religious study from the public school classroom. To make sure his students could assimilate into U.S. culture and successfully process requisite academic content and information about national values, he did not hesitate to employ novel means like instructing students in their native languages—a choice that helped students succeed faster and also established trust among immigrant families hesitant to surrender their home languages to broadly preferred American English.

For Harris, who later served a record term as U.S. Commissioner of Education (1889–1906), all of these efforts to educate and institutionally initiate all of America's young citizens were essential to the well-being of the nation taking shape around him. In the words of educational historian Lawrence A. Cremin, Harris, a student of German idealist philosophy (Hegel in particular), believed "the curriculum was to be the means by which the child would be brought into orderly relationship with his civilization." That "institutions . . . are not opposed to man; they enable man to achieve his truest expression" and "[lead] him away from his primitive self."[11]

The curriculum Harris viewed as ideal for bringing about such an orderly relationship with civilization was concentrated around basic academic pillars: mathematics, geography, history, grammar, literature, and art. What Harris called the "windows of the soul" unfolded in a deliberate sequence from foundation to greater complexity, empowering students with a kind of self-activity that could best process the resources and opportunities of the mainstream institutions.[12]

Nevertheless, reformers at the time found Harris's preferred methods, his beliefs about our relationships to institutions, and his views of how schools should shape individuals accordingly, to be highly unsatisfactory.

In *The Struggle for the American Curriculum, 1893–1958*, historian Herbert M. Kliebard places Harris (and his colleagues in the National Education Association-appointed Committee of Ten, who sought to establish national curricular guidelines that better aligned with varying college entrance requirements[13]) in the category of the humanists—"guardians of an ancient tradition tied to the power of reason and the finest elements of the Western cultural heritage"—and names three forces that sought to blaze very different trails for American education.

Group One: the *developmentalists*, who sought to reform curriculum "along the lines of a natural order of development in the child."

Group Two: the *social efficiency educators*, who believed that schools should more directly and efficiently prepare students for the workforces awaiting them after their educations, thus prioritizing a greater specialization of skills and greater curricular differentiation.

Group Three: the *social meliorists*, who saw in schools "a major . . . force for social change and social justice." Hoping to stave off the social characteristics they saw growing up around them in the fledgling nation, this group pushed for changes that would favor attitudes and ways of being more than sets of academic competency or readiness for further education.[14]

In the decades bridging the late nineteenth and early twentieth centuries, these three groups had profound impacts on the funnel of education. Each initiated engines of reform that are still running in modern school systems. The one that applied the most force and ultimately left the most lasting mark on American education, however, was the Progressive Education movement. Growing out of the overlap between the developmentalists and the social meliorists, this movement collectively heaved the funnel, hoping to turn American education over once and for all.

Many individuals played significant roles in bringing Progressive Education principles into mainstream acceptance as best practice. No single contributor has been associated more essentially with this shift, however, than the American pragmatist philosopher John Dewey.

In actuality, Dewey's advocacy for and actions toward reforming traditional educational methods is fairly modest when compared to those of several others. Ultimately, and rather oddly, a close look at Dewey's work (not to mention his eventual reaction to the Progressive Educators' methods—more on that shortly) would make one question the strength of the ties often assumed between his philosophy and Progressives' beliefs and practices. In *The Struggle for the American Curriculum*, Kliebard goes so far as to say that Dewey's "actual influence on the schools of the nation has been both seriously overestimated and grossly distorted,"[15] a view echoed by multiple chroniclers of this period.

Which is all well and good, except that if you ask pretty much any U.S. educator about how the work of Herbert Spencer, G. Stanley Hall, Colonel Francis W. Parker, Edward Thorndike, William Heard Kilpatrick, Harold Rugg, or any number of other individuals not named John Dewey affects how they teach, it is doubtful they'll have much of a response beyond "Who?" To history, it seems, all of these figures are only bit players in Dewey's show.

Part of this is due to American teacher-preparation programs, where Dewey looms as a towering, near-mythic figure. "Not for nothing has Dewey's picture been found on the wall in so many ed school offices for so many years," wrote Stanford education professor David Labaree in 2004's *The Trouble with Ed Schools*, as "[Dewey's] was a vision of education that could get the blood pumping."

> It called for turning education upside down, by having the purposes and interests of the student drive the curriculum rather than forcing the curriculum onto the student. It offered a way to free schools from artificial constraints and rigid disciplines and unleash the student's natural impulse to learn. It proposed to re-create the classroom as a model democratic community of learners, which could become a way to reduce injustice and enhance democratic equality in the larger society. . . . It offered most education professors the mission they needed in order to infuse meaning into their work as teacher educators and functionaries in the educational machine. They did their teaching and research within the structure defined by [social efficiency-driven leader/reformer Edward] Thorndike, but their hearts and minds belonged to Dewey.[16]

At the beginning of American education's great turning, Dewey's educational writings and professional experiences[17] provided precisely the kind of inspirational charge described by Labaree to educational reformers. For groups hoping to overturn more traditional, humanist educational views and methods in the decades bridging the nineteenth and twentieth centuries—all the dreaded "subject-matter-set-out-to-be-learned," student-expression-muting classroom environments, and the rest—the ideas Dewey issued were echoes of their own hearts' desires. Ideal professional practices, dispositions, and school models were developed around Deweyan ideas and, whether successful or not, were dutifully reinforced over the decades in educational professionals' training.

Despite how charged up many of these Progressives may have been by Dewey's ideas, however, the educational theory Dewey so painstakingly developed ultimately "was either converted into a pitiful caricature . . . or neglected altogether. Dewey was invoked in connection with curriculum and general school reforms of all sorts whether they reflected his ideas or not."[18] (In later chapters, we will take a closer look at how Dewey's basic ideas were translated into modern practice.)

The ideas themselves—the ones that so ignited the passions of late nineteenth- and early twentieth-century "new education" reformers (who later formed the Progressive Education movement) and present-day ed school leaders alike—can be found in four key works by Dewey: *My Pedagogic Creed* (1897), *The School and Society* (1900), *The Child and the Curriculum* (1902), and *Democracy and Education* (1916).[19]

The theories shared in these works rose from Dewey's work in academic psychology and his growing interests in child development and appropriate schooling, and they were especially shaped by the work and ideas of German philosopher and psychologist Johann Friedrich Herbart. Dewey was, in fact, a member (albeit not an enthusiastic one) of the U.S. National Herbart Society that so publicly challenged William T. Harris during his term as commissioner of education.[20] Ultimately, Dewey's work hoped to bridge the divide he observed between the child study movement favored by the developmentalists (as paraphrased by Kliebard, Dewey saw their movement as following "more evangelism than science"[21]) and Herbart's genuinely scientific psychology and pedagogy.

Though each work focuses on unique themes and uses specific arguments to communicate them, three key themes were particularly suitable to the first reformers' agendas:

1. *Education should be directly relevant to the life one lives*: As schools should seek to reflect the life of the larger society, the traditional academic curriculum's abstractions and isolation from the realities of day-to-day living are irrelevant and wasteful. "Introducing the child too abruptly to a number of special studies, of reading, writing, geography, etc., out of relation to [the child's] social life," Dewey wrote, can even "violate the child's nature."[22]
2. *Education's center of gravity should be the individual child, as they are now*: All of schooling's learning activities, subject matter, and habits of being should originate from the instincts of each child, no matter what those instincts may be. Here we see the role of teacher changing from an active learning *leader* to a collaborative learning

facilitator. "The teacher is not in the school to impose certain ideas or to form certain habits in the child," wrote Dewey in *My Pedagogic Creed*, "but is there as a member of the community to select the influences which shall affect the child and to assist him in properly responding to these influences."[23]

3. *Education should—and can—create the society we wish to see*: Running with Harris's ideas about using schools to smooth the way into America's institutions, Dewey pictured schools as the lever through which society could be made, over time, into an ideal one for all. He wanted schools "to inculcate habits that would enable individuals to control their surroundings rather than merely adapt to them. And he wanted each generation to go beyond its predecessors in the quality of behavior it sought to nurture in its children."[24]

Followers of Dewey proceeded outward from his foundational influence, translating the foundational concepts into practical/methodological ideals and promoting their superiority through a number of different channels. This collection of Dewey-inspired thinkers came to be known as the Progressive Education movement, and it is this movement that is most directly responsible for tipping over the funnel.[25]

To illustrate the types of reforms and innovations the Progressive Education movement made based on Dewey's ideas—and in reaction to the original aims of American education—we can look to one individual.

Proceeding directly from Dewey's circle and into American education's subsequent discussions of practice and paradigm was a one-time high school math teacher from Georgia named William Heard Kilpatrick. Kilpatrick's contribution to American education's funnel-turning is instructive for three reasons:

1. His work bridged (and also distorted) Dewey's ideas into the mainstream.
2. His suggestions of practice and pedagogical ideals were embraced and implemented widely in his time, catapulting him to guru-pundit status.
3. His long-term impact is unquestioned, simply because so many of his ideals around students' experiences within and engagements to learning activities can still be observed in today's schools.

Kilpatrick worked as a graduate student under Dewey in the early 1900s, and ample records exist to suggest the two shared a strong mutual appreciation. The historian Cremin even describes Kilpatrick as "unabashedly the disciple, the interpreter of Dewey." Interestingly, however, Cremin also suggests that "in seeking to make Dewey's ideas manageable for mass consumption by the teaching profession, [Kilpatrick] ended by transforming them into versions quite different from the originals."[26]

One such transformation was Kilpatrick's project method, a proposed practical ideal that would set "the purposeful act" at the center of the educational process. In his famed 1918 essay "The Project Method," Kilpatrick outlined and justified a way to work within schooling's strict, compartmentalized structures to achieve Deweyan ends. Accepting that wildly innovative Lab Schools like Dewey's were unlikely to be installed across American education, Kilpatrick devised, through a curriculum reorganized around a succession of projects, a way educators could still "do Progressive Education."[27]

The "purposeful act" that sat at the center of all such projects, Kilpatrick posited, would serve as the projects' essential fuel, in that they would be determined by students. Students would choose their learning projects, in other words, based on personal passions or interests. In the classrooms of Kilpatrick's time or those of today, such might inspire students to beautify a public space with a mural as their project. The learning/experiential exercises would be the total project's execution: from the acquisition of acquiring permissions and materials to designing to painting to hosting a public unveiling ceremony, and so on. Distinguishing between "the typical unit of the worthy life in a democratic society" and "the unit of life for the serf or the slave . . . [who] must in the interest of the overmastering system be habituated to act with a minimum of their own purposing,"[28] Kilpatrick's essay suggested that to do anything but let students choose their own project topics was tantamount to slapping students in manacles and cracking the whip.

Other pieces of the essay assert that if the child is not interested enough in a certain topic to make it the focus of a project, it really only means they're not ready to learn about it. As this piece of content is not yet "a mental possession," it "will pretty effectually quench the glow of thought. Unreadiness will rather characterize his attitude."[29] In other words, if one attempts to make a student learn something he doesn't want to learn, the student may act out. If a teacher finds herself dealing with student-attitude issues, Kilpatrick says this is more than the teacher's *problem*. It's the teacher's *fault*.

"The Project Method" was so well received by American educators at large that it "catapulted [Kilpatrick] to national and international fame. Over 60,000 reprints were destined to circulate during the next twenty-five years."[30] Kilpatrick became a full professor at Teachers College of Columbia University—long considered a leading preparer of American teachers and generator of American education–related thought and research—and spent the remainder of his professional career there.

Not related directly to "The Project Method"—but too closely related in time and content to be purely coincidental—the Progressive Education Association was founded in 1919. Linked strongly in spirit with Kilpatrick's famous essay, the Progressive Education Association's first statement of principles declared the organization committed to the "freest and fullest development of the individual, based on the scientific study of his mental, physical, spiritual, and social characteristics and needs."[31] A far cry, indeed, from William T. Harris's traditionalist views about schooling as bringing the child "into orderly relationship with his civilization" and trusting institutions' abilities to enable "man to achieve his truest expression" and lead man "away from his primitive self."

Formally organized and guided by thought leaders like Kilpatrick, the Progressive Education movement fully and forcefully flipped over the funnel of American education.

The point is that there is a clear and distinct chain linking early thinkers like Pestalozzi, Froebel, and Spencer to the demigod Dewey, his disciple Kilpatrick, and the Progressive movement at large. This chain undoubtedly exerted remarkable force against the original framework of American education. Later, we'll look at how some of their central ideas are the very same ones American education has seen recycled and repackaged multiple times to form the misaligned funnel we see today.

Before launching into this discussion, we need to consider one final point—namely, what might have been.

What if Progressives hadn't succeeded? What if they had not so completely commandeered American education's professional-preparatory infrastructure for the past century and, in the words of Kieran Egan, "progressivism's tenets. . . become the conventional wisdom of American education"?[32] If this had been the case, it might be more widely recognized that one of the movement's greatest champions, *John Dewey himself*, publicly objected to the practices being designed and promoted in the name of his ideas.

For one, Dewey declined membership in the Progressive Education Association from its outset. (He did accept an honorary presidency after the death of Charles Eliot, but this appears to have been little more than a courtesy to his late colleague.)

More telling, however, are the public commentaries Dewey made at the height of the Progressives' momentum. In a 1926 article titled "Individuality and Experience," he slammed the lack of adult guidance he observed in child-centered schools that were supposedly following his guidelines. "Such a method is really stupid," Dewey wrote, "for it attempts the impossible, which is always stupid; and it misconceives the conditions of independent thinking."[33] Also, in 1928, the same year that Harold Rugg and Ann Shumaker's momentous *The Child-Centered School* was released, Dewey addressed the Progressive Education Association. As paraphrased by Cremin, Dewey's address warned the gathered Progressives against forsaking students' systematic exposure to and processing of certain subject matter in that it risks limiting students' ultimate individuality and, quite harshly, failing in one's obligation as an educator.[34]

Unfortunately—and especially so for the children required to pass through the upside-down funnel and the education professionals destined to witness their failure—Dewey's criticism and cautions were not heard. His comments did not slow the implementation of Progressive practices, nor were they included in the body of Deweyan ideas eventually held up as touchstones of instruction and child development.

Maybe if educators at the time had actually listened to what Dewey was saying, the misalignment we see now would never have happened.

NOTES

1. As it sent such considerable waves through all of American education's practices and policies, this transformative period—and the Progressive Education movement, in particular—has been documented very well and by multiple talented historians and thinkers. Recommended resources include Diane Ravitch, *Left Back: A Century of Battles Over School Reforms* (New York: Touchstone, 2000), 162–201, and *The Troubled Crusade: American Education 1945–1980* (New York: Basic Books, 1985), 43–80; Paul A. Zoch, *Doomed to Fail: The Built-In Defects of American Education* (Chicago, IL: Ivan R. Dee, 2004), 47–107; Kieran Egan, *Getting It Wrong from the Beginning: Our Progressive Inheritance from Herbert Spencer, John Dewey, and Jean Piaget* (New Haven, CT: Yale University Press, 2002), 37–148; William J. Reese, *America's Public Schools: From the Common School to "No Child Left Behind"* (Baltimore, MD: Johns Hopkins University Press, 2005), 79–117; Herbert M. Kliebard, *The Struggle for the American Curriculum, 1893–1958,* 3rd ed. (New York: RoutledgeFalmer, 2004); and Lawrence A. Cremin, *The Transformation of the School: Progressivism in American Education 1876–1957* (New York: Random House, 1961). Though not all titles listed above are pure histories, each provides unique, vital insights into the impact of the progressives echoing into the future.
2. Reese, *America's Public Schools*, 80.
3. Ibid., 83–84.
4. Ibid., 88.
5. Ibid., 90.
6. Egan, *Getting It Wrong from the Beginning*, 15.
7. Beatrice Webb, *My Apprenticeship* (1926; reprint, Harmondsworth, UK: Penguin, 1971), 50–51.
8. Egan, *Getting It Wrong from the Beginning*, 15.
9. Herbert Spencer, *Essays on Education, etc.*, introduction by Charles W. Eliot 1911 (London: Dent, reprint 1928), 62.
10. Ibid., 63.
11. Cremin, *The Transformation of the School*, 19.
12. Kliebard, *The Struggle for the American Curriculum*, 32–33.
13. In seeking to agree on such uniform curricular expectations, the Committee of Ten provided a key opponent around which to organize for "new education" loyalists. In *Left Back: A Century of Battles over School Reform* (New York: Touchstone, 2000), historian Diane Ravitch singles out the Committee of Ten's report as oft-used by "new education" (and later Progressive Education) reformers in their arguments as it "gave rise to myths about the American public high school in the late nineteenth century [as an] . . . aristocratic institution, devoted solely to those who were preparing for college." Ravitch then goes on to show how many such myths were actually untrue (Ravitch, *Left Back*, 48).

14. Kliebard, *The Struggle for the American Curriculum*, 23–25. Though membership in any of Kliebard's compartments can overlap, of course, and the dividing lines blur somewhat (between the meliorists and developmentalists, for example, who believe a developmentally appropriate curriculum leads to a more socially just society; many other combinations can be imagined), Kliebard's grouping of three main idea-sets standing opposed to the humanists is a keen and useful arrangement.

15. Ibid., 27.

16. David F. Labaree, *The Trouble with Ed Schools* (New Haven, CT: Yale University Press, 2004), 157–58.

17. In addition to his philosophical writings, Dewey began the University of Chicago Laboratory School to implement and study learning theories, a model that was duplicated across multiple U.S. sites still in operation today.

18. Kliebard, *The Struggle for the American Curriculum*, 27.

19. Though *Experience and Education*, from 1938, also belongs to Dewey's education oeuvre, Cremin describes it as having at the time "little fundamentally new" (Cremin, *Transformation of the School*, 237). It is generally not seen as one of Dewey's Progressive Education idea-catalyzing works as it takes some swipes at the Progressive movement and because the movement was already well underway by the time of its publication.

20. Then-president of the Herbartians, Charles DeGarmo, actually viewed this challenge—a specific debate, in particular, at the 1895 meeting of the National Education Association in Cleveland—as the turning point between traditional and "new" methods of education. See Kliebard, *The Struggle for the American Curriculum*, 15–17.

21. Ibid., 45.

22. John Dewey, *Dewey on Education: Selections*, ed. Lawrence A. Cremin (New York: Bureau of Publications, Teachers College, Columbia University, 1959), 25.

23. Ibid.

24. Cremin, *The Transformation of the School*, 123.

25. Again, for brevity's sake and to not much longer delay our central arguments, comprehensive profiles of these reformers and their innovations will not be launched here. For more information, consult the many excellent histories referenced throughout this chapter.

26. Cremin, *The Transformation of the School*, 221.

27. William H. Kilpatrick, "The Project Method: The Use of the Purposeful Act in the Educative Process," *Teachers College Record* 19 (September 1918), http://historymatters.gmu.edu/d/4954/.

28. Ibid.

29. Ibid.

30. Cremin, *Transformation of the School*, 216–17.

31. Ibid., 240–41.

32. Egan, *Getting It Wrong from the Beginning*, 5–6.

33. John Dewey, "Individuality and Experience," *Forgotten Heroes of American Education: The Great Tradition of Teaching Teachers*, ed. Jo Wesley Null and Diane Ravitch (Greenwich, CT: Information Age Publishing, 2006), Kindle edition (quotation is in paragraph 9 of the essay).

34. Cremin, *Transformation of the School*, 234–35.

Chapter Four

A Meaningless Engagement

Gripping and enduring interests frequently grow out of initial learning efforts that are not appealing or attractive.

—William Chandler Bagley (1874–1946), American educator, in the October 1941 *Journal of the National Education Association*

The Progressive Education movement grew from a set of European-based philosophies about human nature into a set of pedagogical practices that, combined with the Gilded Age's power-wary zeitgeist and the burgeoning organization and professionalization of teachers, gained the inspirational appeal and professional consensus necessary to turn over the funnel of American education. But why did they do it, exactly?

Beneath the movement's complex philosophical layers and political motivations, the Progressives' objectives were simple. In short, the pedagogical side—led by John Dewey, Herbert Spencer, William Heard Kilpatrick, and others—sought a public education experience that wasn't so darn boring, difficult, and indifferent to individuals with diverse needs.

Progressives challenged the traditionalist education establishment of their time, believing it to be obsessed with building knowledge, skills, and dispositions essential to living effective lives and replenishing American institutions. Progressives objected to the idea that any such knowledge, skills, and dispositions should be deemed essential without any regard for the student's perspective. They believed the traditionalists' preferred structures of learning environments, activities, and methods were out of step with children's natural, exploratory impulses. Think desks in rows. Teachers—not students—doing all the talking. Hours spent practicing certain operations or memorizing certain facts. Students rarely given opportunities to express themselves. Believing there was no way children could effectively learn under such conditions, the Progressives wanted to undo this kind of drudgery.

According to their own educational experiences, Progressive Educators knew that humans invest increased effort and learn new things more effectively when they feel personally invested in and connected to tasks. The thought-works of Spencer, Dewey, and their disciples legitimized this view. So, Progressive Educators set out to create an education system that elevated individual student preferences in the planning of instruction. In numerous ways and at every level of the educational enterprise, efforts grew to put each child—not consistent content-proficiency or any particular set of social outcomes—at the center of educational practice. And in order to best teach each child, the thinking went, practitioners needed to know how each child would most effectively become *engaged* in their own learning.

Much as you may despise or be tired of discussions about how to build student engagement to learning, know that it all basically started right here.

This central idea places a high premium on learning experiences students will find engaging. It recommends ways to engage students more deeply by turning learning choices and decisions over to students themselves. From the time of the Progressives until now, almost no instructional stone has been left unturned to better engage students based on their preferred actions and/or developmental abilities.

Kilpatrick's project method provides the implicit foundational ideal for untold numbers of engagement-building academic activities. In it, the student-determined "purposeful act" becomes the center of instructional activity to drive student motivation, exploration, and understanding (or, per Kilpatrick, "readiness"). Since this method's introduction, the idea of the "purposeful act" has provided the basis for countless instructional activities, all hoping for more genuine student engagement or investment in content-learning tasks. Modern educators would say that such instructional choices are based in a *constructivist* approach to teaching and are intended to tap students' *intrinsic motivation*. These two terms were not used by Dewey or Kilpatrick but they sprouted directly from their works.

These kinds of instructional adjustments vary wildly in depth and frequency across the classrooms of American education. A few examples follow to illustrate how U.S. educators alter instructional activities to make them more engaging to greater numbers of students and thereby not, as Kilpatrick would have it, "effectually quench the glow of thought."[1]

- As students are observed disengaging from learning activities based in works from the traditional literary canon ("Dude, Shakespeare is *so* boring"), practitioners remove rigorous canonical selections from Language Arts curricula. To build a lifelong love of reading in students, educators replace canonical and/or generally more challenging works with more accessible, lower-rigor texts or, in many instances, texts chosen by the students themselves ("Dude, *The Walking Dead* is totes a GRAPHIC NOVEL").

- To more effectively engage students in the study of science, schools offer more hands-on instructional activities to replace textbook-driven communication of science concepts.
- In order to replace the "transmission" model of learning social studies content, students complete projects—constructing posters, board games, or electronic slideshow presentations, for example—based on individually assigned or student-selected topics around a particular theme.
- Hoping to build students' comfort with math and their engagement in math-related activities, elementary school teachers substitute two blocks of math instruction per week with "Math Game Time." In these new game blocks, students choose between games with other classmates and games played independently on computers.
- To create classroom environments in which more students will follow expected standards of behavior, teachers allow students to cowrite classroom rules. In theory, each child's deeper personal stake in the classroom's ultimate orderliness—not simply imposed from outside the student by the teacher—will increase students' individual engagement to behaving as desired/expected.

In other settings, adding occasional activities that feature inquiry-based, project-based, or student-selected approaches is not considered sufficiently engaging. On this end of the student-engagement continuum, entire schools' fundamental structures and operations (i.e., scheduling, physical layout, student groupings, course requirements/offerings, etc.) are designed to enable comprehensively more genuine and more individualized student engagement. Open schools and Montessori schools, for example, are full-school models of such engagement-building that, in order to maximize students' self-direction and self-initiated learning, greatly alter the structures, routines, and expectations found in traditional settings.

Similarly, a number of U.S. public charter schools organize around the objective of maximizing student engagement. And like Montessori and open schools, they do not hesitate to strip away traditional school structures and operations to realize this goal. Some charters are designed around a specific theme (e.g., performing arts, the environment, technology, etc.) to attract and engage students who share these interests.

In order to meet student preferences regarding traditional schooling environments and expectations, some sectors in American education are in fact doing without the traditional schooling environment *altogether*. Fully online schools, where students receive instruction and complete coursework at a self-determined pace via the Internet, operate in many districts. In fact, these schools are seeing enrollments skyrocket, which is pushing traditional schools to expand online course offerings.

Preoccupation with student engagement also affects instructional practice. Some schools seek to engage students by differentiating instruction according to each student's ability and learning preferences. In differentiating instruction, practitioners prepare lesson content in ways that will satisfy numerous learning modalities, styles, and intelligences.

The terms "learning modalities," "learning styles," and "intelligences" are derived from the work of developmental psychologist Howard Gardner. In his 1983 *Frames of Mind: The Theory of Multiple Intelligences*, as well as subsequent works, Gardner proposes that humans possess nine discrete intelligences: visual-spatial, verbal-linguistic, logical-mathematical, bodily-kinesthetic, musical-rhythmic, interpersonal, intrapersonal, naturalistic, and existential. According to the theory, all nine intelligences exist to some extent in each of us, but particular intelligences develop more strongly than others owing to heredity, early training, and other factors. But each individual defaults to the strongest intelligence when processing and understanding new phenomena.[2]

To differentiate effectively, then, teachers must present material in a range of formats to satisfy the various default intelligences in a given room. Hoping to understand their classrooms more deeply, some teachers even begin their courses by having students complete "learning style inventories" to obtain a class-wide profile of preferred learning styles.[3] Such profiles ultimately permit the teacher to alter content delivery in ways to better match their learners' identified preferences.

Teachers in these environments also adjust assessments according to students' learning styles and ability levels. Through continual systems of differentiated assessments to ascertain what their students know and understand, teachers adjust instruction and content to provide experiences that are appropriately rigorous and engaging.

Whether it dominates schooling models or is sprinkled throughout programming, the student-engagement ideal prevails across the educational enterprise. This ideal urges practitioners to adjust instruction according to each student's individual abilities and preferences. This is what American education aspires to make manifest, and the enterprise will go to just about any length to make it happen.

Since the time of the Progressives, prioritizing student engagement in learning and learning through so-called "constructivist means"—also known as "student-directed," "student-determined," "student-discovered," or "student-hands-on"—reigns unquestioned as a best pedagogical practice. It's an idea first instilled in practitioners during training/licensure programs, then reinforced continually throughout each teacher's professional experience.

Children learn best by doing, children learn best when they are personally interested, children learn best when they use their imagination, and all the rest.

It is such a pillar of Progressive conventional wisdom that it's doubtful many educators would admit, even if they truly believed it, that other objectives—a strong academic curriculum, for example, or the construction of student work and social habits—should take priority over students' preferences and interests when making instructional decisions.

Here is a particularly telling example of how widely and deeply the constructivist student-engagement ideal is embedded: their widespread inclusion in both professional-evaluative rubrics of teachers and widely adopted standards of effective teaching practices. The construction and implementation of such rubrics and standards, intended to quantify effective teaching in a more objective and reliable way, have risen sharply in recent years, sparked by high-profile, well-publicized research about the relationship between effective teachers and student achievement.[4]

As the *improvement of teacher quality* has emerged as a major reform effort, many states have mobilized resources—and even enacted legislation—to systematically strengthen teacher-evaluation criteria and processes. To unprecedented degrees, states have mandated and overseen the teacher evaluation process at multiple levels. From observation protocols to recommended standards of teaching practice to numbers of required observations per year and beyond, a growing number of states are effectively taking the evaluation of teaching professionals out of the hands of schools and school districts.[5]

Though no national standard of effective instruction is currently in use, teachers' student-engagement-building practices—usually aligned with constructivist ideals—are regularly featured in evaluation systems. The Charlotte Danielson Framework, for example, is a teacher-evaluation system of criteria and processes adapted for use in numerous urban school districts (including megadistricts like New York City, Chicago, and Los Angeles) and across entire states. It sends administrators into classrooms to look for evidence that teachers are engaging students according to student-directed, student-determined guidelines.

In the instructional domain (Domain 3) of the Danielson Framework's 2013 Evaluation Instrument, for example, a full component is dedicated to "Engaging Students in Learning" and is described as "the centerpiece of the Framework for Teaching." For observers gathering evidence in classrooms, indicators that a teacher is successfully engaging students include "Student enthusiasm, interest, thinking, problem solving, etc." and "students highly motivated to work on all tasks and persistent even when the tasks are challenging."

What is most interesting, however, is that observed degrees of students' initiative, self-direction, and expression are ultimately used to determine a teacher's level of effectiveness on Danielson's "Engaging Students" scale. In other words, for a teacher's rating to progress up and up through this domain element's levels of performance, students must be observed exercising more and more control of the classroom environment. (If we take this to a logical extreme, the perfect Danielson teacher is one who does no actual teaching whatsoever.)

To move from "Proficient" to "Distinguished," for example, the separating descriptor is that students will move from "invited to explain their thinking as part of completing tasks" (Proficient performance level) to "taking initiative to improve the lesson by (1) modifying a learning task to make it more meaningful or relevant to their needs, (2) suggesting modifications to the grouping patterns used, and/or (3) suggesting modifications or additions to the materials being used" (Distinguished performance level). Similar student-centered indicators of student-engagement practices are also sought out in performance-level progression in the Danielson Framework's domains 1 (Planning and Preparation) and 2 (The Classroom Environment).[6]

Throughout the Danielson Framework and adaptations of it, the message is clear: while all teachers are expected to bring their students into learning, *great* teachers involve students by getting them to help determine matters of behavior, learning activities, content, and all the rest—while never, of course, losing control of the classroom.

The administrative professionals who select systems like the Danielson Framework do so because they believe these practices are keys to greater success for all the students in their school, district, or state. Having defined effective teaching for all students according to their ideals, the Progressives must be rejoicing.

NO SHORTCUTS: STUDENT ENGAGEMENT THE HARD (AND PRODUCTIVE) WAY

Clearly, student engagement is important. Students should feel engaged in what they are learning and with the tasks and expectations of schooling. A sense of engagement can provide great motivation toward completion and mastery. Engagement encourages higher levels of individual satisfaction and happiness in these tasks, even when the task in question might not be inherently satisfying. Truly, then, it is beyond admirable, when planning learning activities, to explore and activate engaging options along the lines of each child's abilities, preferred learning styles, and interests.

Following constructivist learning theories and doing whatever it takes to engage students is also, unfortunately, not always in each child's best interests. Here's why: engaging activities that lack academic rigor (and do not promote academic growth) are essentially worthless from an institutional-preparatory perspective. Flatly, the systemic expectation to engage students first is too often achieved at the expense of academic rigor and is a major force keeping the funnel of American education upside-down.

Top-performing education systems in other nations—even those routinely cited by U.S. education commentators as models to emulate—are acutely aware of how crucial it is to dial standards of rigor consistently high. To achieve the results that made these nations education superpowers, most did not seek to modify schooling or content to engage more students or make consumption easier. Quite the opposite. Many of these nations earned superpower status after *elevating* standards. They did not pursue magic engagement techniques. They made school *harder*. And their students rose, on average, to the new standard.

So how, the Progressive Educator might ask, did they keep their kids and families *engaged* in the face of expectations that would make all their lives more difficult, expose kids to failure, and require students to master content they don't find intrinsically interesting?

It's a surprisingly simple formula, according to Amanda Ripley's 2013 account, *The Smartest Kids in the World: And How They Got That Way*. After studying and visiting countries that have either consistently topped international measurements of academic aptitude or made impressive growth on these measurements in short periods of time, Ripley found that the systems in question basically do three things:

1. Make school count, usually via mandatory, high-stakes tests prior to graduation.
2. Make school academically challenging.
3. Stick with it.

In contrasting Finland's, South Korea's, and Poland's educational approaches to that of the United States, Ripley noted one difference in particular: each nation's acceptance of what school was for and that school was meant to be hard work. "I started to notice one fundamental theme," she wrote.

> [E]veryone—kids, parents, and teachers—saw getting an education as a serious quest, more important than sports or self-esteem. . . . The fundamental difference was a psychological one. [Korea and Finland] believed in rigor. People in these countries agreed on the purpose of school: School existed to help students master complex academic material. That clarity of purpose meant everyone took school more seriously, especially kids. The most important difference . . . was the drive of students and their families. It was viral, and it mattered more than I'd expected.[7] . . . High school in Finland, Korea, and

> Poland had a purpose, just like high-school football practice in America. There was a big, important contest at the end, and the score counted. . . . [After studying these countries,] [o]ne thing was clear: To give our kids the kind of education they deserved, we had to first agree that rigor mattered most of all; that school existed to help kids learn to think, to work hard, and yes, to fail. That was the core consensus that made everything else possible.[8]

Bucking the engagement-first ideal, more and more American schools are realizing just what Ripley observed across multiple continents and committing to make it come to life within their walls.

National charter organizations like the Knowledge Is Power Program (KIPP), SABIS, and BASIS, as well as many other independents, are re-elevating expectations. Not surprisingly, they are also recording admirable results on everything from state proficiency exams to their students' college-acceptance and college-completion rates, often among populations that have historically found themselves on the wrong side of the achievement gap.[9]

Somewhat predictably, however, these charters also raise concern among some Americans. These charters, often located in American inner cities, frequently couple elevated academic expectations to a "no excuses" model of school culture that includes strict discipline standards and highly prescribed routines. Multiple critics—from Furman University professor P. L. Thomas[10] to many indignant bloggers[11]—accuse the charters of everything from child abuse to modern-day colonialism to Jim Crow revivalism.

The results, however, are indisputable. Controversial "no excuses" practices of aggressively wrangling student behaviors, attitudes, and habits into forms that will help them master complex academic work are successfully channeling more students into post-K–12 institutions. And having gone through these experiences, students emerge from these charters with more viable options and better readiness for mainstream-institutional expectations. Very simply, these schools' funnels are right-side-up.

In some ways, "no excuses" practices help schools like KIPP and others make up for the essential difference between the countries Ripley studied and the United States: a genuinely high-stakes culmination of the experience. Finland, Korea, Poland, and many other countries increase students' engagement by requiring rigorous finishing exams (Finland's, for instance, takes *fifty hours* over three weeks to complete[12]) that have a direct bearing on each student's future. Today, America offers nothing close to this.

For standardized tests enacted under No Child Left Behind, the stakes are far higher for schools than for students. College-entry exams like ACT and SAT are optional, too; and most students not planning on post-secondary study opt out. Even for the college-bound, these scores constitute only one criterion for admission. They are not make or break. And while it's true some states have attempted to embed minimum required graduation standards into exams, these are usually geared to very basic levels, and students get multiple chances to demonstrate mastery.

In several states, even these kinds of minimum requirements for earning diplomas are considered too drastic. Public blowback has made many states question if they're worth all the trouble. Ripley recounts Oklahoma's struggle with this decision in *The Smartest Kids in the World*, for instance.[13] Minnesota, too, recently eliminated embedded minimum-toward-graduation requirements in its year-ending accountability tests.[14]

Let's look at this from the student's perspective. They are required to attend school. But there is no clear, important outcome. They are not working toward an event; they are working toward a document that will either be simple or impossible to attain. It's easy to see why so many U.S. students tune out from work that either challenges them past the point of comfort or does not, in their view, apply to their lives in any meaningful way. In turn, it's easy to see why schools would respond to this dynamic by adjusting schooling to meet student expectations instead of the other way around—and why, when schools take "no excuses" approaches, so much dust gets kicked up. As a society, we have come to accept that schools should provide minimal resistance to students and, ideally, cater to students' individual needs and desires.

This isn't working.

This is the upside-down funnel, both in practice and result.

But why? Why does engaging first and teaching second create the opposite of what it intends?

THE CASUALTIES OF CONSTRUCTIVIST ENGAGEMENT THEORIES

The first and most obvious casualty of constructivist, engagement-first education is students' knowledge of content. When learning activities seek to engage first and put teaching second, the engagement-building exercises themselves too often become the sole focus. The original objectives of content and skill mastery are postponed, forgotten, and lost.

Recall the examples of how engagement-first learning activities might look in a number of academic disciplines. Each of these examples—which can be found readily in any U.S. school—are wonderful options for keeping students engaged. Learning experiences like these can complement the central subject matter, bringing concepts together into a fuller, more complete understanding and appreciation of the topic at hand.

But there is a risk. Unless properly balanced with more intensive academic activity (taught more explicitly and directly, too, for students experiencing difficulty), engagement-first activities shortchange students. Learners are engaged, but they miss out on attaining the academic competencies the activities were designed to transmit.

To demonstrate how the balance can tip, let's focus more closely on one example: the Language Arts classroom that opted to assign larger amounts of high-interest/low-rigor texts in response to students' flagging engagement. However enthusiastically students read and respond to these more popular selections, the choice of reading assignment raises a number of practical questions related to schooling's mission to preparing all students for the post-K–12 world.

First, where in this course will students get outside their comfort zone? Where will they encounter the challenge of texts that surpass their current reading ability and subject matter expertise? College classes tend to emphasize texts that do exactly this. For that matter, so does life after K–12, college or not. Whether reading news stories or job applications or bank statements or insurance forms or reports prepared by a coworker or many other examples routinely encountered in the public sphere, students will be required to make sense of fairly rigorous texts that may not be immediately engaging but are nevertheless critical to their economic and social well-being.

Second, assuming that the high-interest/low-rigor work was chosen in order to fortify students' love of and stamina for reading, will those intended qualities—if students achieve them—be sufficient to power students through assignments that are more challenging and textual analyses that are more rigorous? How will the teacher monitor and make certain that students are attaining such slippery, nebulous concepts as "love of reading" and "reading stamina"?

Third, is it fair to these students (and their future selves) to delay exposing them to high-quality learning experiences with challenging but universally recognized great works of literature? If we deny students opportunities in an environment where professional supports *are already in place to help them* through the inevitable struggles with comprehension and effective analysis, are we limiting their future options? When standardized college-entry exams require them to read and respond to a highly complex passage, will they be sufficiently prepared to record scores that will allow them to compete for admission at a wide range of schools? Or will they be stuck with whatever college will have them?

Finally, if these students choose never to read a book again (and recent research shows as many as one in four of American adults not reading a book in more than a calendar year[15]), which books would teachers want them to have already read? Which will serve them best in the world after schooling?

Some teachers might respond that they have tried to teach more "classic" selections but the effort fell flat. Students wouldn't read the novel or threatened outright revolt. But after adjusting to lower-rigor texts, the situation improved. More students began to cooperate, participate, and actually seem to enjoy class.

The same dynamic is at work when engagement-first adaptations are made in science, social studies, and math coursework; theme-based charter schools; and the like. Once activities are made more hands-on, more project-oriented, and/or more problem-solving in nature, students are more engaged and more likely to participate.

Increased interest in schooling's expectations and activities should absolutely be considered partial victories, especially if class sessions up to that point had been derailed by student inactivity or full-on struggles between teachers and disruptive students.

But at what cost? What are they actually engaged in?

If we sacrifice the student's understanding of target academic concepts for the sake of engagement, then the engagement is an empty and (literally) meaningless gesture with respect to schooling's mission to make all students ready for post-K–12 realities.

When the educational funnel is right-side-up, student satisfaction in the moment is less important than the ability to demonstrate a clear understanding of content and skills. Anything else, it has been shown, actually moves students further away from—not closer to—post-K–12 readiness. The work of educational psychologist Richard E. Clark makes this quite clear. Clark, who identified and analyzed a number of instructional practices that actually *hurt* students' short-term and long-term learning, points out, "No matter if students preferred less guided methods, they learned less from them."[16]

Any science-like activity, after all, does not necessarily package science concepts or promote understanding in ways expected by post-K–12 settings. The same applies for *any reading experience*, *any project relating to social studies*, and so on. If the instructional activity is dialed down to accommodate students' current levels of interest and readiness, it absolutely does not prepare them for what they will face later. Ultimately, it is failing the students it is hoping to assist. Lowering the bar is not helping. It is delaying the inevitable.

A PERILOUS, BLIND IDEALISM

Current educational theory holds two fundamentally flawed assumptions:

1. More genuine investment is all students need to succeed.
2. Genuine investment can be engaged by limiting guidance, reducing cognitive resistance, and eschewing more direct teaching approaches.

These assumptions reveal an educational enterprise that is perilously idealistic. Within various tasks and intended subject-matter understandings, some students—particularly those with larger learning gaps—will need substantially more than increased motivation or personal connection to achieve success.

However engaged or passionate a student may become about concepts of physics, for instance, she will not be able to fully understand or apply them without a reliable command of certain mathematics. However interested a student may become in the history of World War II after a field trip or film clip, he will struggle to understand his new interest if his reading abilities are profoundly limited. Though these students may be able to remain engaged through expectations differentiated to their limitations, the education enterprise fails them when it does not lift them to the genuine understanding they deserve.

To provide this lift, class time and teacher expertise/support (not to mention considerable amounts of educational funding) used for myriad minimally guided engagement-building activities must be repurposed. This time, expertise, and funding would all be much better spent in directly addressing crucial learning gaps where identified and arranging for additional student practice toward mastery. This is especially important in children's earlier grades, before more fundamental gaps become too large to feasibly close.

While studies confirm that more student-centered, indirectly academic attempts to engage students are desirable for learners who are more advanced, substantial research has also confirmed the limitations of these methods for novice learners, suggesting they are the *polar opposite* of what is needed when a student approaches a new concept or struggles to grasp it. Fervent constructivists would strive to design more engaging learning activities in which students are to discover, then construct, authentic and individualized meanings. Multiple studies, however, have shown that more direct, explicitly instructive approaches are much more effective for learners who are new to concepts.[17]

This may seem obvious. But American education has long preferred to believe otherwise. When the methods and ideals first rolled out by Progressives in the late nineteenth and early twentieth centuries are contradicted or come under attack today, professional educators dig in deep to defend them. Or, rather, having little empirical evidence to actually defend these methods and ideals, the education establishment chooses simply to ignore evidence contrary to Progressive ideology.

In addition to discounting standardized tests of proficiency and college/career-readiness that clearly show current approaches and aspirations are not working for all students, advocates of Progressive methods also ignore more objective, scientific evaluations of practice. Take Gardner's theory of multiple intelligences, for example. It is widely considered a scientific engine that can power more individualized instructive approaches. But under actual experiment, it collapses into pseudoscience.[18] Yet the educational enterprise still endorses it. Put another way, this enterprise pretty much believes what its Progressive ideals lead it to believe.

The educational enterprise's use and practical application of a study like Project Follow Through provides another instructive example of its tendency to, in the words of University of Oregon education professor Doug Carnine, have "less respect for evidence than for opinion or ideology."[19] "The world's largest educational experiment," Project Follow Through sought "to break the cycle of poverty through improved education"[20] by studying reams of data collected from nearly two hundred school sites over thirty years (the project began in 1967 and wrapped up in the mid-1990s).

According to Project Follow Through's prodigious evidence, Direct Instruction displayed considerable promise. Developed by the University of Illinois's Siegfried Engelmann in the 1960s, Direct Instruction is a model of teaching that is decidedly more explicitly guided than models favored by Progressives or constructivists. While many other models in the study (which also included constructivist favorites like whole language, open education, and developmentally appropriate practices, among others) had close to zero—and even *negative*—effects on student outcomes, students learning under Direct Instruction's principles of pedagogy recorded growth in basic skills, on deeper comprehension measures, and on social measures. Over longer periods, Direct Instruction–taught students also earned higher scores in mathematics and reading and were twice as likely to graduate from high school.

Project Follow Through could have altered practices forever, or at least caused practitioners to question long-held beliefs. It should have done both. But it did neither. All it really accomplished was justifying more resources for the demonstrably ineffective methods the study's teachers preferred and wished to expand.[21] To this day, Project Follow Through findings are almost never referenced in education professionals' discussions of best practices.

In addition to compromising students' academic achievement, widespread adherence to engagement-first principles is creating false expectations about mainstream-institutional participation. In American schools, students' needs and preferences are gauged and attended to incessantly. The educational enterprise aspires to *meet its students where they are*, effectively absolving students of any individual responsibility and setting them up for devastating "expectation shock" in the world beyond their K–12 education.

Expecting to be entertained during—or simply steered past—some of the more tedious parts of working or learning, disappointed young Americans are currently frustrating a nation of middle managers. They frequently cite a lack of engagement as the reason for poor performance or the choice to quit.

And though every generation of rookie employees frustrates mainstream institutions' veterans to some degree, the most recent one—the "millennials" or "Generation Y"—seems uniquely baffling.

Conduct a Google search of "millennials workplace," "millennials work habits," or "millennials work ethic," for example, and results will return in the dozens of thousands. Demand is high for answers that might help workplace leaders get a handle on this most recent product of American education. The stories themselves cover a wide spectrum, from "things you should know about motivating your millennial employees" to "myths about millennials" (usually written by millennials, by the way) to pretty much everything in between. All are alike, however, in how they attempt to explain this new, alien breed of worker: compared to Baby Boomers or even Gen X-ers, millennials present a weird, troubling stew of strengths, motivations, and expectations.

Similarly frustrating characteristics are seen in post-secondary education. Mark Bauerlein, professor of English at Emory University and former director of research and analysis at the National Endowment for the Arts, is a scholar who has observed and questioned millennials' readiness for post-K–12 institutions. His analyses correctly pin a good share of what makes millennials so frustrating on American schools.

Bauerlein's 2008 book *The Dumbest Generation: How the Digital Age Stupefies Young Americans and Jeopardizes Our Future*, in addition to detailing how this newest generation is unprepared in terms of essential cultural knowledge, skills, and intellectual habits, spends a chapter ("The Betrayal of the Mentors") taking the millennials' elders—schools very much included, of course—to task for failing to help millennials build proper values.

The first value Bauerlein trains his criticism on is one with a distinctly Progressive fingerprint. (Bauerlein even references the writings of G. Stanley Hall, another of Progressive Education's leading early voices.) It's the idea that "a successful adolescence and rightful education entail growing comfortable with yourself"—that "adolescence has claimed an independent value, an integrity all its own."[22] In Bauerlein's view, the main problem with nurturing this value is that children will, over time, develop senses of self that are fully disassociated from the heritages they are joining and—ideally—strengthening for the future.

In a later piece for *Education Week,* based in Bauerlein's first-hand experience with recent college students, he points out how this attitude manifests itself in students' classroom work habits and expectations. Namely, he notes a disturbing tendency toward checking out or quitting when subject matter does not reach the student's ideal interest threshold—and that today's students believe they have full license to not only declare what's worth persisting in but also walk away without consequence from whatever subjects don't turn their crank, so to speak.

Cross-listing this tendency with data from studies conducted in 2006, 2009, and 2010 (by public policy firm Civic Enterprises, Indiana University's Center for Evaluation and Education Policy, and research firm Public Agenda, respectively) of student engagement and performance, Bauerlein connects the same dots suggested here: that this essentially self-centered mindset "raises a disturbing concern about the relevance of student engagement at the high school level. In adjusting curriculum and pedagogy to student interest," Bauerlein continues, "educators may . . . stunt students in preparation for the next level of their education. In telling them, 'You think the material is pointless and musty, but we'll find ways to stimulate you,' high school educators fail to teach them the essential skill of exerting oneself even when bored, even when the material has no direct bearing upon one's future."[23]

To be fair, carping about millennials' work and post-secondary educational habits may come off as stodgy. *Kids* these days! They may seem like a grumpy old coot's garden-variety generational complaints: things were better in the old days, young people today don't know how hard we all had it, they had better buck up and fall in line like we had to, and so on. These concerns, however, come from a much deeper place than pure old-fogeyism.

The concerns originate from the undeniable fact that lots of U.S. kids are failing. They are failing in schools and failing after their schooling, with or without diplomas. To halt the growing divide between America's haves and have-nots, the educational institution must be as equalizing as possible. Though schools have long prioritized and built operations around young people's personal engagement, believing it to be a prime enabler of academic success, the results have not borne this out. At all.

By several accounts, it appears more as though the institution of American education is preparing children for a world it wishes to see, and not the one that truly is. We hear all the time about yet another measure pointing out the mismatch between our students' preparatory experience and the institutional realities they ultimately face. Meanwhile, other nations—and growing numbers of U.S. schools—have been honest with themselves about what schooling is for and have structured themselves accordingly. Most critically, students from these schools routinely outpace average results generated by American education.

However plain this may be (and however plainer still when viewed through the lens of scientific evaluation), the institution of American education refuses to loosen—much less cut—its tether to Progressive ideals and methods. Neither flagging student results nor the lack of empirical proof seem to be effective deterrents. Some Progressive-inspired advocates see these outcomes as proof that schools simply haven't tried hard enough; they actually demand deeper and wider implementations of Progressive ideals/practices.[24]

The divide continues to grow. America's "have-not" students spend much of their school career being coaxed into engaging with learning (and not necessarily learning what will help them academically or institutionally), while the "have" students, pre-engaged in school tasks by virtue of birth into an alignment with mainstream institutional expectations, receive the academic rigor that will propel them into rewarding post-secondary study and lucrative careers.

At the very least, U.S. graduates (and non-graduates) must understand and accept the expectations of mainstream institutions, and they must be prepared to meet these expectations. If these two conditions are not being met—and copious statistical and anecdotal evidence would indicate they are not—then the multitude of engagement-building practices aren't working. At least, they aren't working well enough to effect meaningful changes in the lives of students and the institutions that need them to survive.

In other words, engagement-first practices are about as upside-down as it gets. Effective funnels route material into receiving vessels, catching material at the edges and bringing it safely to the middle. American education, preferring to engage students where they are, does not catch anyone or move them anywhere.

When the funnel is upside-down, the only material with a good chance of making it into the receiving vessel is that which started out on the right course in the first place. With the mouth of the funnel facing downward, away from the pouring container(s), all other material, sadly, is left to spill down the sides.

Considering the institutional mis-preparation of this "other material," it should not come as a great shock that routine indices of post-K–12 institutional success (e.g., standardized measures of academic proficiency,[25] college dropout/completion rates,[26] employment figures[27]) often show the "spilled" students lagging behind their privileged peers. Having gone to schools so committed to engaging learners that actual learning was abandoned, these students really had no other choice.

To prepare individuals for success in the world after K–12, educators must acknowledge and emphasize this world's actual expectations and parameters—even if it means de-emphasizing the individual. The international education systems written about by Ripley do this through high-stakes assessments that can't help but infuse all of school with direct meaning.

As long as the United States resists a similar effort, it must find ways to build post-K–12 awareness and direction among students without resorting to lowering academic or behavioral expectations. U.S. schools employing "no excuses" structures and practices pull students toward these expectations and are seeing promising results, but they are likely not an appropriate answer for all. Not every school can institute "no excuses" systems, but these guiding philosophies can tell us all a lot about the *types of adjustments* we must make to create a regularizing, rigorous, and right-side-up education.

NOTES

1. William H. Kilpatrick, "The Project Method: The Use of the Purposeful Act in the Educative Process," *Teachers College Record* 19 (September 1918), http://historymatters.gmu.edu/d/4954/.

2. Howard Gardner, *Frames of Mind: The Theory of Multiple Intelligences*, 3rd ed. (New York: Basic Books, 2011), 294.

3. Such inventories can be found readily in educational resource materials. Perhaps indicative of their wide use and high demand, a Google search of the term "learning style inventory" (in January 2014) returned nearly 2.5 million results—many offering free, printable learning style quizzes for practitioners to use with their students.

4. Steven Cantrell and Thomas J. Kane, *Ensuring Fair and Reliable Measures of Effective Teaching: Culminating Findings from the MET Project's Three-Year Study*, MET Project/Bill & Melinda Gates Foundation, January 2013, http://www.metproject.org/downloads/MET_Ensuring_Fair_and_Reliable_Measures_Practitioner_Brief.pdf.

5. For more information about what states are requiring in their teacher-evaluation systems and how comprehensively each state is evaluating its teachers, see Jim Hull, "Trends in Teacher Evaluation: How States Are Measuring Teacher Performance" (Alexandria, VA: Center for Public Education, 2013), 20–22.

6. Charlotte Danielson, "2013 Framework for Teaching Evaluation Instrument," The Danielson Group, 2013, http://www.danielsongroup.org/userfiles/files/downloads/2013EvaluationInstrument.pdf.

7. Amanda Ripley, *The Smartest Kids in the World: And How They Got That Way* (New York: Simon & Schuster, 2013), 116–18.

8. Ibid., 193–94.

9. Much has been written about "no excuses" schools like KIPP, SABIS, and BASIS. For more information about positive results being generated, see Joy Resmovits, "Mathematica 2013 Study: KIPP Charter School Students Outperform Public School Peers," *Huffington Post*, February 27, 2013, http://www.huffingtonpost.com/2013/02/27/mathematica-2013-study-kipp_n_2768476.html?utm_hp_ref=@education123; Mary Ann Zehr, "KIPP Middle Schools Found to Spur Learning Gains," *Education Week*, June 22, 2010, http://www.kipp.org/files/dmfile/EdWeek_6_22_10_PDF.pdf; SABIS Educational Systems, *Closing the Achievement Gap—2013* (Eden Prairie, MN: SABIS Educational Systems, 2013), http://www.sabis.net/downloads/systems-brochures/closing-the-achievement-gap-2013-the-sabis-experience.pdf. For more on BASIS, see Ripley's *The Smartest Kids in the World*, 197–98.

10. P. L. Thomas, "Education Reform in the New Jim Crow Era," *Truthout*, May 17, 2013, http://truth-out.org/opinion/item/16406-education-reform-in-the-new-jim-crow-era.

11. For samples, see Russ Walsh, "Colonialism in the Inner City: Charter School Discipline Practices," *Russonreading* blog, October 6, 2013, http://russonreading.blogspot.com/2013/10/colonialism-in-inner-city-charter_6.html; Jonathan Pelto, "Child Abuse in the Form of the 'No Excuses' Education Model," *Wait What* (blog), October 4, 2013, http://jonathanpelto.com/2013/10/04/child-abuse-form-excuses-education-model.

12. Ripley, *The Smartest Kids in the World*, 156.

13. Ibid., 185–86.

14. Joe Nathan, "Did Different Standards Help Increase Minnesota's High School Graduation Rate?" *Hometown Source* (ECM Publishers), February 20, 2014, http://hometownsource.com/2014/02/20/joe-nathan-column-did-different-standards-help-increase-minnesotas-high-school-graduation-rate/.

15. Pew Research Center, "Americans' Reading Habits over Time," *Pew Research Center RSS*, June 25, 2013, http://www.pewresearch.org/2013/06/25/library-readers-book-type/.

16. Richard E. Clark, "When Teaching Kills Learning: Research on Mathemathantics," in *Learning and Instruction: European Research in an International Context*, Vol. 2, ed. H. N. Mandl, N. Bennett, E. de Corte, and H. F. Freidrich (London: Pergamon, 1989), 1–22. Referenced in John Hattie, *Visible Learning: A Synthesis of Over 800 Meta-Analyses Relating to Achievement* (London: Routledge, 2009), 243.

17. For suggestions of multiple relevant studies on this topic, see Paul A. Kirschner, John Sweller, and Richard E. Clark, "Why Minimal Guidance during Instruction Does Not Work: An Analysis of the Failure of Constructivist, Discovery, Problem-Based, Experiential, and Inquiry-Based Teaching," *Educational Psychologist* 41, no. 2 (2006): 78–81. See also Ken Rowe, "Effective Teaching Practices for Students with and without Learning Difficulties: Issues and Implications Surrounding Key Findings and Recommendations from the National Inquiry into the Teaching of Literacy," *Australian Journal of Learning Disabilities* 11, no. 3 (2006): 99–115.

18. Harold Pashler, Mark McDaniel, Doug Rohrer, and Robert Bjork, "Learning Styles: Concepts and Evidence," *Psychological Science in the Public Interest* 9, no. 3 (2008): 105–19.

19. Douglas Carnine, *Why Education Experts Resist Effective Practices (And What It Would Take to Make Education More Like Medicine)* (Washington, DC: Thomas B. Fordham Institute, 2000), http://www.edexcellence.net/sites/default/files/publication/pdfs/carnine_9.pdf.

20. Bonnie Grossen, "The Story behind Project Follow Through," *Effective School Practices* 15, no. 1 (Winter 1995–1996), http://pages.uoregon.edu/adiep/ft/grossen.htm.

21. Hattie, *Visible Learning*, 258.

22. Mark Bauerlein, *The Dumbest Generation: How the Digital Age Stupefies Young Americans and Jeopardizes Our Future, *Or, Don't Trust Anyone under 30* (New York: Jeremy P. Tarcher/Penguin, 2008), 168.

23. Mark Bauerlein, "The Paradox of Classroom Boredom," *Education Week*, August 6, 2013, http://www.edweek.org/ew/articles/2013/08/07/37bauerlein.h32.html.

24. For example, thinkers like Alfie Kohn (who continually preaches that the United States *has not gone Progressive enough* on issues ranging from engagement to homework to standardized testing to modes of content delivery and on and on) are some of American education's most popular and referenced thought leaders/speakers/authors. (For a more complete list of Kohn's preferred topics—and to view his very full calendar of speaking engagements—see http://www.alfiekohn.org.)

25. To illustrate the impact across two large demographic categories, income level and race/ethnicity, two references are suggested here. To review a five-year range (2008–2012) of discrepancies in ACT performance by student income level, see ACT, Inc., *The Condition of College & Career Readiness: Low Income Students* (Iowa City: ACT, 2012), http://www.act.org/newsroom/data/2012/states/pdf/LowIncomeStudents.pdf. For comparisons by race/ethnicity, see Allie Grasgreen, "ACT Scores Fall to Lowest Level in Five Years," *Inside Higher Ed*, August 21, 2013, http://www.insidehighered.com/news/2013/08/21/act-scores-fall-lowest-level-five-years. Three demographic groups that historically struggle similarly in the United States would include students with programmatic designations like English Language Learners, Special Education students, and Homeless/Highly Mobile.

26. For analysis of college degree completion by income level, see Tami Luh, "Income Gap Continues to Affect College Graduation Rates," *CNNMoney*, November 21, 2011, http://money.cnn.com/2011/11/21/news/economy/income_college/. For an analysis of college degree completion by race/ethnicity, see Duncan Hsu, "U.S. College Graduation Rates by Race by State," *EdPond—Education Pondered*, April 23, 2012, http://edpond.blogspot.com/2012/04/us-college-graduation-rates-by-race-by.html.

27. For unemployment disparities between black Americans (who are historically underserved in U.S. education via low academic expectations) and white Americans over time, see Brad Plumer, "These Ten Charts Show the Black-White Economic Gap Hasn't Budged in 50 Years," *Wonkblog* (blog), *Washington Post*, August 28, 2013, http://www.washingtonpost.com/blogs/wonkblog/wp/2013/08/28/these-seven-charts-show-the-black-white-economic-gap-hasnt-budged-in-50-years. Plumer's analysis also contains several intriguing data sets comparing employment figures over time for multiple U.S. races/ethnicities, trends in segregated-school enrollment, and so forth.

Chapter Five

Building Skyscrapers on Sand

> You wish to be great, begin from the least. You are thinking to construct some mighty fabric in height; first think of the foundation of humility. And how great soever a mass of building one may wish and design to place above it, the greater the building is to be, the deeper does he dig his foundation.
>
> —St. Augustine of Hippo (354–430), early Christian theologian

Read the passage below and answer the questions that follow.

We couldn't get weak lead going because the 5 was slanting into B at the snap, with Will pressing the alley hard and Mike reacting to flow. We decided to make four changes:

1. The PST invited the 5 across-face and washed down through B.
2. On a combo with the C, the PSG released up to Mike when sure the 2i couldn't get penetration.
3. H showed B but then was to banana weak and cover—sealing inside, if there was leverage—Will.
4. T threatened B but bounced hard weak just before PST's heel marks, hopefully to get Mike to step B, at least deep enough that (1) PSG could get there and get position or (2) the trash from PST-5 would knock off and alter from path.

If these four things could happen against the look we got, we were confident that we could get the corner for big gains.

POST-READING QUESTIONS

1. What is the above passage describing? What is its main idea?

2. Draw a diagram to represent the changes the narrator made in order to solve the problem described in the passage.
3. Based on your answer to #1, infer the following: Who is likely narrating the passage? What is his/her field of expertise?
4. In your judgment, are the changes the narrator made effective for solving the issue faced? Explain why or why not.
5. On a scale of 1–10, rate the level of confidence you have in your responses to questions 1, 2, and 3.
6. Make a list of any words, acronyms, and/or phrases from the passage that you find confusing or that you need better definitions of to make you more confident of the passage's meaning.

Try using this passage and questions with teacher or administrator workshops for improving reading instruction. Together, they illustrate the important relationship between a reader's background knowledge and the reader's ability to comprehend text.

What you may notice right away is that the sample passage does not contain much domain-exclusive technical vocabulary.[1] However confused many readers find themselves while working through the passage, it's not because they don't know the raw meanings of the words. For anyone reading at a fourth-grade level or above, the only mysteries are the acronyms (*PST*, *C*, etc.). Aside from these, the passage includes words adult readers know very well: *snap*, *five*, *banana*, *will*, *trash*, and so on.

What makes these words confusing is the context. In the passage, familiar words become meaningless. In workshop groups where this exercise has been used, participants have confessed to being so rattled by the context that, despite several re-readings, they couldn't even get through the first sentence with any confidence. "Is the narrator talking about getting weak *lead* like rhymes with *bead*?" they ask. "Or does *lead* rhyme with *bread*? Without knowing that, I couldn't find anything to grab onto."

These thinkers certainly have nothing to be ashamed of, because this passage intentionally leaves them to dangle. Reading in this highly specialized context, the only spark that could possibly infuse the vocabulary with useful meaning is some (and, in this case, more than some) background knowledge about the subject at hand. Without this knowledge, the narrator's use of familiar words gets canceled out by the sheer amount of content understanding he/she assumes the audience already has.

In case you're wondering, the passage is narrated by a football coach describing a series of mid-game adjustments his offense made to counter a defensive strategy deployed by the opposing team. The familiar words having their common meanings erased, then, have been re-purposed for footballese: *lead* (rhyming with *bead* here, incidentally) is the name of the play, *snap* is the center-quarterback exchange, *banana* is the curve-shaped path the indicated player must follow in this particular adjustment, *Will* is the defense's weak-side linebacker, *2i* is a term denoting the weak-side defensive tackle's alignment, and so on. (And yes, this is just how coaches speak to one another. If you're skeptical, eavesdrop sometime on a varsity high school locker room's halftime meeting.)

In most real-world reading experiences, writers typically leave similarly large contextual gaps for the sake of presenting lean arguments and evidence. Without some assumption of the reader's understanding, all writing would be packed with so many definitions, clarifications, and examples that it would seriously test the reader's patience.

Because the gaps in this particular passage are so huge, the combined reading-related expertise of all the adults in these literacy workshops doesn't help them comprehend the text. Even if they can get to a general sense of the main idea (i.e., the narrator is describing a problem he/she faced and the adjustments made to overcome it), true comprehension about the problem and the adjustments simply isn't possible.

The point is that context, or background knowledge, does so much of the work in reading comprehension that its absence can literally *erase meaning* from words most readers already know.

The intent of this exercise is not to irritate workshop participants who are not familiar with football vernacular. Rather, it is to encourage discussion of some important philosophical and practical questions.

For instance, considering how crucial relevant context is to accurate, meaningful comprehension of text, why do we dedicate so little of our reading-instructional time to building readers' background knowledge?

And isn't it strange that we *devalue* knowledge-building as a "lower-order thinking skill," coasting past it while urging students toward "higher-order" act-of-reading strategies and activities such as making inferences and/or predictions, divining and/or evaluating main ideas, and making cross-textual and/or text-to-self connections?

Also, are we losing students when our reading-instructional preferences and choices omit knowledge building? Considering which students will fall the furthest behind without additional background knowledge (namely, those coming from homes less likely to have already provided the basics), are we failing to serve these students?

Finally, if background knowledge is so powerful that its absence will easily confound college-educated, professionally certified adults, why do we make it such a low priority in our work with younger, inexperienced readers?

Finding answers to these questions is difficult for many practitioners, precisely because they have been taught to focus on coaching act-of-reading skills instead of building background knowledge.

This phenomenon is not unique to reading instruction. Due to the fact that the upside-down funnel of instructional practice emphasizes higher-order-thinking theories of learning, these constructivist theories drive instructional models across all academic disciplines. Whether teachers are organizing leveled groups for "Balanced Literacy" programs like Reader's Workshops, urging students to describe their mental processes as part of a Thinking Mathematics lesson, coaching students to Think Like a Historian, or coordinating Inquiry-Based Science experiments, foundational skills and thought considered "lower-order" are typically skipped over as a matter of (so-called) "best practice."

Few in the education establishment would challenge this type of practice ("It is simply *sound pedagogy*!"). The passion for these theories is fierce, imbuing them with the power to persist despite *scant proof that they do what they are supposed to do*. When proven ineffective, they even have a terrifying zombie-like habit of rising from the dead with different names.

This is another practical expression of education's upside-down funnel. Specifically, Progressive philosophies of learning that de-emphasize the building of foundational skills and capacities have a devastating impact on short- and long-term learning potential.

LOWER ORDER = *ESSENTIAL* ORDER

Any educator practicing today will be familiar with Bloom's Taxonomy, the intellectual skills categorization compiled by academic Benjamin Bloom in the mid-1950s. Commonly used to make instructional decisions in appropriate sequence, the cognitive domains of the taxonomy are divided into six levels of skill.[2] From least to most difficult, these levels are:

Knowledge (Remembering)—recall data or information

Comprehension (Understanding)—understand the meaning, translation, interpolation, and interpretation of instructions and problems; state a problem in one's own words

Application (Applying)—use a concept in a new situation or unprompted use of an abstraction; apply classroom learning to novel workplace situations

Analysis (Analyzing)—separate material or concepts into component parts to understand its organizational structure; distinguish between facts and inferences

Synthesis (Creating)—build a structure or pattern from diverse elements; put parts together to form a whole, with emphasis on creating a new meaning or structure

Evaluation (Evaluating)—make judgments about the value of ideas or materials[3]

Bloom's arrangement came with the caveat that mastery of its lower or more basic levels must be demonstrated *before* progressing into the higher or more complex levels. In many instructional choices, however, this important warning is downplayed or ignored. Though the levels of the taxonomy are not intended to represent a hierarchy of value, many practitioners make this assumption: the first level is the least valuable, the sixth is the most. As a result, they choose to focus more energy on the "better" levels (often referred to as "higher-order thinking" or "critical thinking" skills) than on the levels they characterize as overly simplistic—the rote-learning faculties outlined at the lower end.

This is plainly ridiculous. Is "species" inherently superior to "family" in the biological taxonomy? Is a molecule more important than an electron? Is a state better than a city? Clearly not. Nevertheless, scores of educators design individual activities—entire terms and years of curricula, even—around just such false value judgments, often spurred on by education advisory groups and think tanks.[4]

The workshop exercise described earlier was adapted from the work of educational thinkers who have been questioning this misapplication of Bloom's Taxonomy for the past two and a half decades. Many have offered ideas that so oppose the establishment's Progressive ideology that their work has had difficulty finding traction. Sadly, individuals emphasizing the importance of the taxonomy's earlier levels are often dismissed as hyperbolic handwringers from the "back-to-basics" cult—stubborn dead-enders seeking to "drill and kill" children into robots, who are woefully out of touch about how children learn, or driven by ultraconservative politics.

As difficult as it is for non-Progressive views to gain acceptance among practitioners, it's made worse by influential education-advisory organizations (like the Partnership for 21st Century Skills [P21]) and resource groups (like the George Lucas Educational Foundation/Edutopia).[5] Their interference amplifies Progressive notions about learning, though usually not through research that verifies the effectiveness of these practices. Rather, they rely on claims about the future: what it will be like, what it will want from us, and how our current practices are not aligning with it. P21, in particular, wants America's students to do more group work, design more community-based projects, and participate in more technologically based instruction that will better prepare them for the needs of the twenty-first century[6]—a time when, they assure us, institutions will be looking for new kinds of learners and thinkers.

The first chapter of Bernie Trilling and Charles Fadel's book-length P21 white paper, *21st Century Skills: Learning for Life in Our Times*, provides an effective illustration. To give readers an appropriate grasp on their current lives and times, Trilling and Fadel provide a quick tour of quaint agrarian- and industrial-societal realities before reaching the infinitely connected wonderland of the twenty-first century: a magical place where all previous rules cannot apply—one that demands professional and personal skills that old ways of teaching could never provide.[7]

Though they don't go so far as to call knowledge-building obsolete, they give it little more than a brief glance in the learning priorities they envision:

> To be a productive contributor in our 21st century, you need to be able to quickly learn the core content of a field of knowledge while also mastering a broad portfolio of essential learning, innovation, technology, and career skills needed for work and life. And when you apply these skills to today's knowledge and innovation work, you are participating in a global network in which, for example, a product may be designed in California, manufactured in China, assembled in the Czech Republic, and sold in chain stores in cities across the world.[8]

Note how the authors breeze past "quickly learning the core content of a field of knowledge" in order to giddily get to the "broad portfolio of . . . skills . . . for work and life." This passage is indicative of the messages constantly hammering American educators and citizens. It's the way knowledge-building has been portrayed since the time of the Progressives: simple stuff that was important to schools of bygone eras but just isn't suitable for our times. The authors insist that while raw knowledge-building once served its purpose, a modern world with built-in shortcuts to huge stores of information doesn't much need people who know lots of things. The only way this brave new world can run efficiently, according to influential organizations like P21, is if schools provide the proper training toward highly critical thought and creative capacity—not all that outdated, fact-based stuff.

In this culture, you can see how difficult it is for concepts like "don't ignore lower-order intellectual capacities" to be given serious consideration. (Or heard at all, for that matter.) Between future anxiety and the historical heft of Progressive ideals and practices, any answer arising from a more traditional source is instantly branded as backward. It's a reality that, when viewed in the light of the past three decades of cognitive science, is woefully unfortunate, if not a touch ironic.

In the late 1980s, E. D. Hirsch, an English professor turned education scholar (and eventual founder of the Core Knowledge Foundation), caused considerable controversy when he suggested that American students were lagging behind those in other nations[9] because educators had an unhealthy preoccupation with teaching skills over knowledge. Hirsch's *Cultural Literacy: What Every American Needs to Know* turned nearly eighty years of accepted pedagogical wisdom and reform rhetoric on its head, positing that in the rush to prepare graduates for the future, American education had underestimated the necessity of content knowledge.

Hirsch argued that strong content knowledge is the crucial active ingredient in thinking processes from reading comprehension to forming critical judgments to producing original creative work. Because of this, the key to fixing much of what wasn't working in education would not be found in some innovative model of teaching or schooling, but rather in the past—a past that once dedicated considerably more energy toward knowledge-building.

Among those who built careers deriding knowledge-building as obsolete or inappropriate for today's learners and tomorrow's world, Hirsch's ideas were, rather obviously, not warmly received.[10] Even those who disagreed, however, found Hirsch's supporting evidence difficult to dismiss out of hand because he bucked education thinkers' typical rhetorical pattern. Eschewing idealistic intuitions and observations/surveys of educators and students, Hirsch rested his arguments on supports provided by neighboring fields of scholarship.

Namely, he relied on recent research about how humans learn from cognitive science and from the then-emerging field of artificial intelligence (AI), which had been working to re-create human reasoning with computers. The work of such scientists, Hirsch concluded, "should induce a deep skepticism toward the belief that our schools can teach reading, writing, and critical thinking as all-purpose general skills applicable to novel problems."[11]

The more the AI researchers studied humans, Hirsch said, the more they were able to observe content experts outperforming content novices "not because they have more powerful and better oiled intellectual machinery but because they have more relevant and quickly available information."[12]

At the time, Hirsch's ideas were ignored, dismissed, and resented. Since then, however, knowledge-building advocates have continued to study and publish. In recent years, perhaps no such advocate has attracted notice like cognitive scientist Daniel Willingham. Commanding a multimedia presence that includes newspaper and education journal articles, blogs, videos, and multiple books, Willingham has breathed new life into Hirsch's central premise with a healthy dose of common (and scientifically supported) sense.

Using the current understanding of how humans learn (which, unlike others, he freely admits is incomplete) as his platform for informing educators' pedagogical choices, Willingham takes on topics from the cognitive processes of effective study[13] to debunking the purported cognitive impacts of vendors' latest instructional aids.[14]

On the importance of factual knowledge to later learning and critical thinking, Willingham's *Why Don't Students Like School*, published in 2009, clearly echoes Hirsch circa 1987:

> Data from the last thirty years lead to a conclusion that is not scientifically challengeable: thinking well requires knowing facts, and that's true not simply

> because you need something to think *about*. The very processes that teachers care about most—critical thinking processes such as reasoning and problem solving—are intimately intertwined with factual knowledge that is stored in long-term memory (not just found in the environment).[15]

Using the quarter-century's worth of study between his work and Hirsch's, Willingham digs further beneath the surface than Hirsch was able to in *Cultural Literacy*. Though he confirms the assertions Hirsch made based on AI research, he elaborates by explaining some processes that have been scientifically verified since Hirsch's early work.

He cites a 2006 study of expert chess players by cognitive-scientific researchers from Cambridge University, for instance, that showed the act of problem-solving to be almost solely a function of one's long-term memory stores (how well stocked and efficiently accessed they are, to be more precise), not a skill that can be learned, practiced, and sharpened in isolation.[16] He also breaks down how cognitive scientists explain efficient decision making (chiefly as a matter of accessing working memory efficiently[17]) and how, by increasing the number of connection-ready cues to new pieces of information, increasing one's factual knowledge actually improves one's memory.[18]

For a moment, let's set aside all of the data, research, and scholarly examinations. Anyone reading this can use personal experience to verify Hirsch's and Willingham's points about the necessity of background knowledge for original critical thought.

Think of a time when you fell behind on a significant news topic. When you tried to catch up, you likely encountered multiple levels of frustration: TV pundits discussing the issue constantly referred to events and ideas that were unfamiliar to you. Colleagues and friends, all versed at varying levels, fuzzed your understanding with contradictory bits of information and analysis. Even your independent, Internet-assisted research attempts did not go smoothly, because an appropriate starting point and a view of the total timeline were difficult to pinpoint.

If you've ever hung in there to become an expert on a topic after arriving late in the game, you are (in addition to being a remarkably driven person with a very strong personal connection to the subject) a walking testament to the necessity of background knowledge with respect to making sense of new information in a personal and critical way. You know firsthand just how difficult it is to slog through an overwhelming amount of fact and opinion to know enough to form your own opinion. More important, you know that you would never have arrived at your superior understanding without knowledge of the issue's origins, evolution, and nuances.

The Relationship of Bloom's Lower-Order Abilities to Effective Reading

Education's lack of emphasis on foundational intellectual blocks is hindering American learners' future critical and analytical capacities. But that's not all that's going on. Cognitive scientific studies are also showing troubling repercussions at the most fundamental levels of education. Specifically, cognitive science continues to find evidence that, just as with critical thinking, the ability to read effectively depends very heavily on explicit teaching, practice, and mastery of word-sound awareness (or phonics/phonemic awareness) in one's early reading years as well as the amount and depth of the content knowledge one possesses.

This may seem like common sense. But many of our nation's teachers would disagree. The past century of American education has run away from this kind of thinking, even when it is backed by empirical evidence.[19] Instead, many of today's schools respond to sagging reading scores with a purely skill-building approach that moves from organic in the early grades to downright robotic in the upper grades. All the while, the ideal refuses to become reality.

Across U.S. education, it's difficult to find early-grade educators who believe that focusing on the "raw materials" of reading—such as phonics for decoding and a broad base of knowledge for comprehension—is the right way to build effective readers. Commonly, early-grade teachers utilize "Reader's Workshop" instructional formats to accomplish the following tasks: emphasize act-of-reading skills good readers use as they read, like "making text-to-text, text-to-self, and text-to-world connections" and regularly making text-based inferences; enhance students' confidence as readers through high-interest, "just right" (and often student-selected) texts; monitor students' proficiency in discrete reading skills and coach as necessary through difficult patches; and move students through levels to offer progressive challenges in reading and idea complexity as they exhibit promotion-readiness.

Working within these frameworks, individual students who lag behind their peers or do not reach pre-established benchmarks continue on in lower reading groups and receive more intensive skill-building exercise. When larger groups or entire schools full of students fall short of benchmarks, a common adjustment is to severely truncate—*or eliminate altogether*—time spent building general knowledge through subjects like social studies and science, so students can spend more time working on act-of-reading skills.[20]

When their confidence fails to appear and their love of reading stubbornly refuses to blossom, the neediest students are tracked into remedial reading classes and placed in front of computers (and/or unlicensed tutors) as interventions. Here, they continue to work intensively with expensive, time- and resource-inefficient software packages that drill them with mind-numbing—and often statistically fruitless[21]—act-of-reading exercises like locating main ideas, sequencing, and summarizing.[22]

As you may have guessed, one of E. D. Hirsch's most important contributions to the field was explaining the connection between the student's general knowledge bases and reading skill. He writes in *Cultural Literacy* that working with college students in the 1970s first piqued his interest in the "widening knowledge gap" and its impact on the students' overall effectiveness as learners. Intrigued by the negative effects this lack of knowledge was having on his students' abilities to understand texts, he chose to turn away from his primary research interest at the time (relative readability in composition) to study the knowledge gap more closely.[23]

What he found was that the two preceding decades' worth of research on reading comprehension had converged to define reading as a more complex and active process than many at the time considered it to be. To effectively decode the words in a piece of text or understand a text's different components, Hirsch said, is but "the tip of an iceberg of meaning; the larger part lies below the surface of the text and is composed of the reader's own relevant knowledge."[24]

In his 2006 *The Knowledge Deficit: Closing the Shocking Education Gap for American Children*, Hirsch illustrates this statement by leaning on the findings of educational psychologists studying the actual mental mechanisms of reading comprehension and recall:

> One elegant experiment was conducted to find out how important domain-specific knowledge is in actual reading tasks. . . . In two of the four groups studied, one had good decoding skills but poor knowledge of the subject, baseball, while the poor-decoding group knew a lot about baseball. As predicted, the reading comprehension of the low-skills, baseball-knowing group proved superior to the reading comprehension of the high-skills, baseball-ignorant group for that particular text. These results have been replicated in other situations and knowledge domains and show the powerful effect of prior knowledge on actual reading skill.[25]

Not surprisingly, Daniel Willingham has piled on to Hirsch's ideas in recent years, energizing the conversation with his cognitive-scientific credentials and his choice to deliver ideas through online channels. A YouTube video called "Teaching Content Is Teaching Reading"[26] takes just under ten low-impact, witty minutes to explain the key points detailed in the "Knowledge Is Essential to Reading Comprehension" section of his 2009 book.[27]

Willingham may be most often cited, however, for a 2009 blog post titled "Reading Is Not a Skill—And Why This Is a Problem for the Draft National Standards," which was written for *The Washington Post*'s online education commentary page *The Answer Sheet*.[28] The post took on the then-fledgling national core reading standards (more about those in chapter 6), and it has practically become the stuff of legend among pro-knowledge-building edu-wonks.[29]

In the post, Willingham asserted that, by setting standards based on the idea of building students' act-of-reading and reading-comprehension skills, the drafters had basically created a path to reading failure. The issue, according to Willingham,

> is that teachers and administrators are likely to read those . . . standards and to try to teach to them. But reading comprehension is not a "skill" that can be taught directly. We tend to teach comprehension as a series of "reading strategies" that can be practiced and mastered. Unfortunately it really doesn't work that way. The mainspring of comprehension is prior knowledge—the stuff readers already know that enables them to create understanding as they read. Prior knowledge is vital to comprehension because writers omit information. . . . A writer who doesn't assume some prior knowledge on the part of her readers will write very boring prose.

However reluctant American educators and writers of education standards may be to embrace this idea, reading researcher Tom Sticht claimed in a 2011 article that the American Armed Services have been aware and respectful of the difference between individuals' general reading ability and possession of specialized knowledge for years. In fact, he said, the Armed Services Vocational Aptitude Battery (ASVAB), given to scores of American high school students each year, purposefully scores and considers reading ability and general knowledge separately in an effort to place future service members appropriately. Dividing the two proficiencies was a continual consideration, he said, in professional development work he and his colleagues handled for the Navy. Working to build sailors' reading ability and career-progression knowledge concurrently, Sticht and his colleagues developed separate assessments to gauge each. And upon analyzing the results, they found that

> with low background Navy knowledge, a person needed a general reading ability of about the eleventh grade to comprehend with 70 percent accuracy. But highly knowledgeable personnel needed only a sixth grade level of general reading to comprehend Navy-related material with 70 percent accuracy. In this case, then, *high levels of background knowledge substituted for some five grade levels of general reading ability.* (Emphasis not in original.)[30]

And what of U.S. schools that subscribe to right-side-up ideas like Hirsch's, Willingham's, and Sticht's? Do these schools, after widening their instructional funnels to give students with less background knowledge stronger foundations, actually generate the kinds of results promised?

Karin Chenoweth, education researcher and senior writer for the Education Trust, singles out several of these schools in two books about achieving academic success in the face of long demographic odds.[31] One of the educators featured in these works is principal Valarie Lewis, who led the 96 percent minority/90 percent poor Osmond Church Middle School in Queens, New York, to reading and math scores that soundly outpaced state averages in all demographic subgroups. Lewis openly credits the Hirsch-driven Core Knowledge curriculum as key to her school's dramatic, historically unlikely success.

Before implementing Core Knowledge, Lewis said, it was precisely the "knowledge gap" Hirsch describes that hindered the progress of students and teachers: "Teachers were teaching 150 percent but they weren't getting the results. The children weren't strong readers. They didn't have the background knowledge—up to the point of not knowing what animals they liked. Teachers would teach skills, but if [the children] didn't have background knowledge, it didn't stick."[32]

This kind of success has been seen on a wider scale as well, and has even been measured directly against pure skills-building approaches to reading. In 2008, desperately reaching for a reading instruction platform that would cost-effectively increase proficiencies across his city, New York schools chancellor Joel Klein launched an experiment to test Core Knowledge's potential. He paid for Core Knowledge materials and training in a handful of city schools, then embarked on a three-year measurement of those schools' results compared to demographically similar schools using the predominant Balanced Literacy/Reader's Workshop model. "After the first year," wrote columnist Sol Stern in the *New York Daily News*, "the kindergartners in the Core Knowledge program had achieved gains five times greater than those of students in the control group. The second-year study showed that the Core Knowledge kids, now in first grade, made reading gains twice as great as those of students in the control group."[33]

Some may dismiss the work of Hirsch and the Core Knowledge Foundation as "lower order" and out of step with twenty-first-century realities. But thinkers like the twenty-first-century-skills-advocating Linda Darling-Hammond have repeatedly lauded Core Knowledge schools for their educational promise. Bucking the persistent and pernicious myth that Hirsch/Core Knowledge returns students to a short-sighted, limiting brand of "back-to-basics" instruction, Darling-Hammond has written favorably of how well Core Knowledge schools support sophisticated thought with broad knowledge foundations. "They are living proof," Darling-Hammond says,

> that strong disciplinary (and interdisciplinary) learning is not at odds with the development of twenty-first-century skills, such as problem solving, critical and creative thinking, the capacity for independent learning, reflection, and

> communication. Indeed . . . aside from the uses of new technologies, most of these skills have been central to the definition of a well-educated person for centuries, although they are in higher demand in today's economy.[34]

The Relationship of Bloom's Lower-Order Abilities to Mathematical Understanding

Just like reading comprehension, math instruction has been dominated by a constructivist philosophy of how young people learn. From the perspective of constructivist math proponents, teachers should not be overly concerned with students finding answers. Rather, teachers should guide students toward transferrable understanding of the processes and concepts working beneath the surface of correct answers, preferably through self-discovery.

In the early grades, constructivist math teachers avoid moving students toward memorized mastery of math fundamentals (e.g., numerical sense and operational automaticity), urging students instead to explore and understand how the operations work. They lay out challenges and encourage students to problem-solve before discussing basic-level procedures, all the while reminding students to continually verbalize or describe in writing the procedures they're executing.

Constructivist math teachers avoid funneling students toward any standard way of doing math. (Among these teachers, incidentally, the phrase "standard algorithm" is treated with a level of disdain that borders on the pathological.) Instead, they focus on teaching multiple possible calculation strategies, having students work through problems using each one and, after students have found their individual "best fits," encouraging each individual to choose and permanently adopt the strategy that works best. They show no answers, but rather coax students toward solutions through sequences of questions designed to help students verbalize their thinking.

Traditional methods of math instruction, on the other hand, seek first to have students master basic processes and work up to applying these processes in more and more complex problems. Constructivist math teachers hold off on standard arithmetical work until students have had ample opportunities to explore. The ultimate goal is not to apply mathematical operations toward mathematical problem-solving. Rather, constructivist math aims for students to truly understand *how numbers work*, and it strives for them to demonstrate their understanding through written, verbal, and graphic representations alongside more traditional math problems.

Accordingly, drill-based practice to achieve mastery of basic facts of addition, subtraction, multiplication, and division is strictly de-emphasized. In the constructivist frame, this practice does not allow students to truly *learn* mathematics. As constructivist math educators view stored facts as only having been memorized to satisfy timed tests, they consider any facts learned through memorization to be impotent and useless in novel, applicative problem-solving environments.[35]

Constructivist mathematics advocates have often been challenged on this stance by defenders of traditional methods. These defenders argue that history is filled with traditionally educated math experts who have solved unthinkably complex problems of science, engineering, finance, and on and on. And indeed, society would have never reached its current technology-dependent, Higgs-boson-confirming, deep-space-exploring state without generation after generation of traditionally taught math specialists applying their gifts to novel problems.

Based on their understanding of how children learn, however, constructivists believe we can do better. Conceding that history has produced many mathematical leaps and powered almost exclusively by traditional instructional methods, constructivists maintain that these same methods have left many, many students feeling disinvited from succeeding in math.

At bottom, then, constructivist math educators' chief aspiration is a methodology capable of reaching more students—one that will produce even more of the advanced problem-solvers who have helped civilization progress. If these methods are faithfully applied, constructivists say, they will drastically slash the number of students who, frustrated with all the "drill and kill" tactics used to learn "mere facts," check out of math early on and never come back.

Although this is a noble idea, little proof exists that constructivist methods are yielding the intended results. In fact, these efforts may actually be slowing the progress of potential pace-setters and leaving behind more of the kids they originally aspired to help.

Progressive/constructivist principles have influenced American math instruction for a century. Their broad acceptance as best practice has accelerated in the past two-and-a-half decades, spurred by the National Council of Teachers of Mathematics (NCTM)'s 1989 publication, *Curriculum and Evaluation Standards for School Mathematics*. Since that work was published, best practices for math instruction have urged more problem-solving, more emphasis on deep conceptual understanding, and markedly less preference for direct instruction of math facts and algorithms previously favored as "standard."

Math-instructional reforms set in motion by *Curriculum and Evaluation Standards* triggered a violent backlash from many U.S. professors of mathematics. Taking shots at the NCTM's reform efforts from bunkers like scholarly journals, legislative hearings, and grassroots websites (mathematically-correct.com and wheresthemath.com, to name two), these critics argued that the new terminologies, procedures, and objectives outlined by NCTM were—despite the intent to create a more inclusive, engaging, and immediately applicable study of mathematics—actually out of step with the demands of entry-level college math.

Further, the critics argued that while "reform math" might help keep students engaged throughout their elementary and secondary years, it was setting them up for certain, costly failure once they reached college. Once over the collegiate threshold, students of reform math would be ill prepared and consequently required to complete remedial math courses (read: no-credit, full-cost) to reach minimum college proficiency.

The controversy became particularly heated in the late 1990s and early 2000s, after the U.S. Department of Education officially endorsed *Curriculum and Evaluation Standards*–based curricula. A month following a 1999 U.S. Department of Education report designating ten "exemplary" or "promising" math programs, a group of four prominent mathematics professors (and more than two hundred cosigners, including Nobel laureates and Fields Medal recipients) coauthored an open letter to then-Secretary of Education Richard Riley urging him to withdraw his recommendations. The group was so concerned about the situation that they got funding from the Packard Humanities Institute to publish the letter as a full-page ad in the *Washington Post*.[36]

Also, a 2000 paper by three academics from outside mathematics—from Carnegie Mellon's psychology department, that is—branded the constructivist reforms as lacking "genuine empirical support" and "based in large part on folk psychology."[37]

Academic objectors were energized at the local level, as well. Early in 2001 Lawrence Gray, a professor of mathematics at the University of Minnesota and the director of undergraduate studies, went before the Minnesota state legislature to share his concerns about the reforms' effects on the students and families that he and his colleagues worked with daily. Speaking before the Higher Education and Public Policy Joint Committee, Gray argued against the new curricula. He suggested it would be unwise for secondary schools to turn their backs on traditional math courses, first because these courses traditionally produced great successes for technology- and science-inclined students; and second because so little reliable data existed to justify replacing them.

Echoing the Carnegie researchers and fortified by his practical experiences with frustrated undergraduates and their parents, Gray had little reason to believe in the promise of the so-called New Math. "While the content and emphasis found in 'integrated math' courses have almost universal support within the math education academic community," Gray said, "they are viewed with widespread suspicion among scientists, research mathematicians, and engineers. In our disciplines, we expect our students to be comfortable with basic mathematical skills, both with and *without* calculators. Indeed, we find that the students that have the most difficulty in our courses are typically those that are weak in this area. But recent trends in K–12 math education put low priorities on these kinds of skills."[38]

Having no ironclad proof that the shifts they had encouraged were worth it, the NCTM was ultimately unable to stem the criticism from science and mathematics professionals or the mounting frustration of other critics.

The Council decided to backtrack. First, it issued the 2000 *Principles and Standards for School Mathematics* (*PSSM*). Though the 402-page revision of *Curriculum and Evaluation Standards* included some of the balance the Council's critics demanded, it left most cold. One of these was math professor Bill Quirk, who maintained that NCTM was still missing the point. After reviewing the revised standards he claimed the pervasive lack of focus, specificity, and measurability actually disqualified them from being considered standards at all. Worse, he charged that the goals stated in *PSSM* were more related to sociology and psychology than they were to genuine math.[39]

NCTM's next step backward included returning the dreaded "standard algorithms" to 2006's *Curriculum Focal Points*,[40] which newspapers like the *Chicago Sun-Times* equated with "the council [admitting], more or less, that it goofed."[41]

The flap ultimately resulted in President George W. Bush's formation of the National Mathematics Advisory Panel in 2006. Tasked with getting to the heart of American students' sinking math performance with respect to both international comparisons and the demands of American industry, the panel ultimately concluded that the NCTM's inquiry-based approach lacked the strength to turn results around by itself.[42]

It is hard to pinpoint exactly why the constructivist approach to math falls short. Its focus on problem-solving and student ownership of concepts is admirable. Indeed, much of what the approach emphasizes appears to align directly with the proficiencies emphasized by current assessments, content standards, and American industry. The only problem is it doesn't get results.

Conclusive proof of success simply has never surfaced, leaving advocates to either retreat (as NCTM has since 1989) or pass the buck to instructional front-liners like teachers and administrators. When challenged, constructivists tend to rely on excuses much like those deployed by mid-twentieth-century Progressive Educators, maintaining that the methods are fine; it's the inability (or refusal) of practitioners to implement them properly—or practitioners' substandard mathematical proficiency—that is ultimately to blame for the lack of positive empirical evidence.[43]

The battle isn't over. As the wars rage on about the best ways to teach math, however, researchers in the field of cognitive science continue to uncover more learner-based reasons why constructivist mathematical instructional methods tend to fall flat. Much like the works of Daniel Willingham, E. D. Hirsch, and others related to reading, scientists studying how humans understand math find that working memory (i.e., solidity of content knowledge and facility accessing it) plays a critical role when we perform complex mathematical tasks.

A 2006 study by researchers Paul Kirschner, John Sweller, and Richard Clark, for instance, points out more precisely how constructivist approaches to mathematics instruction hinder meaning making. They do so by requiring

> the learner to search a problem space for problem-relevant information. All problem-based searching makes heavy demands on working memory. Furthermore, that working memory load does not contribute to the accumulation of knowledge in long-term memory because while working memory is being used to search for problem solutions, it is not available and cannot be used to learn. Indeed, it is possible to search for extended periods of time with quite minimal alterations to long-term memory. . . The consequences of requiring novice learners to search for problem solutions using a limited working memory or the mechanisms by which unguided or minimally guided instruction might facilitate change in long-term memory appear to be routinely ignored. The result is a set of differently named but similar instructional approaches requiring minimal guidance that are disconnected from much that we know of human cognition.[44]

Sadly, the consequences repeatedly pointed out by Kirschner, Sweller, Clark, Hirsch, Willingham, Sticht, and others remain widely ignored by American education's practitioners and leaders. Hoping to accelerate student performance with respect to established content standards and motivated by industry leaders' demands for a fluidly reasoning, innovative workforce, current practitioners and leaders continue to turn their instructional funnels upside-down, pushing students faster and more intensely toward the upper levels of Bloom's Taxonomy—levels that, it must again be pointed out, are not inherently more important than the levels that precede them.

Despite all the evidence cognitive researchers present about the importance of sturdy learning foundations for upper-level cognition, and despite how well right-side-up approaches work, most people in education believe they can build cognitive skyscrapers on sand. Clinging doggedly to the idea that "rote memorization of facts," "viewing children as passive knowledge containers," and "drill-and-kill exercises" will surely stunt children's personal and academic growth, they reject anything that even comes close to knowledge-building or skill-reinforcing drill—then find themselves puzzled when positive results fail to materialize.

This upside-down approach to student learning—this refusal to turn the funnel right-side-up and focus on foundational knowledge and skills *before* moving into higher-order interactions with content—is what holds students back. It gives many of them the distinct impression that they cannot learn what teachers are asking them to learn. When students have gaps in fundamental knowledge, constructivists deliberately refuse to give it to them. This approach is not only baffling, it also denies all students a fair chance to succeed during the K–12 journey and in post-K–12 institutions.

NOTES

1. To qualify: the provided passage has nowhere near the amount of domain-exclusive vocabulary found in most highly specialized fields, where experts actually invent new terms to label certain phenomena. In particle physics, for example, libraries of terms (like *gluons*, *muons*, *quarks*, etc.) have been created—not simply borrowed from the common lexicon—over time to describe newly observed realities. In comparison to a passage from such a field as particle physics, then, the passage here has very few such terms.

2. Two other educational domains—the Affective and Psychomotor—are included in Bloom's, but are not often referenced in making academic decisions.

3. D. R. Clark, "Bloom's Taxonomy of Learning Domains," Performance Juxtaposition, 1999, accessed July 26, 2010, http://nwlink.com/~donclark/hrd/bloom.html. The taxonomy was given a subtle facelift in the 1990s by Lorin Anderson, a onetime student of Bloom. Though the taxonomy largely retained its fundamental essences, the revision included two levels trading places in the complexity-hierarchy (Synthesis and Evaluation, with Synthesis renamed to "Creating") and all levels' labels made more active with -ing endings (*Knowledge* to *Knowing*, *Application* to *Applying*, and so on). The order of levels here reflects Bloom's original order, with revised titles/orders noted in parentheses.

4. Alliance for Excellent Education, "A Time for Deeper Learning: Preparing Students for a Changing World," *Alliance for Excellent Education*, May 26, 2011, http://www.all4ed.org/files/DeeperLearning.pdf.

5. P21's influence has become so strong, as a matter of fact, that its operating principles are being adopted by some of America's longest-standing defenders of content-rich curriculum and academic standards. In July 2011, the College Board's Advanced Placement Program announced that it had joined P21, publicly calling the Partnership a "guiding light" for their program. ("Four Leading Education Organizations Join Partnership for 21st Century Skills," *Reuters/PR Newswire*, July 12, 2011, http://www.reuters.com/article/2011/07/12/idUS151518+12-Jul-2011+PRN20110712.)

6. In P21's case, the technology recommendations deserve scrutiny. Essentially a front organization for the education divisions of some of the world's largest tech providers, P21 offers research-based advice that some suspect is really just marketing dressed in altruistic clothes. (For more, see Stephen Sawchuk, "Motives of 21st-Century-Skills Group Questioned," *Education Week*, December 4, 2009, http://www.edweek.org/ew/articles/2009/12/09/14partnership_ep.h29.html?tkn=LOLFOt7k4DAGb2J88qtnXPi3D6weTWzi%2FXiL).

7. Bernie Trilling and Charles Fadel, *21st Century Skills: Learning for Life in Our Times* (San Francisco, CA: Jossey-Bass, 2009), 12–19. It should be noted that when Trilling and Fadel wrote this book, they were board members of P21 with full-time leadership positions at Oracle and Cisco Systems, respectively, two of the world's largest technology companies.

8. Ibid., 16.

9. And this is a concern that continues to dog education nearly three decades after Hirsch first wrote. See Sam Dillon, "In PISA Test, Top Scores from Shanghai Stun Educators," *New York Times*, December 7, 2010, http://www.nytimes.com/2010/12/07/education/07education.html.

10. Hirsch acknowledges his arguments' chilly reception in *The Making of Americans: Democracy and Our Schools* (New Haven, CT: Yale University Press, 2009), 12–13.

11. E. D. Hirsch, *Cultural Literacy: What Every American Needs to Know*, rev. ed. (New York: Random House, 1987), 60.

12. Ibid., 61.

13. Daniel Willingham, "How We Learn: Ask the Cognitive Scientist, Allocating Student Study Time: 'Massed' vs. 'Distributed' Practice." *American Educator*, Summer 2002, http://www.aft.org/newspubs/periodicals/ae/summer2002/willingham.cfm.

14. Daniel Willingham, "Hall of Shame: Willingham Uses Science to Blast 'EyeQ,'" *The Answer Sheet* (blog), *Washington Post*, November 10, 2009, http://voices.washingtonpost.com/answer-sheet/checking-it-out/hall-of-shame-willingham-uses.html?wprss=answer-sheet.

15. Daniel Willingham, *Why Don't Students Like School? A Cognitive Scientist Answers Questions about How the Mind Works and What It Means for the Classroom* (San Francisco, CA: Jossey-Bass, 2009), 22–23.

16. Ibid., 29–30.

17. Namely, through a process called *chunking*, which streamlines one's decision making by arranging pieces of information into associated chunks of information. These chunks aid thinkers by cataloging pieces of understood information into familiar, rationally determined places, much as the Dewey Decimal System does for books in a library, thus making their retrieval more accurate and timely.

18. Ibid., 30–34. For more recent research on and specific illustrations of how background knowledge and memory factor into human learning, see chapters 2 and 3 ("How Experts Differ from Novices" and "Learning and Transfer," respectively) of John D. Bransford, Ann L. Brown, and Rodney R. Cocking, eds., *How People Learn: Brain, Mind, Experience, and School* (Washington, DC: National Academy Press, 2000), 31–78.

19. For a succinct, enlightening summary of the "Reading Wars," phases 1 and 2, see Daniel Willingham, *When Can You Trust the Experts? How to Tell Good Science from Bad in Education* (San Francisco, CA: Jossey-Bass, 2012), 13–16.

20. Though several examples of such trade-offs have been reported in recent years, a particularly egregious example came out of Dallas in 2011 (see Tawnell D. Hobbs, "'Exemplary' Dallas ISD School Skipped Science, Social Studies for 3rd-Graders," *Dallas Morning News*, November 18, 2011, www.dallasnews.com/news/education/headlines/20111118-exemplary-dallas-isd-school-skipped-science-social-studies-for-3rd-graders.ece).

For an idea of how high up such isolated-reading-skill-building thought is accepted, see Todd Alan Wilson, "Senate Supports Limiting Testing for 3rd Graders," *Daily Press* (Newport News, VA), January 24, 2012, http://articles.dailypress.com/2012-01-24/news/dp-nws-miller-sol-bill-20120124_1_science-and-history-tests-sols-graders. There, Virginia state senator John Miller, explaining the Senate's 33–7 decision to remove science and history tests from third-graders' annual schedule, says it makes "common sense to concentrate on reading and math, and give a good basic foundation in those two core subjects for our students."

21. Mathematica Policy Research, Inc., and SRI International, *Effectiveness of Reading and Mathematics Software Products: Findings from the First Student Cohort* (Washington, DC: National Center for Education Evaluation and Regional Assistance, March 2007), Rep. ERIC document reproduction service no. ED496015, http://www.eric.ed.gov/PDFS/ED496015.pdf. See also Robert E. Slavin, Alan Cheung, Cynthia Groff, and Cynthia Lake, "Effective Reading Programs for Middle and High Schools: A Best-Evidence Synthesis," *Reading Research Quarterly* 43, no. 3 (2008), 290+, accessed at Best Evidence Encyclopedia, http://www.bestevidence.org/word/mhs_read_Jul_2008_RRQ.pdf.

22. It should be noted that the problem of low-ability readers in advanced grades sprouts from seeds planted in the early grades, when students are still learning to decode written language. As so many who teach and choose curriculum in American education's early grades turn their noses up at research around building effective readers (the NICHD's National Reading Panel in the late 1990s is one oft-dismissed example), preferring instead to deploy whole language–inspired approaches like Balanced Literacy to teach primary-grade readers, scores of students are sent into the upper-elementary grades with nothing close to mastery of reading's basic requirements. For more on the United States' early-grades "reading wars," see Robert Kolker, "A is for Apple, B is for Brawl: Why New York's Reading Wars Are So Contentious," *New York Magazine*, May 1, 2006, http://nymag.com/news/features/16775/.

23. Hirsch, *Cultural Literacy*, 8.

24. Ibid., 34.

25. E. D. Hirsch, *The Knowledge Deficit: Closing the Shocking Education Gap for American Children* (Boston, MA: Houghton Mifflin, 2006), 37. For the studies Hirsch refers to, see Donna R. Recht and Lauren Leslie, "Effect of Prior Knowledge on Good and Poor Readers' Memory of Text," *Journal of Educational Psychology* 80, no. 1 (March 1988): 16–20, and Wolfgang Schneider and Joachim Körkel, "The Knowledge Base and Text Recall: Evidence from a Short-Term Longitudinal Study," *Contemporary Educational Psychology* 14 (1989): 382–93.

26. Daniel Willingham, "Teaching Content Is Teaching Reading." YouTube video, January 9, 2009, http://www.youtube.com/watch?v=RiP-ijdxqEc.

27. Willingham, *Why Don't Students Like School?*, 23–28.

28. Daniel Willingham, "Reading Is Not a Skill—And Why This Is a Problem for the Draft National Standards," *The Answer Sheet* (blog), *Washington Post*, September 28, 2009, http://voices.washingtonpost.com/answer-sheet/daniel-willingham/willingham-reading-is-not-a-sk.html.

29. A Google search of "'Reading Is Not a Skill,' Willingham" produces well over 1,000 results, with most references appearing on education-related policy sites and blogs. Though not all writers citing Willingham agree with his assertions, a majority appear to use his argument in attacking reading standards and strategies being implemented across the United States.

30. Tom Sticht, "Confusing Ignorance with Illiteracy," *EducationNews.org*, February 20, 2011, http://www.educationnews.org/commentaries/108159.html.

31. Karin Chenoweth, *It's Being Done: Academic Success in Unexpected Schools* (Cambridge, MA: Harvard Educational Publishing Group, 2007), 163–73. Karin Chenoweth, *How It's Being Done: Urgent Lessons from Unexpected Schools* (Cambridge, MA: Harvard Educational Publishing Group, 2009), 41, 44–45, 46, 47, 49, 195, 204.

32. Chenoweth, *How It's Being Done*, 44–45.

33. Sol Stern, "A Brilliant Experiment in Reading: But Will New Schools Chancellor Fund Revolutionary Program?" *New York Daily News*, July 14, 2011, http://articles.nydailynews.com/2011-07-14/news/29788729_1_reading-test-reading-program-naep. For more on the results of the comparative study, see Anna M. Phillips, "Nonfiction Curriculum Enhanced Reading Skills, Study Finds," *New York Times*, March 11, 2012, http://www.nytimes.com/2012/03/12/nyregion/nonfiction-curriculum-enhanced-reading-skills-in-new-york-city-schools.html?_r=1&emc=tnt&tntemail1=y.

34. Linda Darling-Hammond, *The Flat World and Education: How America's Commitment to Equity Will Determine Our Future* (New York: Teachers College, Columbia University, 2010), 235.

35. D. A. Bernstein et al., *Psychology*, 6th ed. (Boston, MA: Houghton Mifflin, 2003), 221.

36. David Klein, "Math Problems: Why the U.S. Department of Education's Recommended Math Programs Don't Add Up," *American School Board Journal* 187, no. 4 (April 2000): 52–57.

37. J. R. Anderson, L. M. Reder, and H. A. Simon, "Applications and Misapplications of Cognitive Psychology to Mathematics Education," *Texas Educational Review* (Summer 2000), http://memory.psy.cmu.edu/downloadPaper.php?name=Applic.MisApp.

38. Lawrence Gray, "Public Statement on Math Reform," Speech to Minnesota State Higher Education and Public Policy Joint Committee, February 18, 2013, http://www.math.umn.edu/~gray/testimony.html.

39. William G. Quirk, "The NCTM Calls It 'Learning Math,'" *Understanding the Original NCTM Standards*, accessed February 24, 2013, http://wgquirk.com/chap4.html.

40. National Council of Teachers of Mathematics, "Welcome to the Curriculum Focal Points" (2006), accessed March 2, 2013. http://www.nctm.org/standards/content.aspx?id=270.

41. Students First Illinois, "*Chicago Sun Times* Editorial: Fuzzy Teaching Ideas Never Added Up," Students First Illinois, September 13, 2006, http://www.studentsfirst.us/news/contentview.asp?c=184307.

42. U.S. Department of Education, "National Mathematics Advisory Panel, Preliminary Report," U.S. Department of Education, January 2007, http://www2.ed.gov/about/bdscomm/list/mathpanel/pre-report.pdf.

43. Though examples of such criticisms can be found far and wide, a few can be found in John Allen Paulos's *Innumeracy: Mathematical Illiteracy and Its Consequences*, rev. ed. (New York: Hill and Wang, 2001), 99–102, 104; Deborah Loewenberg Ball, Heather C. Hill, and Hyman Bass's "Knowing Mathematics for Teaching," *American Educator* 29, no. 3 (Fall 2005): 14–17, 20–22, 43–46; Lee Shulman's "Those Who Understand: Knowledge Growth in Teaching," *Educational Researcher* 15, no. 2 (February 1986): 4–14; and Fritz Staub and Elsbeth Stern's "The Nature of Teachers' Pedagogical Content Beliefs Matters for Students' Achievement Gains," *Journal of Educational Psychology* 94, no. 2 (2002): 344–55.

44. Paul A. Kirschner, John Sweller, and Richard E. Clark, "Why Minimal Guidance during Instruction Does Not Work: An Analysis of the Failure of Constructivist, Discovery, Problem-Based, Experiential, and Inquiry-Based Teaching," *Educational Psychologist* 41, no. 2 (2006): 75–86 (quote from 77).

Chapter Six

How (Schools Should Help) Children Succeed

> The highest ideal of a civilization is that of a civilization that is engaged constantly in elevating lower classes of people into participation of all that is good and reasonable and perpetually increasing at the same time their self-activity. Such a civilization we have a right to enforce on this earth.
>
> —William Torrey Harris (1835–1909), American educator and philosopher

For the past century, American education has followed the philosophies and ideals of the Progressive Education movement to the letter. It has allowed students' individual learning tendencies and preferences to drive pedagogy. It has subverted proven sequences of human learning in an effort to create critical thinkers and able problem solvers more quickly. These instructional and programmatic design choices were intended to engage more children and deliver on public education's equalizing promise more consistently.

One hundred years in, they are doing anything but. In fact, these design choices downplay or neglect crucial considerations about the construction of effective intellectual function and post-K–12-institutional expectations. And the equalizing effect remains unseen.

Plainly, these ideals and practices turned the funnel of American schooling upside-down.

Though the ideal intent of education's funnel is to route the diverse expanse of American youth into the nation's mainstream institutions, the one we've seen for a century or so only really works for the children who would make it with little resistance anyway—those who start the whole endeavor already familiar with the knowledge, expectations, values, and habits of mainstream American institutions. Children entering the funnel from further away—in terms of class, language, race, socioeconomic status—continue to spill down the sides, away from college, careers, and civic involvement and toward decidedly less mainstream institutions like chronic unemployment, addiction, poverty, and prison.

It's an effect that worsens in direct proportion to one's original position. The further away from the mainstream you start, the lower the odds that K–12 schooling, in its current orientation, will help you enter mainstream institutions at all. Having received very little help from their school years, disadvantaged young citizens must rely on their wits and wherewithal to gain access to these institutions. Few enter, and even fewer succeed.

Keep in mind, this is not a one-way problem. It's creating havoc within the institutions themselves. Accommodating large numbers of institutionally unready people is extremely difficult, and the institutions struggle to fulfill basic functions. One primary goal of the public education system is to replenish these institutions continuously and consistently, so it is important to keep this reality top of mind.

So, if we did manage to set the funnel right again, what would it look like?

An effective funnel would harness available research about how to pull students toward successful, productive experiences with challenging, academic content.

An effective funnel would acknowledge the expectations of the mainstream institutions, moving children toward clearly defined knowledge, skills, and personal qualities.

Educators committed to Progressive ideals resist all of these ideas vehemently, so much so that they are rarely even considered as instructional or programmatic options. Despite multiple decades of evidence about effective instructional methods and the failure of the current model, practitioners are deeply resistant to changing what they've always done.

U.S. SCHOOLING'S GUARANTEE: TWO VIEWS

So here we are. We know American education is (supposed to be) a funneling institution. Its job is to move young citizens into college, into careers, into trades, into government, into science, into research, into industry, into the arts, into small business, into successful and fulfilling lives. And we've seen that, despite good intentions and hard work, it is both practically and philosophically upside-down—which raises some specific questions.

What could a right-side-up funnel do that the upside-down one can't?

What should students expect to gain from it if they invest the time and energy?

What should the panoply of post-K–12 institutions expect from these graduates?

And how do we make it happen? What exactly will it take to help students succeed?

These are not exactly new questions. Indeed, the enterprise of American education has wrestled with them since its inception. As we saw earlier, the Progressive Education movement gained its power from the heat of these debates.

In the current era, the debate is even more volatile. For more than a decade, the educational enterprise has been under the influence of reformers who have very clear, decidedly non-Progressive ideas about what schools should accomplish. These reformers don't offer much in the way of counter-philosophies or alternative teaching practices, however, as they don't deeply understand the practical limitations and flaws described in chapters 4 and 5.

They don't really *care* to understand, to be frank. Few of these reformers bother themselves with the root causes of education's struggles because they've already made up their minds about what's wrong: they believe American education is not delivering on its promise because incompetent, dangerously complacent teachers have been allowed to work unchecked for too long. And, operating from the U.S. Department of Education, these reformers are attempting to correct the system by instituting actions and policies designed to hold educators *more accountable for their actions.* You break it, you buy it. But the only thing accountability reform is truly measuring is how close they can push educators to the breaking point.

The reason why, of course, is because the funnel is still upside-down. Which leaves Progressive-leaning educators with a nasty bout of cognitive dissonance. Education professionals hope to answer reformers' data-driven charge with results, but they are repeatedly frustrated when everything they've been taught—building student engagement, creating welcoming learning environments, avoiding the lower end of Bloom's Taxonomy, and all the other chapters in the Progressive gospel—fails to deliver the outcomes accountability-based reformers demand. Unsure why this is happening, but desperately needing proof that will justify their beliefs about what children need to succeed (and the practices they've chosen to make it so), educators are shifting the debate, moving it even further away from the realm of the academic than it was before.

These are the two factions currently at war in public education. It's a bloody battle with heavy casualties, and it unfortunately shows no signs of stopping.

The "Cognitive Hypothesis" and Accountability-Based Reformers

To borrow a term from journalist Paul Tough (more on him soon), the accountability-based reformers currently shaping U.S. education policy begin from the "cognitive hypothesis."[1] To them, the unquestionable key to individual success in today's world is *demonstrated cognitive ability*, or "the kind of intelligence that gets measured on IQ tests," per Tough. This same cognitive skill or content competency is what reformers believe is the fuel that will keep national engines running. In short, if our nation is going to maintain its solvency and global competitiveness, the average American is going to have to get a whole lot smarter.

Accordingly, accountability-based reformers believe that the purpose of schooling should be to deliver content competency and build students' cognitive capacity. To motivate schools in this regard, accountability-based reformers use more measurement, steeper professional consequences, and sharper competition as their spurs. Their logic is fairly straightforward:

- *Premise One*: For schools to be considered successful, they must reliably deliver content competency.
- *Premise Two*: Competencies aren't ambiguous; they can be measured by annual tests of students' content understanding.
- *Conclusion*: Performance on tests defines a school's success with respect to content competency.
- *Necessary Action*: Policymakers should use test performances to hold lower-performing schools and teachers accountable. For chronically lower-performing schools, drastic oversight or restructuring may be necessary.
- *Important Qualifier*: "Drastic oversight or restructuring" may include reexamining hiring and tenure structures, then circumventing or dismantling them altogether. It may also involve replacing ineffective schools and teachers with shinier, more efficient, and/or more genuinely invested schools and teachers.[2]

In short, the cognitive hypothesis steers all policies toward student assessment, school-quality evaluation and sanctioning, and professional development and evaluation.[3]

When this happens, it deeply affects all educational operations. Longstanding rules that schools once developed and managed independently are now dictated by outside forces that, many practitioners contend, don't fully understand or appreciate education's challenges, workings, and mission. Plus, when a school's effectiveness is made far more public, and in a far more detailed way than ever before, public pressure weighs on schools much more heavily.

Accountability-based reforms of measurement, reporting, and sanctioning are typically accompanied by reformers' expansion of available school choices, which means enrollments are also affected. Hoping to improve schools' accountability by creating competition, reformers are pushing for more charter school options and/or supplying tuition vouchers to be cashed in at private-school or home-school settings. This kind of competition for students, the market-inspired theory goes, will ultimately force public schools to either improve their educational product or "go out of business" when "customers" enroll elsewhere.

Under the influence of cognitive-hypothesis-driven reforms, plainly, educators' very livelihoods are at greater risk than ever before.

The "Noncognitive Hypothesis" Pushes Back

Opposition to accountability-based reform is strong, and has surfaced multiple times in various forms over the past century. Today, that opposition is led by those who seek to discredit the logic of the cognitive-hypothesis-driven reform and its attendant practices of student-measurement and professional consequences. In honor of their Progressive Education–based, child-centered educational foundations (and likely out of answers about how to produce positive results from those foundations), these professionals believe the most effective way to prepare children for the academic and non-academic environments that follow K–12 education is developing students' *noncognitive* skills.

They maintain that American education will only improve when it stops believing in content über alles. They say content knowledge does not predict post-K–12 success, and they have their own data to prove it. Accordingly, they believe that resources spent on better standards and testing, and designing improvements around test results, are misguided.

This side's current intellectual and moral center is Paul Tough, a one-time editor at the *New York Times Magazine* and *This American Life* radio program. In his 2012 book, *How Children Succeed: Grit, Curiosity, and the Hidden Power of Character*, Tough counters the notion of the cognitive hypothesis, asserting that "a disparate congregation of economists, educators, psychologists, and neuroscientists have begun to produce evidence that

> what matters most in a child's development . . . is not how much information we can stuff into her brain. . . . What matters, instead, is whether we are able to help her develop a very different set of qualities, a list that includes persistence, self-control, curiosity, conscientiousness, grit, and self-confidence. Economists refer to these as noncognitive skills, psychologists call them personality traits, and the rest of us sometimes think of them as character.[4]

Tough's book explores a series of psychological factors important to the development of young people and complements them with case studies of individuals who rely on their character to pull themselves through challenges. Ultimately, *How Children Succeed* argues that a particular set of noncognitive skills should be given higher priority than purely cognitive ones if we are to effectively prepare children for life after school.

And though no one is exactly sure how to teach these qualities or how to determine if students are learning them (two realities Tough fully acknowledges), many education professionals—especially those with deep Progressive roots—are responding to Tough's themes in force. In schools where practitioners fear accountability culture and testing are causing professionals to miss "out on some serious parts of what it means to be a successful human,"[5] a full-scale over-correction is in motion.

Inspired by Tough's work and related research, socio-emotional learning elements are finding their ways back into school improvement plans and mission statements across the nation. Schools are scrambling to provide programming that will, explicitly or implicitly, build students' character skills and, where applicable, more effectively account for students' traumatic pasts.

This is especially true in poor-performing, high-poverty schools that have struggled for years, schools that typically work with larger concentrations of students carrying significant *allostatic load*—or physical and neurological effects of continual, pronounced stress management.[6] These schools recognize that their students have considerable socio-emotional ground to make up and are intensely committed to helping students acquire the qualities Tough shows as truly predictive of future success. In this way, these schools feel justified when they kick rigorous academic experiences down the list of priorities.

So who is right? What *do* American children need to succeed in post-K–12 institutions? Is it content-understanding and skills measured by standardized tests? Or is it the harder-to-assess, slipperier character skills identified by writers like Tough?

NOT AN "EITHER-OR"

Once and for all, American children need *both*. And American education must abandon this false choice. Even working within considerable constraints, it is possible for educators to build students' cognitive *and* noncognitive abilities—if and only if they view the two as vitally intertwined. In fact, understanding this relationship is the first step toward righting the upside-down funnel.

To quickly recap:

We've seen how prioritizing student preferences over real-world expectations created a mismatch between what K–12 schools were teaching and what America's mainstream institutions demanded of graduates.

And we've seen how de-emphasizing foundational learning capacities compromises students' ability to master the second half of Bloom's Taxonomy—especially students entering school with less foundational learning.

These choices are detrimental to both students' mastery of content and the strength of their character—or, the noncognitive skills that we will call *institutional virtues.*[7] (In other words, virtues that will serve students well no matter what mainstream institutions they want to join.)

In fact, cognitive skills and institutional virtues are so tightly connected that these choices are multiply damaging to the development of both. Even worse, the damage is deeper and more compounding if one or the other (or both) is not established very early in the educational journey.

Simply, if a student's institutional virtues are not shaped in ways that enable effective learning of rigorous content, they will almost certainly fail to meet the expectations of mainstream institutions. Children who do not attain these institutional virtues fall behind early and often struggle as academic expectations escalate. Similarly, students exiting K–12 schools without having acquired these institutional virtues struggle just as much with mainstream institutions.

It's an especially damaging reality for students emerging from schools that award grade point averages and diplomas based on, say, displays of effort or work habits as opposed to genuine mastery of content, who then matriculate into post-secondary study. When this happens, students gain admission to post-secondary schools with a false sense of what they can accomplish.[8] Fortunately, many who find themselves in this dilemma manage to overcome their deficits precisely because their institutional virtues (or their strong financial backing—a variable that proves crucial) help them withstand the necessary *full-cost, no-credit remedial coursework.* Unfortunately, far too many do not.

It's up to American K–12 education to prepare all students equally for effective participation in life after school. That means institutional virtues and academic competency are equally important and must be prioritized as such. Whether students want to attend college or not, the virtues and knowledge they gain through a right-side-up funnel will channel them into a multitude of mainstream American institutions. Institutionally ready individuals will also strengthen, over time, the institutions themselves, creating better workplaces, communities, and even personal relationships.

To illustrate how academics and institutional virtues intertwine, let's picture a classroom of seventh-graders from Anywhere Middle School who are reluctant readers. (A stretch, for sure, but please do your best.) Now picture an English teacher who designs, in response to his class's low tolerance for reading, a course built around film adaptations of acknowledged great works of American literature. As rationale, the teacher presents some compelling arguments.

First, he asserts that many more students give the videos a chance, whereas they would have given reading no chance at all.

Plus, he can show all the texts in class. (Each film only takes up two or three class periods, so he can cover more titles per term.) This means he can monitor students' consumption of each title and how well they pay attention, information he could never have gotten if he had assigned the readings as nightly homework.

Finally, because he knows precisely which students consumed the content and how actively they did it, he is confident he can engage students in higher-order, free-form class discussions about the films.

These justifications sound convincing. But the teacher is missing several important opportunities to help his students improve their academics and their character. To see this more clearly, let's take a closer look at this teacher's methods through the lens of future workplace and college expectations.

First, the institutional virtues: by failing to find a reasonable way to overcome his students' resistance to reading, he sends a clear message that the students' personal preferences and overall comfort are what is really most important here. This is a poor preparation for real-world institutions. Representatives of these institutions—employers, landlords, professors, life partners, banks, government agencies, law enforcement, and the list goes on—regularly require people to conform to experiences that have very little regard for any one individual's preferences and comforts.[9] (DMV, I'm looking at you.)

Second, the academics: by allowing students to watch instead of read, he denies students the opportunity to build reading stamina, acquire new vocabulary, and increase tolerance for a task that will be a daily essential in post-secondary education (research and discussion preparation), the workplace (absorbing background material for a new product or service), and their personal lives (understanding a smartphone contract).

The deeper students like these get into their K–12 careers—and the more experiences they have with well-meaning, student-centered teachers like the one spotlighted here—the more difficulty they will have with work of increasing rigor. Sadly, when they reach these upper levels—even in settings that consistently provide access to challenging coursework[10]—students neither learn this content (and its attendant academic skills) nor build the upper-level institutional virtues that ramp up in parallel with academic intensity.

Now let's look at another example of how cognitive growth and character development are inextricably linked. Consider the experience of upper-level secondary mathematics study. Though few who have ventured into Algebra II/Trigonometry used the content very often after passing the class, the simple fact that they did pass the class tells everyone who reads their transcripts all of the following:

1. The student can understand, recall, employ and appreciate the value of smaller, more fundamental procedures on the way to solving complex problems.
2. The student can see even the most time- and frustration-intensive problems through to completion.
3. Even when the student can't complete these problems independently, she is willing to do what it takes (seek experts for assistance or attend support sessions, outside of the school day if necessary) to reach solutions and meet expectations.
4. The student is willing to put aside her own interests and questions like "Why should I do this?!" or "What is this even for?!" so she can achieve the first three items in this list.

Attaining and demonstrating these *virtues* is what makes studying mathematics predictive of future success. It's not necessarily the content of the class, although this content is absolutely necessary for high school students who ultimately pursue careers in medicine, information technology, finance, engineering, and other math-dependent fields. But these career choices are not always on students' minds during high school. What makes the study of mathematics important, useful, and valuable for every student is the way it builds character.

At bottom, this is why longitudinal studies of students' collegiate success clearly and consistently indicate that students' "academic intensity"—and passage of Algebra II, in particular—during high school is a unifying predictor: not because certain pieces of essential content were mastered in an academically intense class, but because of what mastering this content says about them as people.[11]

Amanda Ripley captures this well in *The Smartest Kids in the World: And How They Got That Way*: "Math is not just math," she writes. Math "is the language of logic." She then goes on to say,

> It is a disciplined, organized way of thinking. There is a right answer; there are rules that must be followed. More than any other subject, math is rigor distilled. Mastering the language of logic helps to embed higher-order habits in kids' minds: the ability to reason, for example, to detect patterns and to make informed guesses. Those kinds of skills had rising value in a world in which information was cheap and messy.[12]

It is also why, when we see representatives from American College Testing (ACT, the test-production company) testifying to Congress about how their tests are capturing low college-readiness levels of U.S. students, we should pay particularly close attention. (ACT chief operating officer Cynthia Schmeiser did exactly this in April 2010.[13]) This tells us who will likely be paying for remedial coursework once they get to college, which is helpful for predicting who will drop out of college without a degree.

When we fail to equip students with a strong foundation of cognitive skills and institutional virtues, they don't get what they need to process complex and demanding content. We effectively deny them the chance to strengthen the upper-level institutional virtues that will one day be expected of them by college admissions teams and staffing professionals alike. Each one affects the other. Academic work is the resistance medium students work through in order to exercise and strengthen content proficiency and institutional virtues. Neither institutional virtues nor high-level academic mastery alone are the ultimate destination of one's K–12 journey; *both, working together, very much are*.

Practitioners may read these examples and feel a familiar exasperation. And to be fair, the examples do seem like one more consideration to incorporate into an already-overflowing plate, another new concept the public will expect them to deliver (later calling for their resignation when it doesn't happen to their satisfaction), another workshop binder at another hastily thrown together training session, one more half-baked concept administration will expect them to deliver without a complete understanding of how or why, and all the rest. (Ask any educator; they've been there.)

Here's the main point: the enterprise of education must move toward an agreement of practice and philosophy that unifies academics and character-building, especially for students who start out further away from the mainstream. For those students, and also for the mainstream institutions that need them to thrive, it is imperative that American education use research-affirmed principles and practices of effective academic mastery—not research-deficient Progressive ideals—to pull students toward meaningful institutional participation.

The Common Core State Standards: A Source of Hope—Warts, Bruises, and All

In 2010, a source of hope for this imperative appeared: the Common Core State Standards (CCSS)[14] that spread like a brush fire across the country's schools. For those who recognize the importance of Bloom's lower levels to all future learning, the potential of solidifying these levels for all students, and the need to clearly define the steady ramp-up into expectations of post-secondary study, Common Core holds great promise. Thanks to its foundational principles and structures, it is the tool with the single greatest potential to repair American education.

Robert Pondiscio, executive director of Citizenship First (a nationally reaching civic education organization) and a former member of the E. D. Hirsch–founded Core Knowledge Foundation, went so far as to deem the

CCSS a "defibrillator" capable of shocking America out of a flatline that is more than forty years old.[15] Pondiscio's great enthusiasm about the CCSS stems from the standards' obvious basis in ideas he and the Core Knowledge Foundation had championed for years.

The English/Language Arts standards in CCSS, for instance, organize themselves around the idea that effective reading is not a set of skills, but rather an interaction between readers and texts that depends in large part on background knowledge. They place greater emphasis on students' exposure to nonfiction and informational text and, mapping backward from the academic rigor expected in post-secondary study, suggest the kinds of texts students should be able to successfully navigate to remain "on the ramp" through each grade from K to 12.[16]

Appendix A of the Standards justifies this design, citing considerable research about declining expectations of text complexity in K–12 classrooms over the past half-century, as well as about students' declining ability to comprehend complex texts independently, in particular nonfiction. The CCSS framers contend that this mismatch has sent so many students into post-secondary study unprepared that addressing it directly was a prime driver of all subsequent design choices.[17]

This marks a drastic shift away from how standards have typically been constructed. As such, the scores children record on CCSS-aligned tests in the coming years will speak volumes about how well long-standing methods are equipping students with foundational academic capacities like broad knowledge bases and the ability to truly comprehend—not simply decode—complex texts.

In 2014, only a few states have generated a full round of CCSS-based assessment scores to follow up on the standards' adoption and implementation. Kentucky was the first to get its results back, and that first round of results suggests that we should all brace ourselves for massive gaps and system-wide panic: the November 2012 reporting of scores showed student proficiency dropping by well over twenty-five points across all tested subjects and ages.[18] Similarly precipitous drops have been recorded in states like New York and Minnesota, causing all adopting states to prepare for the worst.

In addition to this early panic, the Common Core's rollout and implementation methods are experiencing considerable blowback.

Some protests come from predictable sources in light of the huge shifts in philosophy and practice the CCSS represent. Examples include practitioner advocates like former National Council of Teachers of English president Joanne Yatvin,[19] uniformity-averse state legislative bodies,[20] and the National Education Association, America's largest teachers union.[21] Influential political thinkers like George Will, too, have weighed in with doubts.[22] One state—Indiana—has formally "voided" their prior adoption of the standards,[23] and diehard progressive educators see the CCSS as an attack on their most deeply held ideals.[24]

Other objections, however, are coming from experts who had previously voiced support: Daniel Willingham, Diane Ravitch, and influential education writer Jay Mathews,[25] to name three. Though this group still largely supports the spirit and goals of the CCSS, several of them have expressed reservations about how the standards were introduced, fearful that American schools were not ready to accommodate the paradigm shift in a meaningful way.

Ravitch, perhaps the most visible of these critics, has been particularly harsh on the implementation process. Though still a proponent of a deep and rigorous liberal arts curriculum for all students, she makes it clear that her reservations about the standards' implementation are soaked with a deep suspicion of the Common Core's authors, funders, and advocates—groups she believes are working to subvert and ultimately dismantle American public education.

One very justified fear that all these critics share, however, is that as schools are rushed into monumental shifts in practice without proper training or time to prepare, teachers, leaders, and advisers will misread and misapply the standards' new and radically realigned emphases. Then, desperate for quick answers, schools and districts will, true to historical form, abandon any effort to understand the spirit and intention of the CCSS and turn to private-sector providers for help,[26] setting into motion another cycle of blame for reforms failed by flawed implementation.

With so much stacked against the Common Core standards, it feels dicey at this stage to put much hope into their transformative promise. After all the objectors have weighed in, it's quite possible that a whittled-down and wimpy version of the CCSS will lack any of the substance that so excited supporters like Robert Pondiscio in the first place.

Still, the new standards are a step in the right direction if American education's true wish is to optimally and consistently develop students toward meaningful activity in the post-K–12 world. Academically, the CCSS provide a direct, sequenced ramp into future institutional expectations for all K–12 students, replete with models of appropriate rigor.

This explicit expression of uniformly expected rigor can have a significant effect on students' development of noncognitive, institutional virtues. Within a common frame of expectations, students should learn, in a phased progression (and given lots of appropriate support where necessary, of course), the personal qualities necessary to achieve success with respect to post-K–12 cognitive and academic standards.

The noncognitivists, like Tough, may argue against the CCSS on the basis that individuals' levels of noncognitive development are better determinants of students' ultimate success in college and the workplace. Again, however, development of noncognitive institutional virtues should not be viewed as completely separate from content or deserving of targeted, content-stripped focus.

Content *does* matter, chiefly because the experiences required to master content demand considerable noncognitive strength. The students who make it through sufficiently challenging academic resistance prove, over and over, to be much more capable of post-secondary success. Viewed in this way—and not as a hyper-academic exercise that will neglect the development of students' institutional virtues—Common Core has the potential to help educators use content to build character, and vice versa, in a continuous, symbiotic cycle.

When your education can move you into places where more difficult content can be accessed, experienced, and eventually mastered, it allows you to form, practice, and strengthen institutional virtues that ultimately make you more assessment-capable, more employable, and better able to navigate post-secondary challenges. This is how academics and institutional virtues intersect and intertwine to build successful, well-rounded, institution-ready graduates.

If the Common Core standards can put American education on the path toward this destination, it is most definitely a reform to be excited about—growing pains and all.

Now that we've seen how academics and institutional virtues are more closely related than many educators assume, let's circle back to those earlier questions:

1. What should students expect to gain from their education if they invest the necessary time and energy?
2. What should post-K–12 institutions expect from the system's graduates?
3. What is the best way for schools to meet both sets of expectations?

The answers lie in how American education views its product and its practices. What has greatly complicated these issues is the continued compartmentalization of academic- and character-based teaching and learning, from both inside and outside the enterprise. If we are going to find answers that work, all stakeholders in American education need to stop regarding academic competency and institutional virtues as separate or conflicting challenges. It's not a zero-sum game, and that should be seen as good news for everyone.

These two concepts are not separate entities, but rather two halves of the same whole—two components of the same system. Academic study provides the *resistance medium* that builds character, in the same way that a swimming pool's water provides the resistance medium that builds strength and stamina. Taking it further, the stronger a person becomes through this exercise, the more work they can do. The work and the outcome are not isolated events with no connection. Quite the opposite. Rigorous academic study produces students with stronger institutional virtues, and those virtues enable the same students to take on even more challenging academics—and succeed.

To reconcile itself with this reality, American education must be honest with itself about a number of points, all of which are interconnected and all of which will be painful to address.

1. We can't teach every student everything. The educational institution must recognize that schools are not the sole preparatory institution between students and all the specific possibilities that await them after the K–12 journey. Rather, schools should provide an essential, generalizing preparation that helps students succeed *regardless of the path they choose*. Each step beyond K–12 will shape graduates further and more specifically according to a unique set of desired skills and virtues, whether the setting is college, small business, a vocational school, an apprenticeship, marriage, home-ownership, or anything else. To be clear, meeting all stakeholders' possible interests during the K–12 years is flatly impossible. Our schools should not be seen as the one place where all skills and institutional virtues can—and will—be acquired and all possible interests satisfied.
2. We can teach every student what they need to succeed. American education should not be in the business of providing direct-to-job training. (The impulse is understandable, given the clear connection between education and employment.) What we can provide, however, is universally effective training for any post-K–12 setting: show up on time, do your best, cooperate, be responsible and accountable, find opportunity in adversity. This training also necessarily includes fundamental academic competencies that are essential for participating in our society. In other words, American education is not a factory, but a refinery of our nation's most important natural resources. We are not manufacturing college students or citizens. Rather, we are making the "raw materials" of each incoming class more valuable—and inherently useful—to higher education, industry, U.S. communities, and the U.S. democracy.

If all of this seems implausible, call to mind a figure from chapter 3—nineteenth-century education leader William T. Harris. Specifically, call to mind how Harris viewed academic study: not as a tiresome mechanism for delivering essential content, but rather as the "windows of the soul."

In Harris's ideal academic program, the "windows" were five academic disciplines (mathematics, geography, literature, grammar, and history) representing five points at which citizens "see into" (and join) their civilizations. To Harris, the only reason academic study was even worthwhile was because it helped people access, understand, and improve the institutions they would one day enter. At bottom, the challenge of building institution-ready individuals is precisely what Harris hoped to solve through an academic curriculum that is effectively sequenced and based in the liberal arts.

And it must be said that before it was overtaken by Progressive enthusiasm, American education accomplished some pretty incredible things when it was structured around this mission and philosophy of practice. As we saw earlier, this same mission is generating awe-inspiring results in the nations we frequently look to for ideas about how to improve our own system.

Clearly, the time for these ideas has come again.

THE MARATHON AND THE SWIMMING POOL

Are you ready for another analogy? Seems like we're due.

The dilemma American education finds itself in is not unlike coaching kids to run a marathon, but with only a swimming pool as the training ground. No track, no cross-country trails, just a pool. Actual, full-on running isn't permitted. But you can swim as hard as you want. Many would find themselves frustrated by this reality, and rightfully so. It is indeed a tough challenge, if not an occasionally absurd situation. The pool, however, can actually work well toward the goal at hand if used properly and creatively.

Water provides a wonderful resistance medium, after all. Swimming through it can build full-body muscle strength, perhaps even more effectively than running alone. Learning the various swimming strokes gives kids an appreciation for both precision of movement and conservation of energy—two crucial qualities of marathon runners. Of course, physical stamina and mental toughness can be improved in the pool, too. As a coach, you could even get creative and have students run in the shallow end or alternate high-intensity bursts with extended-interval swims, or. . . you get the idea.

The point is that while the available training ground can't authentically replicate the conditions of competition, it can still build the strengths runners will need to compete. In some ways, training for a marathon in the pool may be preferable to an exclusive running regimen because it accomplishes two goals. Pool-trained marathoners, after all, will not only have the mental toughness, physical stamina, and overall muscular strength necessary to run a marathon, they will also be more skilled swimmers.

In this analogy, water is academic study. The marathon is the student's journey into mainstream American institutions. All the marathoning skills they build in the pool are institutional virtues, while swimming better represents academic competency. The student who completes her training in the pool is physically strong, mentally tough, and definitely more ready to run a marathon than when she started. In other words, she is institutionally ready. She can also swim really well, meaning she's earned measurable amounts of academic ability.

In short, if viewed in the right way and used well, the training ground that once seemed so inauthentic and limited can bring individuals much closer to a competitive level while also giving them substantial competency in other important areas. Schooling can build multiple strengths simultaneously. But you do have to get in the pool.

One of the most important questions here is what to do about students who can't (or don't want to) swim. Maybe they are in poor physical shape, or live with physical disabilities, or are afraid of the water. How should we coach them, keeping in mind that the end goal for all of them—running the marathon with all the other pool-trained kids—remains the same?

If you're the coach, do you put their natural desires to play and explore above their obvious need for training? To honor their preference, do you release them from any requirement to get in the pool? Or do you maybe give them an exercise that makes use of the pool, but doesn't necessarily strengthen their marathon skills in a meaningful way—observing the water to write a poem about it, or having free play time in the shallow end?

Not if you truly want to help these students prepare for their lives' next steps, you don't.

Knowing they will have to run the marathon eventually, it is up to you to figure out a way to improve their stamina and conditioning, however difficult it may be.

Improving their stamina and conditioning the hard way—the only way, that is—is the best way to prepare them for the marathon that can't be avoided. Even if we set aside any thought of a competitive finish in the marathon, the choice you make in this situation is a matter of the student's personal safety. If you decline to help them build their stamina, the marathon they must run could get *very* ugly.

The choice may seem obvious. But it's one many educators resist making all the time, both in day-to-day practice and in overall programmatic ways. Practitioners do not put some students through their academic paces. Or they attempt to find workarounds that absolutely do not help students prepare for the future, academically or in terms of institutional virtues.

A working funnel would pull, however painfully, less-able students into better shape. It would better prepare them for the task that awaits, the marathon they can't decide not to run. But the current funnel of American education, situated upside-down for so many decades, can't do this. It is more likely to forego using academics, escalating in rigor, to strengthen students in multiple ways. Instead, the neediest students remain roughly where they began: at a severe disadvantage compared to students who get in and swim.

To create able "marathoners" out of all students—and to give those who begin their training "out of shape" a chance to succeed—American education should refuse to make academic work easier. Less resistance will only perpetuate the huge gaps at the finish line. In addition to helping more students understand—and buy into—how important rigorous academic instruction is with regard to their journey after graduation, this approach should form the core of reform efforts across the United States if we hope to see actual, self-perpetuating systemic improvement.

Aside from the Common Core State Standards, with all their warts and all the abuse they're (somewhat justifiably) absorbing, the educational enterprise has no interest in turning the funnel right-side-up. Reformers are far too busy measuring performance, ensuring practitioners are held accountable, streamlining learning through unproven innovations, and turning education into a buyer's market to institute the changes that truly need to be made.

Next, we will more closely examine these reformers—and why their solutions will not deliver the desired results.

NOTES

1. Paul Tough, *How Children Succeed: Grit, Curiosity, and the Hidden Power of Character* (New York: Houghton Mifflin, 2012), xiii–xiv.

2. To be fair, not all accountability-based reformers ultimately believe in this qualifier. Even when they do not, however, they do use the cognitive hypothesis to power gentler reform efforts like data-based decision-making processes and building schools' tiered systems of student support. While these gentler reform efforts may not cause bald panic and outrage as the contract-busting, tenure-stripping, school-restructuring reformers have, the time, effort, and paradigmatic shifts necessary to implement them are causing frustration levels to rise in schools all across the United States.

3. Chapters 7, 8, and 9 will explore such private-sector-inspired reform efforts—and their limited reform potential—in greater depth.

4. Tough, *How Children Succeed*, xiv–xv.

5. Ibid., 56, quote from educator Dominic Randolph.

6. Ibid., 12–13.

7. The term *institutional virtues* will be used over *character* or *noncognitive skills* or *soft skills* from this point for two main reasons: First, because qualities like perseverance, grit, teamwork, self-restraint, and so forth are not technically *skills* like shoe tying or computer programming. Second, as they are indeed qualities that enhance individuals' eventual abilities to thrive within mainstream institutions, this term is more appropriate than merely "qualities"—all without the ethical/moral connotations accompanying *character*.

8. Joy Resmovits, "College Dropout Crisis Revealed In 'American Dream 2.0' Report," *Huffington Post*, January 24, 2013, http://www.huffingtonpost.com/2013/01/24/college-dropout-crisis-american-dream-20_n_2538311.html.

9. This is not to say, of course, that the teacher in this illustration is solely responsible for creating all of his students' systems of institutional virtues. In this one instance, however, when he had the opportunity to reinforce key messages and expectations that would reflect the messages and expectations of the post-K–12 world and institutions, he put the child first.

Consider how many such choices are made in the life of every U.S. student over the course of a public education, and the underlying messages become quite definite for many, many kids: in school, *your* engagement, *on your terms*, matters first; adults who do not initially cater to this engagement can be worn down into giving you whatever will keep you engaged, even if the exercise becomes so watered down as to provide no strengthening challenge.

10. Stephanie Simon, "Advanced Placement Classes Failing Students," *Politico*, August 21, 2013, http://www.politico.com/story/2013/08/education-advanced-placement-classes-tests-95723.html.

11. Clifford Adelman, *Answers in the Tool Box: Academic Intensity, Attendance Patterns, and Bachelor's Degree Attainment* (Washington, DC: U.S. Department of Education, 1999). See also Clifford Adelman, *The Toolbox Revisited: Paths to Degree Completion from High School through College* (Washington, DC: U.S. Department of Education, 2006).

12. Amanda Ripley, *The Smartest Kids in the World: And How They Got That Way* (New York: Simon & Schuster, 2013), 70.

13. Valerie Strauss, "What Does Being 'College and Career Ready' Mean?" *The Answer Sheet* (blog), *Washington Post*, April 29, 2010, http://voices.washingtonpost.com/answer-sheet/no-child-left-behind/what-is-being-college-and-care.html.

14. Catherine Gewertz, "Final Version of Common Standards Unveiled," *Education Week*, June 2, 2010, http://www.edweek.org/ew/articles/2010/06/02/33common.h29.html.

15. Robert Pondiscio, "The 57 Most Important Words in Education Reform. Ever," *Core Knowledge Blog*, Core Knowledge Foundation, September 20, 2012, http://blog.coreknowledge.org/2012/09/20/the-57-most-important-words-in-education-reform-ever/.

16. Common Core State Standards Initiative, "Common Core State Standards for English Language Arts & Literacy in History/Social Studies, Science, and Technical Subjects: Appendix B: Text Exemplars and Sample Performance Tasks," Common Core State Standards Initiative, accessed March 23, 2013, http://www.corestandards.org/assets/Appendix_B.pdf.

17. Common Core State Standards Initiative, "Common Core State Standards for English Language Arts & Literacy in History/Social Studies, Science, and Technical Subjects: Appendix A: Research Supporting Key Elements of the Standards/Glossary of Key Terms," Common Core State Standards Initiative, accessed March 23, 2013, http://www.corestandards.org/assets/Appendix_A.pdf.

18. Andrew Ujifusa, "Scores Drop on Ky.'s Common Core-Aligned Tests," *Education Week*, November 2, 2012, accessed March 24, 2013, http://www.edweek.org/ew/articles/2012/11/02/11standards.h32.html?r=1746345602.

19. Joanne Yatvin, "A Flawed Approach to Reading in the Common-Core Standards," *Education Week*, February 27, 2012, http://www.edweek.org/ew/articles/2012/02/29/22yatvin.h31.html?tkn=PRWFzRBijMBBvGLwtLADnxtlOjLWbhDgIH%2FI&cmp=ENL-EU-VIEWS1.

20. Catherine Gewertz, "Common-Standards Rumblings in Utah and South Carolina," *Curriculum Matters* (blog), *Education Week*, March 1, 2012, http://blogs.edweek.org/edweek/curriculum/2012/03/cato_on_south_carolina_fair.html.

21. Joy Resmovits, "Common Core Stakes Moratorium Proposed by Unions as National Standards Face Backlash," *Huffington Post*, April 30, 2013, http://www.huffingtonpost.com/2013/04/30/common-core-moratorium-teacher-evaluations_n_3187419.html.

22. George F. Will, "Doubts over Common Core," *Washington Post*, January 15, 2014, http://www.washingtonpost.com/opinions/george-will-doubts-over-common-core-wont-be-easily-dismissed/2014/01/15/68cecb88-7df3-11e3-93c1-0e888170b723_story.html?hpid=z5.

23. Though Indiana governor Mike Pence effectively voided Common Core in Indiana amid heavy political tension, the move seems more for appearances than for substance: an early version of the revised standards to take the previous CCSS-aligned standards' place has been described as little more than a "warmed over version" of the Common Core by Sandra Stotsky, a retired University of Arkansas education professor who was brought in to supervise the switch. See Eric Weddle, "How Common Core Disintegrated in Indiana," *Indianapolis Star*, March 29, 2014, http://www.indystar.com/story/news/education/2014/03/29/common-core-disintegrated-indiana/7051891/.

24. Lisa Nielsen, "Is the Common Core an Attack on Progressive Education?" *Huffington Post*, March 3, 2013, www.huffingtonpost.com/lisa-nielsen/common-core-cirriculum_b_2802147.html.

25. For Willingham's perspective, see "The Cognitive Science of Skills and Learning," Common Core, accessed April 21, 2014, https://www.commoncore.org/maps/documents/reports/willingham.pdf. For Mathews's, see "Why Common Core Standards Will Fail," *Class Struggle* (blog), *Washington Post*, February 23, 2012, www.washingtonpost.com/blogs/class-struggle/post/why-common-core-standards-will-fail/2012/02/23/gIQATLgbUR_blog.html. For Ravitch's—long a key supporter of standards to enable wide, broad content knowledge—see "Why I Cannot Support the Common Core Standards," *Diane Ravitch's Blog*, February 26, 2013, http://dianeravitch.net/2013/02/26/why-i-cannot-support-the-common-core-standards, and numerous related posts on her blog.

26. To see how the CCSS has invigorated vendors seeking to profit off educators' new standards-based needs, conduct Google searches for terms like "common core resources" and "common core materials." A 2014 search of "common core resources" retrieved well over 51 million results, and in scanning a few pages of these results, at least half were from education publishing companies and consultants.

Chapter Seven

What Gets Measured Gets Done (. . . But Won't Necessarily Change Anything)

> Holy Postulate #3 in Conservatives' Theory of Institutional Change:
>
> The Path of Business Is the True Path—Leadership, decision-making, and organizational functioning should all mirror what is found in the American business community, renowned for its efficiency and hard-headedness. One result is the fetishizing of privatization, often without any regard to context or process or attention to the instructional core.
>
> —Charles M. Payne, American academic and educator, in *So Much Reform, So Little Change* (2008)

Let's now focus our attention on current reform efforts and the people behind them. Though they have appeared a few times up to this point, we haven't explored what they are doing in any detail beyond the assertion that they are off the mark, adding unproductive interference, and keeping the funnel upside-down.

Here's the short version. For all the changes current reformers are making in American education, they aren't affecting the funnel much, if at all.

In most ways, today's reformers don't recognize the funnel is upside-down, period. Not that they would necessarily be familiar with the analogy we're using here. But they simply don't see education in the same way: as a way to prepare as many kids as possible to succeed in mainstream institutions. More than anything, they see the education enterprise as an overgrown, inefficient factory that should have, based on its results, been shuttered decades ago. The thing is, they're basing this stance solely on net margins and faulty assumptions; they never toured the factory in an effort to understand the operation and why it was running inefficiently. Rather, they jumped straight to "motivating" the employees by issuing pink slips more freely and opening smaller factories so as to attract unsatisfied customers—and the associated revenue.

In other words, they are trying to solve the wrong problem. Accordingly, they are highly unlikely to realize the improvements they seek.

Let's make one thing clear right away: many current reforms, while ineffective, are not absolutely wrong, much less evil or purely self-serving, as some critics charge. On the contrary, several reforms of the past decade-plus have heightened enterprise-wide focus, efficiency, and urgency.

The standards and testing movement, for all its flaws, has absolutely steered schools into being more strategic with operations, budgets, and continual improvement efforts. The construction and implementation of the Common Core State Standards is another reform moving in the right direction; the CCSS's illustrations of appropriate rigor and emphasis on broad content knowledge could supply significant force against the upside-down practices and philosophies that have been with us for a century.

From a student-performance perspective, multiple key metrics on the National Assessment of Educational Progress (NAEP) are higher than they've been in twenty years. Granted, not by much in most cases, and still riddled with large success gaps between historically underprivileged and privileged groups. Still, improvement is there, even among the subgroups most disfavored by the achievement gap.[1] Some improvement is always better than none. If current reforms are even partially responsible,[2] they deserve some credit.

That being said, if U.S. policymakers hope to create an education system that produces the results that they openly desire—our nation moving up in international comparisons of academic performance like the Programme for International Student Assessment (PISA), slowing the numbers of college dropouts and their demographic predictability—they are choosing the wrong reform strategies.

Current large-scale reforms that are effectively re-facing American education do not concentrate nearly enough on correcting the upside-down mission and practices discussed earlier. The true root causes of our collective struggles are not being addressed. Period.

Among the funnel-ignoring strategies preferred by modern reformers, a particular favorite is imposing private-sector-inspired processes of performance measurement and holding practitioners more tangibly accountable. This improvement strategy is based on numerous faulty hypotheses about the true problems in American education, and as a result, it is succeeding only in getting practitioners to throw flawed instructional practices at students harder and faster.

THE ACCOUNTABILITY ERA

Early in the new millennium's first decade, educators suddenly began hearing a set of new, somewhat alien-sounding, terms. Administrators warned of "good becoming the enemy of great," and they seemed remarkably occupied with getting the "right people in the right seats" of apparent "buses" they were driving. Schools' mission statements were torn up, and new ones written to ensure these metaphorical buses were driving in the right directions—directions provided by each school's "core values." Teachers were urged to think more like "hedgehogs" and less like "foxes," something they could do if they routinely used data to "confront the brutal facts of reality" and set "big, hairy, audacious goals."

Along with these new buzzwords came new procedures and expectations. School administrations began setting aside time for teacher collaboration and prescribing the formats of how this work would proceed. The collaborative groups were branded with names like "Professional Learning Communities" or "Data Teams," and their meetings were guided by documents that had to be completed in detail and submitted to administration.

It was all enough to make many wonder what was up. The new lingo sounded a little silly, but really not all that strange. Anyone who had been around education a while had seen multiple waves of change crash in (and, naturally, recede), and new buzzwords—even odd ones like these that didn't have much to do with teaching and learning—were always part of the deal. But mandatory, supervised, explicitly structured, and *documented* meetings? And all this data mania and common assessments and SMART goals? Is *everyone* being asked to do this?!

This wave was noticeably different, and it made many educators edgy.

As all in education know well by now, these alarming operational changes were byproducts of the No Child Left Behind (NCLB) Act, a game-changing piece of federal school-reform legislation enacted early in 2002.

NCLB required annual measurements of student achievement via standardized tests and subsequently tied unprecedented consequences to these metrics. For an endpoint, NCLB specified that schools set their proficiency targets to 100 percent for the 2013–2014 academic year.

Basically, this put all American schools on a strict timeline to figure this whole thing out: stop screwing around, set your targets, work toward them. Phase adjustments and rising student results in over a few years if necessary, but get all students, everywhere, to grade-level proficiency by 2014. You will be measured annually, your progress will be monitored, and consequences will be meted out to schools that miss targets. Ten-*hut*!

NCLB guidelines outlined how student results could get schools officially and publicly labeled as failures, and they prescribed an escalating series of improvement actions for schools with chronically low results. At the highest end of this escalator—that is, for schools receiving federal Title I funds, five consecutive years of missing Annual Yearly Progress (AYP) targets—a school could be dismantled and restructured: all staff let go and required to reapply for their positions, for instance, or the school converted into a charter school.

No previous reforms had been as top-down or far-reaching as NCLB. Also, no reforms before NCLB had seemed so rigidly focused on schools' most basic bottom lines: test-harvested proficiencies in competencies like reading, math, and science. And no other reforms showed so little concern for teachers' ideals or teachers' professional growth.

What really separated NCLB from preceding reforms, of course, was the severity of punishment it threatened. Failing to meet NCLB guidelines would cause lots of people, in some cases, to lose autonomy and/or their jobs. Funding could be restricted, meaning cuts to resources and positions. District and state oversight of schools could increase. Improvement plans would need to be constructed and followed to the letter. Leadership—entire school staffs, even—could be fired all at once.

With NCLB as its cornerstone, the Accountability Era had begun. Building from NCLB's base, related reforms emerged to create an environment that operates more according to private-sector principles than ever before.

For example, educational leaders are expected to drive their organizations more like CEOs run businesses, with student test results representing the bottom line. Leaders are professionally evaluated according to their ability to do this. No longer simply overseers of school operations and student-discipline or family-involvement issues requiring final authoritative positions, administrators are now expected to forecast results, make data-driven decisions, create highly collaborative and entrepreneurial staff cultures, and succinctly report progress to stakeholders and superiors. These revised expectations likely explain administrators' sudden fascination, starting around 2003–2004, with organizational change-leadership and all its attendant jargon.[3] (*Flywheel*, anyone?)

In the era of NCLB, teacher and administrator performances are evaluated much more closely. Student results (each year's state test data plus tracking individual student growth with value-added data models, for example), observation-obtained reviews of practice, and even student surveys may be used to assess educator effectiveness according to state mandates.[4] These evaluations play a role, depending on the state, in everything from compensation to license renewal to recognitions for exceptional performance. In some states, evaluations must be publicly reported,[5] actually ranking teachers from best to worst across entire systems according to their (still statistically sketchy[6]) value-added results,[7] a circumstance that very few enterprises, public or private, have been subject to.

Yet another reform in the Accountability Era is the expansion of school choice through open-enrollment policies, public charters, and, in some regions, school vouchers. All of these are designed to supply market pressure. Expanded school options threaten schools with losing per-pupil funding if students elect to leave in search of a better educational fit. If enrollment and operating dollars ultimately shrink to the point that the school must "go out of business," so be it: the market will have spoken.

Finally, independent nonprofit school-reform organizations, acting in the name of increased accountability, are riding education's free-market frenzy to overtly (and covertly) challenge teachers' unions, groups long perceived as obstructing positive change in the enterprise. This is not technically a government-sponsored reform, but it is a clear side effect of NCLB. These organizations (including Democrats For Education Reform, 50CAN, Teach For America, Stand For Children, StudentsFirst, and many more) are actively pushing battles into the policymaking sphere, influencing school board decision making and membership. In Rhode Island, for example, a state where the state chapter of 50CAN has particularly deep roots, school boards have recently—and not coincidentally—attempted a novel way of subverting unions and teachers' rights: staging mass terminations to bypass seniority rules en route to full staff restructuring.[8]

The real death blow to teacher-tenure policies and other traditional union protections, however, may have come in June 2014 with the *Vergara v. California* lawsuit brought by Students Matter, another (millionaire-backed) grassroots education reform group. Students Matter fielded an elite team of lawyers to represent nine student plaintiffs who claimed that they had received terrible educations from terrible teachers. (These claims seem somewhat dubious; a post-trial brief suggests that none of the plaintiffs was ever assigned to a documented "grossly ineffective" teacher.[9]) A California superior court judge agreed with the plaintiffs, tentatively overturning five state laws related to the employment of teachers and declaring them unconstitutional because they created unequal educational quality.[10] The victory for Students Matter provides a roadmap for like-minded reformers in other states, who will likely soon follow it and may see similar results.

GARBAGE IN, GARBAGE OUT: BAD HYPOTHESES IN ACCOUNTABILITY

In light of all these reforms, it's clear that highly influential decision makers have determined schools need more of the accountability, strategic organization, and competition that have made America's business sector a world power. Extrapolating backward toward the kinds of beliefs that could generate such policies, it's clear that the Accountability Era and its attendant reforms spring from two hypotheses about the U.S. education system: the *cognitive hypothesis* and *the lazy bum hypothesis*.

The cognitive hypothesis, as coined by writer Paul Tough, says that, because content competencies help students compete and contribute to the nation's economic strength, delivering these competencies should be schooling's primary goal. With reforms inspired by the private sector, the cognitive hypothesis justifies the objective and regular measurement of students' content outcomes. If you can't measure it, how do you know it's improving?

The lazy bum hypothesis, meanwhile, justifies the teeth in these reforms. This hypothesis says that American kids don't succeed after K–12 because their teachers are lazy bums. They may be lazy bums who achieve tenure, stop caring, and go on professional auto-pilot. Or they could be lazy bums who are no-talent do-nothings—the type that inspire sayings like "Those who can't do, *teach*." Lazy bum hypothesizers believe American education is overrun with lazy bums who have hidden for too long behind unfair, union-erected tenure structures. Stuck with so many lazy bums for teachers, the thinking goes, students don't stand a chance to learn the content they need to succeed in post-K–12 environments.

Reformers wired with these ideologies believe the education system needs two things: one, to measure students' academic progress as tightly as possible; and two, to carry much bigger sticks—ones that will beat lazy teachers into working harder, talentless teachers into becoming more effective, and autopilot teachers into retirement.

You know, just like they do in *real jobs*.

With the expectations—if not the realities—of their environment revised to reflect private sector thinking, many education leaders are pushing their staffs to become as corporate-minded as possible, as quickly as possible. Heavy emphases are placed on regular data review to monitor student progress and plan appropriate reactions, evaluating teachers' day-to-day instructional effectiveness, and increasing leadership capacity within staff.

One of the biggest levers used to these ends is controlled collaborative structures. They may be called Professional Learning Communities (PLCs), Data Teams (DTs), Instructional Leadership Teams (ILTs), or some other purposefully opaque name. Highly structured teacher teaming of this sort seems to address multiple school-improvement imperatives simultaneously. Which is why the idea exploded across the country as a *necessary* improvement.

In many ways, teacher teaming makes sense. After all, as structured teams work in coordinated lines toward the results students ultimately record, they allow school personnel to monitor student progress more efficiently and actionably. According to collaborative protocols and ideals, practitioners align instructional activities to the standards on which students will be tested, assess students' growth toward standards mastery more reliably, and figure out remediation plans more cooperatively when students fall off (or fly past) expectations.

Also, the models of teacher collaboration help individual schools develop the strength of their *entrepreneurial cultures*, a common and essential quality of thriving organizations according to the leadership treatises school administrators are reading. Without a space for strong professional discussion and debate, leadership experts say, education will struggle to find new solutions to familiar organizational issues and remain unable to build the collective, positive attitudes toward risk-taking that Fortune 500 companies possess.

Third, structured and documented collaborative processes have the potential to help administrators with ongoing, high-stakes staffing efforts. Dividing teachers into smaller teams to focus on student results and work with colleagues to improve these results, and then documenting the entire process, can—with hard evidence—clearly show which teachers "are (or aren't) on the bus," "should be in a different seat on the bus," or "should be thrown off the bus altogether" (to borrow from Jim Collins's *Good to Great* [see note 3]). These processes also create space for the cream to rise: a place where leaders outside the immediate administrative team can be identified and groomed to provide more staff-level torque to improvement initiatives.

For district and school-site administrators, teacher-teaming structures like PLCs offer a concrete way to pull together and meet the staff-collaboration objectives of accountability-oriented reforms. While organizational leadership gurus tell schools which qualities great organizations have in common, leaders of teacher-teaming groups provide the playbook for schools to practice and realize such qualities through effective collaboration.

After several districts and schools realized this, and word spread about the promise of teacher teaming to meet NCLB objectives in the early 2000s, an entire industry sprang up to support these concepts with marketable products. Companies cropped up overnight, offering everything from professional development workshops to operations-guiding tools (like meeting-accountability forms) to implementation self-monitoring instruments, to motivational speakers for kicking off implementations of these required models. By 2010, this industry also featured riffs on and build-outs of foundational PLC concepts (like the Leadership and Learning Center's "Data Teams," for example) to help schools get the results they were seeking.

So how is it all going? Are the reforms actually working? Now that effective teaching is more quantifiable and systematically evaluated, some barriers to removing ineffective teachers have been removed, more choice has created competition, and assessment habits have become stronger, are we seeing the results accountability-oriented reformers believed we would see? Do their hypotheses about what has so dogged American education, in other words, appear to be correct?

In any bottom-line-driven organization, the fairest place to look for an assessment is student results. After all, these results are the only thing motivating the mobilization of so many people, the reorganization of their professional interaction, and the dedication of so much funding to enable it all.

Unfortunately for everyone, the results suggest that reforms based on the cognitive and lazy bum hypotheses aren't doing much good at all.

Students are nowhere near the initial long-term reading and math proficiency target of 100 percent across all student subgroups. They are so far away from those original targets, in fact, that in 2011 the Department of Education began moving the goalposts, offering flexibility from the stipulations of NCLB. (Or, more accurately, the Elementary and Secondary Education Act [ESEA]—NCLB is the name of the ESEA's reauthorization in 2002, its seventh since being introduced in 1965.[11]) By late 2013, forty-two states and select districts had been granted this flexibility, taking ESEA waivers in exchange for refinements to accountability practices.[12]

Pulling back from NCLB's nationwide, bottom-line focus, the federal government gave waivers to states committing more resources to preferred improvements from the Department of Education. (The decision was justifiable, given how few states recorded anything notably positive under a decade of NCLB.) Though more than 80 percent of U.S. schools no longer have to sweat over the target of 100 percent student proficiency, they still must implement private-sector-inspired reform actions: improving teacher evaluation systems, ratcheting up academic standards, defining and enforcing professional accountabilities, and more. And to remain in compliance (and avoid similar oversight and funding penalties of prewaiver NCLB specs), they must do all of this more deeply, systematically, and accountably.

Some steady progress has been made on the internal assessment of academic progress, the National Assessment of Educational Progress (NAEP), since NCLB kicked off the Accountability Era. These figures are widely touted by proponents of reformers as proof their ideas are working—but they are far from anything worth celebrating. The gains that have been recorded are quite small, for instance, and some demographic groups are actually moving *backward* on the NAEP (see note 1).

On international measurements of student performance, including the Programme of International Student Assessment (PISA) from the Organisation for Economic Co-operation and Development (OECD), the United States is hardly climbing up the ranks. Putting the United States' (rather scary) rankings among other nations aside, a phrase that comes up far too often in reports of PISA results is "not measurably different." As in, no matter where U.S. students rank internationally in mathematics, science, and reading, their average scores don't progress much between assessments—

and especially between assessments given during the Accountability Era. Indeed, observing the last decade's worth of PISA results, it would be difficult to tell that anything different was happening in American education policy.[13]

Adding insult to the injury of NCLB's mixed-at-best yields, the dearth of positive results has triggered a number of highly publicized results-doctoring scandals across the United States. Occurring everywhere from charter chains to major U.S. districts, and even implicating one of the accountability reform movement's most visible figures (Michelle Rhee, the former chancellor of Washington, DC, schools and founder of education lobby group Students-First), multiple instances of rigging enrollment and erasing-and-replacing test answers have been uncovered.[14]

However shameful and unfortunate these cheating scandals are, they could be considered a sort of victory to private-sector-inspired reformers: now that American education has its own little Enrons, it's clear the "whatever it takes" corporate mentality is starting to take hold.

Viewing this decade-plus's worth of results in light of the Accountability Era's massive amounts of reform-related upheaval, it seems clear that there is something faulty about either the reformers' hypotheses or the execution—or both.

But the reformers appear undeterred. At the time of this writing, accountabilities, school choice expansion, and required actions show no signs of slowing. By all indications, reformers stand by their hypotheses about education's deepest issues, believing absolutely that they will succeed if those stubborn school-level professionals just start executing things properly.

This is a belief in vain—and not because teachers and administrators are stubbornly resistant or just plain incompetent, as so many of the reformers prefer to think. Instead, this belief is in vain because most of the accountability reformers just don't know enough about the education enterprise—what makes it work, what defines and/or constrains it, and how its funnel is upside-down. If they genuinely understood, they would recognize that education is so fundamentally unlike the private sector that purely corporate operating principles would never take hold, and that all the threats and incentives in the world can't create effective practice alone.

Education's boots on the ground may leave a lot to be desired. Certainly, anyone who's been schooled can think of a few "lazy bum" teachers who could use serious reformation or who should just be shown the door. But assuming most teachers are like this paints the whole enterprise with much too broad a brush. And reform actions based on this assumption are inherently unfair to all educators.

Accountability-based reformers' energies and resources would be much better spent fully exploring why and how educators' practices are upside-down. Then, based on their new understanding, reformers should spend their energies on systematically tipping things right-side-up. Without righting the upside-down funnel of mission and practice, our institution stands very little chance of significantly changing its outcomes beyond the incremental, up-and-down, inconsistent results we've seen to date in the Accountability Era.

EDUCATION ≠ BUSINESS

One very important reason that private-sector-inspired principles generate such meager results is because education is not a business. Yes, there are employees and executives and operating budgets. Yes, students produce results that can be measured, and so on. But the two enterprises diverge in a number of obvious and important ways.

Business serves the profit motive. Education serves the greater good by meeting what all agree is a critical societal-institutional need—but there isn't any money in it. Businesses get to choose who they employ and who their customers are, and if something goes awry they can decide to hire other people or pursue a different market. Education must, by law, educate all U.S. citizens, regardless of their background, experience and personal situation, whether they speak English or three other languages, whether they are excited to come to school or refuse to participate. Business is free to solve problems any way they want within the law; they can dream up innovations that support their mission, and if the CEO says to do it, it gets done. Education makes all of its policy decisions within an interlocking stack of four regulatory bodies and four sets of guidelines: district, municipal, state, and federal.

Although it should be obvious that a school is not a business and can't run according to corporate operating principles, this is anything but obvious to accountability-oriented reformers.

The differences become even more apparent if we get a bit more granular. Specifically, let's look carefully at four factors that are critical to both enterprises: human capital, prioritization of effort, products and services, and customers.[15] As much as free-market education critics want to make it so, a straight comparison between businesses and schools does not hold up. And as such, it shouldn't be surprising when the rules of the marketplace don't suddenly transform classrooms, schools, and districts for the better.

Human Capital in the Education and Private Sectors

Regarding human capital in the private sector and education, an overwhelming belief exists among corporate reformers that when the lazy bum hypothesis is put to the test—ineffective teachers are labeled as such and then let go—deposed staff will be summarily replaced with much more able replacements. This is a flawed assumption, to say the least.

Though teachers' rights and union influence are weakening thanks to efforts by various accountability interest groups, teacher contracts are still remarkably difficult to change or override. Traditional controls regarding seniority, tenure, and transfer are still fully operational in most districts. The private sector, which can (usually) hire and fire at will, simply can't relate to these policies. (And while the landmark *Vergara* decision is still quite fresh and its appeals will take months or years to play out, its reception and aftershocks will be an instructive test as to how deeply entrenched these union influences actually are.) Believing a free flow of superior teachers would deluge schools if the union dam were broken (getting Jim Collins's vaunted "right people in the right seats") is at best wishful thinking. Even if such a free flow were possible, all potential replacements are inculcated through the same training and professional development programs, a majority of which approach teaching from a strongly Progressive perspective.

Surely you remember those teacher-licensure programs mentioned earlier: the ones described as upside-down, teaching from unproven philosophical ideals, ignoring evidence about effective practices, and telling all those eager pre-teachers about the best constructivist methods? Trained in this way, new, more preferred teachers will likely teach in much the same way as those they would be replacing.

Additionally, as Amanda Ripley points out in *The Smartest Kids in the World: And How They Got That Way*, the minimum standard necessary to become a teacher in America is profoundly low, especially compared to the nations we seek to emulate. Citing studies from the National Council on Teacher Quality, Ripley reminds us, "Just one out of every twenty education schools was located at a highly selective institution in the United States. Far more than that had no admission standards at all. In other words, to educate our children, we invited anyone—no matter how poorly educated they were—to give it a try . . . a bit like recruiting flight instructors who had never successfully landed a plane, then wondering why so many planes were crashing."[16]

In sum, even if the accountability reformers can use assessment data, evaluations, union-busting, and whatever else to unseat the lazy bums they believe are obstructing success, the teachers filling the lazy bums' empty seats may not be more knowledgeable, committed, or pedagogically sound than the lazy bums themselves. Nothing has changed at teacher-preparation levels to change this dynamic.

Reform organizations like Teach For America (TFA) seek to ameliorate the situation by recruiting top young talent from some of America's most selective institutions, hoping to bring an improved brand of educators into the field through alternative licensing pathways (which, by design, subsequently route many TFA corps members to posts within education's policy-making sphere). An FAQ on the organization's website reports a total of thirty-two thousand alumni, "about a third" of whom are still teaching.[17] In other words, with ten thousand or so members still teaching after nearly twenty-five years in operation, Teach For America had better get busy if they hope to cover the United States' nearly four million full-time teaching posts.[18] Even if they only wanted to fill four hundred thousand positions and cover the bottom 10 percent—the certified worst of the lazy bums, that is—they still have a long way to go.

Human capital can't be strictly compared between the private sector and public education in terms of quality personnel's recruiting, availability, and retention. However much transformative potential reformers see in swapping out less effective people with more effective ones, the realities of education's workforce are more limiting than reformers seem to have estimated. These limits must be acknowledged and planned *around* instead of planned *for*.

Setting Priorities in the Education and Private Sectors

The second major disconnect between private-sector and educational operating principles is in how each is able to prioritize its efforts. Where each private-sector organization (and pretty well every nonprofit, for that matter) has the freedom to seek out its own competitive niche—narrowing its focus as a "hedgehog" would, again per *Good to Great*—almost no schools have this luxury.

A national chain of sporting goods stores may decide to shutter poor-performing locations in one region and better train their "laser-like focus" on the Southwest. Schools can't do this. Though schools can be shuttered and/or consolidated to more efficiently use district resources (a fairly common occurrence in large urban districts), the net outcome has to stay constant. Schools can't shut down service to first and second graders to focus more intensely on grades 3–5, or declare that they will dismiss all special-education personnel and stop providing services to special-education students to free up resources for technology upgrades. Private-sector reformers must realize, as business executive Jamie Vollmer did in 2002, that schools must be far less mercenary in their priorities; to improve their end product they can't just "send their blueberries back" when they're not of acceptable quality.[19]

As much as a given school may want to focus on any single aspect of improvement—and, no doubt, many do a remarkable job focusing on particular areas without losing their overall balance—this is incredibly tricky to pull off. Staff turnover, persistent issues, enrollment shifts, and timing of assessment results are just a few of the factors that make it incredibly difficult to set priorities and allocate resources consistently. In schools with numerous and profound issues, just *identifying* the top priority feels like playing a shell game.

Funding for programming, staffing, and continual improvement is another critical factor that separates schools from private businesses in terms of organizational focus and issue-prioritization. To provide the best-possible mandated and community-preferred educational services, after all, schools must work within strict publicly regulated guidelines and timeframes. Indeed, school leaders' annual races to finalize their schools' budgets, those budgets' dependence on property taxes, and the inherent injustice of such a funding structure could fill a book on its own.

Naturally, restrictive guidelines and timeframes are also considerations for private-sector organizations. Limited liquidity for budget planning, though, makes matters—urgent and unexpected matters, especially—far stickier for schools than for businesses. As schools are funded, funds for the upcoming school year are typically allocated according to preregistration numbers and forecasted enrollments from the previous spring. Even the most forward-looking and well-prepared principal will be forced to scramble for additional resources if her school experiences a significant demographic shift that was not anticipated six months prior to opening day. In many large urban districts, this happens with alarming frequency.

Unexpected surges of demand happen in the private sector as well, of course, moving businesses to pursue capital to fund their responses. Lines of credit are opened, bonds are issued, or stock sold to add facilities, equipment, or people. But individual schools can't work this way. With students present to be taught and teachers locked into place by contracts, staff can't easily be moved around from their appointed spots. Though business leaders and private-sector-inspired reformers see this lack of agility and call it poor management or insufficient vision or a lack of creativity, this completely disregards the financial and operational realities within which education leaders are legally required to work.

Products and Customers in the Education and Private Sectors

The final two differentiators between business and schools are their respective products and services, and their customers. These will be discussed here as a single factor because, in education, they are one and the same. While business offers a certain product or service aimed at specific customer segments, education's service is designed to transform its customers. To earn a high school diploma, students must work according to the directives of the enterprise to become measurably different from when they entered. The credential signifies a satisfactory transformation.

Education's product is not necessarily its content or its teaching methods, but rather each satisfactorily transformed customer. Both the customer and post-K–12 institutions benefit equally from this transformation, and each utilizes the product to their respective optimum benefit.

Some businesses work the same way, transforming individuals in a way and that requires some effort on the customer's part: self-help, health care, and fitness, to name three. The major difference between these organizations and schools, however, is what is at stake if customers choose to not invest the effort required to transform.

If someone voluntarily signs a health club contract and pays the monthly membership fees but chooses never to check in or exercise at the club, he will likely not achieve the desired transformation. The health club, however, still profits from the customer's money. Despite recording this profit, the club is under no obligation to complete the transformation. The agreement between the club and the customer stipulates that the customer is ultimately accountable to himself to achieve the transformation—and, of course, pay the monthly bill.

This works in exactly the opposite way for schools on two fronts.

First, students do not attend school voluntarily. Though choices exist about where you can get your education, compulsory education laws mandate that no American citizen can elect to go wholly uneducated, with minimum dropout ages—differing from state to state—averaging around sixteen years old nationwide.

Next, when a student emerges from schooling without having earned the desired transformation of skills, knowledge, and institutional virtues, *schooling* is seen to have failed. It doesn't matter at all whether the student elected to show up and "exercise" or not. (In fact, when students choose not to show up, schools must expend even more resources tracking them down and forcing them to return.)

Schools are obligated—increasingly, painfully obligated in the Accountability Era—to transform all of their customers. All of these customers—whether they follow school directives or earn the transformation or not—are tested to see how well schools are performing, but only the school pays the price. Of course, students who put forth no effort likely suffer future losses, but in terms of the accountability test, students have no stake. Unlike the lazy health club member, students who do not put in the work are not in any way held accountable for their lack of transformation. To finish the comparison off, the penalties schools must endure in these cases are akin to health clubs being sued for negligence when members who never exercise don't lose significant amounts of weight or win bodybuilding competitions.

Education commentator and historian Diane Ravitch captured this flaw in the accountability system very well in 2010's *The Death and Life of the Great American School System.* "NCLB neglected to acknowledge that students share in the responsibility for their academic performance and that they are not merely passive recipients of their teachers' influence," Ravitch wrote. She continued: "Nowhere in the federal accountability scheme are there measures or indicators of students' diligence, effort, and motivation. Do they attend school regularly? Do they do their homework? Do they pay attention in class? Are they motivated to succeed? These factors affect their school performance as much or more than their teachers' skill."[20]

The market-informed view of education sees students purely as customers instead of integral parts of the process. In the same way, it sees students' personal preferences as their consumer rights—expectations to which the school, or "vendor," needs to cater. This thinking simply does not apply to schooling. To help students gain the academic competencies and character traits that will serve them best in future, schools must occasionally put students through experiences that are not exactly satisfying. (Hard work rarely is, at the time it's being done.) It's the school's responsibility to drive students toward rewarding, enriching experiences and away from experiences that could compromise or slow their academic development.

When a student drops a class because they don't feel a teacher is accommodating his learning style or drops out of one school to attend a charter that a friend told him was much more laid back, educators should not simply shrug and say, "Well, the market has spoken." Education should steer students toward choices that are demonstrably better for them over the long term.

The intertwined nature of American schooling's product and customer, as well as the minimal, unenforced responsibility of the students to contribute to the process, presents conditions and limitations that are unique to schooling and will forever frustrate market-inspired, accountability-based improvement. These reforms may work after some very crucial considerations are adjusted, including compulsory education laws/dropout ages and graduation and competency-demonstration standards, for starters. But certainly not before.

The fact that education and business are fundamentally incongruent endeavors does not necessarily mean that all accountability-driven attempts to improve teaching, strategic planning, and professional collaboration should be called off. All of these have considerable potential for improving American education when combined with other crucial pieces, like a revised expectation contract for the enterprise's customer-products and a more right-side-up mission and instructional practices.

The only results market-inspired reforms have accomplished so far, however, is more accurately measuring the poor state of American education and informing practitioners that they're on notice. To truly begin the work of improving it, reformers must turn their attention to the most fundamental problem: the upside-down funnel.

To make this clear, let's examine the impact of market-inspired reforms on the enterprise of education with respect to the funnel analogy.

- First, picture a person in her driveway pouring gasoline into the tank of a car using an upside-down funnel. Imagine the dangerous mess it creates.
- Now picture an accountant with a clipboard standing beside this person, recording what he sees and periodically informing the neighborhood about the state of the mess.
- Next to the accountant is a coach who repeatedly tells the funnel holder what the accountant's data says about the spilled gas—regularly interspersed, of course, with lots of inspirational quotes and slogans: how the holder must more truly believe in the gas's ability to make it into the tank, how the holder's quality is the main determinant of the gas's successful transition, and so on.
- Occasionally, the accountant acquires a grant for a second upside-down funnel that fits over the first. Gasoline continues to spill with this second funnel in place. When the grant expires and the second funnel is removed, not much changes.
- When the mess gets *really* bad, the accountant makes the funnel holder more uncomfortable. (He makes the funnel holder wear a fur coat. And stand on one foot. And only use her thumbs.) Then he takes up his post with the clipboard to observe, document, and occasionally report on the funnel's performance.
- At the accountant's headquarters, data support staff work feverishly to update the clipboard's recording forms for greater efficiency and accuracy, electronically warehouse the data he's bringing back from this and other places where funnels are making a mess, convene an executive leadership team, and so forth.

You get the idea. It's the teacher trying to use the poorly positioned funnel and market-inspired reformers holding the clipboard. You can understand why teachers and reformers alike find the situation so frustrating. It should also be clear why neither of them is likely to get what they want anytime soon.

To improve American education, reformers must recognize that the funnel is upside-down, understand why this is a problem for everyone involved, and focus their efforts on turning the funnel right-side-up.

This will no doubt require a great deal of research, planning, and fortitude. The good news is that the data and research already exist. We can find them in schools around the world that use their funnels more effectively, to see what might work and what actions the enterprise should take. These approaches may be very different from what American practitioners have been trained to believe are best practices. But if we look at the data about our own current situation—our international standing, graduates' college-dropout rate, our tragic demographic achievement gaps, and all the rest—how can we justify staying the course? How can we continue leaning on best practices that have delivered anything but the best?

Of course, private-sector reformers have not yet considered this approach. If they attempted it, reformers may find themselves surprised by how cooperative the enterprise would be. Imagine a reform effort that takes a more cooperative mindset, one that says, "it's a big change, but let's work on this together" instead of leaning so heavily on the cognitive and lazy bum hypotheses that are failing to produce anything except disappointment and aggravation all around.

Let's not forget that teachers are saddened when education doesn't work for kids. This sadness becomes frustration—and confusion and feeling "lost"—when the techniques and practices they were told would be best for kids don't work. This happens far too often, precisely because the instructional funnel is still upside-down. Unless we address our upside-down practices, even the most effective PLC meetings or the most accurate assessment and data-harvesting systems won't make a meaningful difference. Even if teachers follow through faithfully with explicit PLC structure, and submit all the requisite forms, and comply with administrators' directives, teachers will still fail to push students to mastery if they are using inherently flawed practices in the classroom.

Practitioners do the best with what they know how to do, plain and simple. And what they know how to do well, thanks to their training and the education establishment's continued dismissal of anything but Progressive pedagogical principles, is fundamentally flawed.

Reformers could accomplish much more for American education if they did not assume practitioners were either lazy or talentless and then punish them senseless as a result. As we've seen, this approach changes very little. Instead, reformers should work to help teachers know what right-side-up education looks like—all students are prepared for meaningful participation in America's mainstream institutions—and how this change can be accomplished.

Here are four broad but essential corrective actions reformers must work into short- and long-term improvement matrices to do just that. Without them, all the Accountability Era's measuring, punishing, strategic planning, teacher teaming, and the rest will continue to generate the lackluster results we have seen to date.

1. *Examine and reform the ways in which teaching is improved.* Perform studies of ideal and effective pedagogical principles, especially with regard to local student data. At the teacher-licensure and licensure-renewal levels, revise field-entry criteria prospective teachers need to meet. Consider the mechanisms for evaluating, coaching, and retaining practitioners. Look at how practitioners learn best and incorporate

revised ideals of practice both through ongoing professional development and teacher-licensure programs.

2. *Increase every student's personal stake in his or her educational transformation.* Build a clearer sense of schooling's relationship to future institutional participation through policies and school programming/counseling (attendance requirements, minimum dropout ages, graduation requirements, grading). Without this connection, students will never make the personal investment that is necessary in order to transform themselves. The current one-sided accountability model creates far too many false negatives; yet schools are effectively powerless to change it.
3. *Make true commitments to finding the best local answers—and follow through.* Balance measurement/consequence culture by investing in strong solutions to improving local student achievement. To set priorities and resolve conflicting commitments, consider internal district structures to be built, rebuilt, and/or sustained to assess issues effectively, shape instructional policy, and provide necessary support. Make long-term, genuine commitments to the work of these structures (backed financially and contractually where necessary), tasking them to find solutions before handing over responsibility to outside experts. Resolve to seek outside input only after careful vetting to ensure tight alignment with organizational missions and objectives.
4. *Prescribe and monitor curricular balances and effectiveness of delivery before results.* End corrective actions proven to be ineffective, such as increasing act-of-reading instruction or additional technology-based math interventions at the expense of other subjects. Prescribe, support, and monitor effective delivery of comprehensive liberal arts education for all students.

Reform can happen, and it doesn't need to take a generation or more. The answer to effective reform, however, has never been purely about accountability. This would be like shouting at an upside-down funnel in an effort to get it to move. This is, in effect, what current reformers are doing. If they really want to improve education, they need to tip the funnel into its only effective orientation.

Great organizations, though, don't just measure and demand results (or so all the management rah-rah literature tells us). They also seek innovative answers continuously. Next, we will see how market-inspired reformers' preoccupation with "innovative solutions" adds even more complexity to system-wide improvement. Though the apparent hope is that we can deliver superior education if we can harness our world-renowned creativity (and business acumen), the only thing this mindset has produced is pushing educators ever closer to the breaking point.

NOTES

1. To interactively review 2013 NAEP data and historical progress by multiple demographics, other student classifications, and state, see NAEP, "2013 Mathematics and Reading," National Center for Education Statistics, November 7, 2013, http://nationsreportcard.gov/reading_math_2013/#/.

2. A point that is certainly up for debate: NAEP data suggests that positive results generated in the reform era post-2001 really just build onto an already-positive trend.

3. Incidentally, all these expectations were the base reason for all the new lingo and slogans of a few pages ago. Needing help with how to organize their sites to be as corporate as possible as quickly as possible, leaders began turning in force to the ideas of renowned corporate figures for guidance. One of these, management guru Jim Collins, provided just such terms in his book *Good to Great: Why Some Companies Make the Leap . . . and Others Don't* (New York: HarperCollins, 2001), the top-selling business title of 2001, the year before NCLB's passage. For *Good to Great*, Collins studied over fourteen hundred companies and found eleven that, owing to a set of specific qualities, moved from merely "good" to verifiably "great" performance. In response to the social sector's—and particularly school leaders'—growing needs to better understand and more aptly guide bottom-line-driven organizations, Collins himself began appearing and speaking on the education-leadership conference circuit, and leaders and consultants across the United States began translating it for the school setting. School principals and district officials summarily returned to schools, signed copies of *Good to Great* in their swag bags, ready to lead schools more like CEOs lead their organizations, and unleashing all the Collins-isms (even when they didn't much apply to improving teaching and learning).

4. Jim Hull, "Trends in Teacher Evaluation: How States Are Measuring Teacher Performance" (Alexandria, VA: Center for Public Education, 2013), 1–3.

5. Ibid., 28–30.

6. American Statistical Association, "ASA Statement on Using Value-Added Models for Educational Assessment," American Statistical Association, April 8, 2014, https://www.amstat.org/policy/pdfs/ASA_VAM_Statement.pdf.

7. Fernanda Santos, "City Teacher Data Reports Are Released," WNYC, February 24, 2012, http://www.wnyc.org/story/301783-teacher-data-reports-are-released.

8. Abby Goodnough, "Mayor Tries to Reassure Providence Teachers as Furor Grows over Firing Notices," *New York Times*, February 25, 2011,http://www.nytimes.com/2011/02/26/us/26providence.html. See also Katie Zezima, "A Vote to Fire All Teachers at a Failing High School," *New York Times*, February 24, 2010, http://www.nytimes.com/2010/02/24/education/24teacher.html.

9. Diane Ravitch, "The Vergara Trial Teachers Were Not 'Grossly Ineffective,'" *Diane Ravitch's Blog*, June 11, 2014, http://dianeravitch.net/2014/06/11/were-the-vergara-trial-teachers-grossly-ineffective-no/. For the brief itself, see it stored at thevergaratrial.com: http://www.vergaratrial.com/storage/documents/2014.04.10.Intervenors_Post-Trial_Brief.pdf.

10. For good analyses and summaries of the Vergara decision, see Andy Smarick, "10 Things to Know about the Vergara Decision," *Flypaper* (blog), Thomas B. Fordham Institute, June 10, 2014, http://edexcellence.net/articles/10-things-to-know-about-the-vergara-decision, and Valerie Strauss, "Is This the Beginning of the End of Teacher Tenure?" *The Answer Sheet* (blog), *Washington Post*, June 11, 2014, http://www.washingtonpost.com/blogs/answer-sheet/wp/2014/06/11/is-this-the-beginning-of-the-end-of-teacher-tenure/.

11. U.S. Department of Education, "The Opportunity of ESEA Flexibility: Protecting Students and Supporting Local Education Solutions" (Washington, DC: U.S. Department of Education, 2012), www2.ed.gov/policy/elsec/guid/esea-flexibility/resources/esea-flex-brochure.pdf.

12. Allie Bidwell, "Education Department Loosens NCLB Requirements," *U.S. News & World Report*, November 14, 2013, http://www.usnews.com/news/articles/2013/11/14/education-department-loosens-nclb-waiver-requirements.

13. Valerie Strauss, "Key PISA Test Results for U.S. Students," *The Answer Sheet* (blog), *Washington Post*, December 3, 2013, http://www.washingtonpost.com/blogs/answer-sheet/wp/2013/12/03/key-pisa-test-results-for-u-s-students.

14. For a list of recent test-cheating scandals with links to related published accounts, see Lois Beckett, "America's Most Outrageous Teacher Cheating Scandals," *Propublica.org*, April 1, 2013, www.propublica.org/article/americas-most-outrageous-teacher-cheating-scandals.

15. And even these four factors—plus the introductory ones above—still barely scratch the surface, saying as they do nothing about considerations buried deeper in each's fabric: the historical culture and values of each's professionals, professionals' relative standing in public opinion, relative compensation, and so forth.

16. Amanda Ripley, *The Smartest Kids in the World: And How They Got That Way* (New York: Simon & Schuster, 2013), 85.

17. Teach For America requires a two-year service commitment; participants may elect to leave the classroom after said term. Though many do stay in education in some capacity, a great majority of TFA alumni do not become lifelong classroom practitioners. See "Facts about TFA," Teach For America website, accessed February 8, 2014, http://www.teachforamerica.org/our-organization/faq.

18. "Fast Facts," National Center for Education Statistics, U.S. Department of Education, accessed February 8, 2014, http://nces.ed.gov/fastfacts/display.asp?id=28.

19. In 2002, Vollmer wrote a piece for Education Week that has become the stuff of legend in education training circles. See online at Jamie R. Vollmer, "The Blueberry Story: A Business Leader Learns His Lesson," *Education Week*, March 6, 2002, http://www.edweek.org/ew/articles/2002/03/06/25vollmer.h21.html.

20. Diane Ravitch, *The Death and Life of the Great American School System: How Testing and Choice Are Undermining Education* (New York: Basic Books, 2010), 162–63.

Chapter Eight

Outside the Box, But Standing Still

Success doesn't necessarily come from breakthrough innovation but from flawless execution. A great strategy alone won't win a game or a battle; the win comes from basic blocking and tackling.

—Naveen Jain, business executive and entrepreneur, in a 2012 leadership article for *Inc.* magazine

Innovation. It's the defining characteristic of successful, breakthrough, pioneering, game-changing companies. It's the future, the next big thing, the new new thing. So of course, no attempt to remake schools in the image of the private sector would be complete without it.

In the United States especially—where fresh ideas have created countless jobs, made people's lives more fulfilling, and lined the pockets of those who brought them to life—any organization that wants to compete effectively must innovate continuously. No matter how successful they already are, companies cannot stand pat and hope to stay that way. Strong organizations, we are told, live by the no-nuance mantra, "Innovate or Die."

Yes, indeed, the zipper, air conditioning, candy corn, the airplane, iPods, Tupperware, Post-It Notes, and buffalo wings are all dreams Americans made real, and along the way injected billions of dollars into the economy and improved the lives of millions. And all of these innovations came from a singular creative spark. Sparks like these have pulled entire global companies back from the brink of financial ruin. Single ideas!

Innovations like these didn't stop when they made our lives better. They inspired competitors to one-up them and showed everyone else that it was possible to bring an idea to life, both of which helped set the stage for further innovation. To borrow from Henry Adams's famous quote about inspirational teachers, it is impossible to tell where the influence of one great innovation truly stops.

Plain and simple, new ideas are what America does. Because this is self-evident, no comprehensive heave into a private-sector paradigm would be complete without all kinds of attempts at innovation.

Along with closer measurement of results, more stringent consequences, and more structured strategic planning, "fresh ideas" are a hallmark of private-sector-inspired reformers' attempts to improve system performance. Of course, "fresh ideas" are not necessarily good ones.

Hoping to save the educational enterprise from its general lack of private-sector vision and creativity—and intensely dedicated to the good of all American children, of course—the accountability reformers have set complex machinery into motion. Government offices, nonprofit organizations, divisions of for-profit organizations, and university education department subdivisions have been established to study and recommend the kinds of innovations American education needs to better meet the demands of the twenty-first-century marketplace. Regional and national conferences host inventors of (technology-based, usually) educational innovations in order to facilitate love-connections with investors who can bring these ideas to life and bring them to the marketpl—er, classrooms—more quickly.

The emphasis on innovative thinking in education is by no means limited to these task groups and vendors. Indeed, it runs throughout the educational enterprise: from the federal policy level to the state/district level, and into each classroom's methods and desired student outcomes, education professionals are less concerned with improving the fundamentals (the "blocking and tackling," per the epigraph by master-innovator Naveen Jain) and more enchanted with remaking education using as-yet-unproven improvement strategies and instructional techniques.

Below are quick overviews of the kinds of innovations currently at work in American education. (Some overlaps will be noted between these samples and ideas covered earlier, particularly in chapters 4, 5, and 7.)

- Through the Race to the Top (RTTT) and Investing in Innovation (i3) grant programs, the U.S. Department of Education has earmarked and distributed well over five billion dollars—awarded through application-based contests instead of a more uniform manner—to fund *innovative* education improvements at the state, district, and school levels.
- *Innovative* school models like charters—decoupled, as they are, from many state laws and the restrictions of teacher unions and similar organizing groups—are being expanded. In the time since the charter concept was introduced twenty years ago, more than 80 percent of U.S. states have passed legislation authorizing charters; students are leaving traditional schools in higher numbers each year to enroll in brick-and-mortar and online charter schools.

- In classrooms, instructional technology *innovations* are exploding in popularity. Teachers are encouraged—professionally expected, even, according to some recent evaluation rubrics—to regularly incorporate advanced technology into their instruction. The technologies are used to assess students more accurately and more often, to provide more intensive and student-specific interventions for struggling and/or disengaged students, to give all students greater access to (and proficiency with) the Internet and various devices, and to operationally aid lessons to build student engagement.
- To improve teacher performance, districts are using more *innovative* approaches and strategies. Some of these are accountability-based (value-added modeling to measure students' growth with certain teachers), while others use altered models of professional development (explicit collaborative structures like PLCs toward a job-embedded development structure). Still other means of improving teacher performance (e.g., "merit pay" arrangements to incentivize performance and the creation of alternative or streamlined licensure pathways for mid-career professionals to enter the teaching profession) are being implemented in a number of U.S. districts and states.[1]

Unfortunately, when it comes to improving American education, innovations like these have only as much potential as the accountability-based reforms discussed earlier. Which is to say: very, very little.

Despite all the cheerleading performed by their proponents, these innovations tend to fall into one of three categories: accountability-based reforms framed as innovations for no other reason than that they are new; reforms based more on hunches than on firm evidence about sound teaching and learning; or reforms that are so costly and structurally upsetting as to render them unfeasible. (There is also the combo platter: a new-in-name-only accountability reform that is both unproven and unworkably expensive.)

Worse, several of them—namely, those that seek to augment and expand on the principles and practices heretofore we've identified as institutionally upside-down—may actually effect the *opposite* of improvement if fully carried out. If the educational enterprise isn't careful and simply agrees with the recommendations of the futurists and innovators who are studying (but not always genuinely comprehending) education, it will end up implementing shinier, re-tooled, and highly costly versions of the same things it has done for a century or so but that have not worked.

Put another way, implementing certain innovations is like substituting the upside-down funnel for a different upside-down funnel, one constructed from some space-age, frictionless polymer. Such a system will only continue to produce more student spillage and weaker U.S. institutions.

INNOVATIVE IN NAME ONLY

A fairly obvious point about a number of the innovations mentioned here is that they're not very innovative at all, at least not in the sense of an utterly new idea that can solve a stubborn issue. They are more like strategic ways for top government officials to expand, implement, and monitor the private-sector-inspired reforms discussed in chapter 7.

For example, the intent of U.S. Department of Education programs to spur innovation—like RTTT and i3—has never been to provide an *American Idol*–like venue for unearthing and nurturing the next great educational ideas. Though the Department of Education's public communications insist it has transformed its methods of driving improvement (i.e., from setting rules and enforcing compliance to using incentives to jumpstart new ways of thinking about instruction[2]), its innovation-incentive programs are far from wide open. Really, these programs are focused on providing money to states that commit to reforming education the way the Department of Ed wants them to.

And probably not surprisingly (in light of points covered in chapter 7), several of the Department of Education's preferred, grant-worthy actions under RTTT and i3 are ones that lubricate the mechanisms of private-sector-inspired reform: better statewide data systems for improving student measurement, improved assessments to increase accuracy of student measurement, strengthened systems of teacher-evaluation and hiring to improve teaching and leadership forces, increased partnership with philanthropic and private-sector entities to execute all of the above, and so forth.[3]

Admittedly, programs like RTTT and i3 are unquestionably innovative in how they get private-sector consultants and vendors on the inside to effectively privatize vast swaths of U.S. public education—one of the surest and quickest ways, remember, to finally make education operate more efficiently. It works like this:

1. Seeing that education funds are available through new federal programs and, naturally, always in need of extra funding, states and districts study the criteria and prepare applications according to the specifications—not necessarily according to their "must do, but can't currently afford" lists. Let's say that again: they are applying for money to fund projects they don't necessarily believe are important.
2. After winning grants to fund improvement initiatives the federal government prefers, states and districts are assigned schedules for monitoring and reporting. This is when they get to read the fine print.
3. Grant-winning states and districts discover they don't actually have the capacity to see these initiatives through. What is important is getting the money, so many states and districts make promises they can't

keep, have no hope of keeping, and often have no idea how to keep. Unless . . .

4. Unless private-sector companies come to the rescue. When grants are awarded, astute entrepreneurs flood local districts, peddling exactly what schools need to deliver what they have promised. (What a coincidence!) It can be everything from improved student data systems to teacher-evaluation tools to STEM (science, technology, engineering, mathematics) curricula and partnerships with local colleges and on and on.
5. Vendors make out handsomely, whether they deliver results or not. And the Department of Ed gets to inject the system with a powerfully high dose of private-sector vitality serum.

Though this sequence begs the question of why states would apply for grants to fund initiatives they don't want, the short answer is self-defense. State-level departments of education and districts that opt out of applying for these grants risk getting excoriated in the press, both as stubbornly squandering a rich education-improving opportunity and unwilling to innovate—two charges few leaders in American education's current climate are willing to bear.

This is indeed an innovative way to make the education sector operate more like the private sector: convince districts they have manufactured needs, give them the money to pay for the solutions, and then see that they contract with private-sector providers who conveniently offer products and services specifically designed around these new needs.[4]

Charter schools in the United States also represent a great bastion of innovative potential. As first imagined by charter-school founding father and long-time American Federation of Teachers president Albert Shanker, charter schools were supposed to be teacher-designed "laboratory schools" that would experiment with new ways to connect with hard-to-reach students. Shanker's vision sought to free teachers from the typical contractual constraints, required curricula, and traditional policies to teach targeted students in whatever ways they deemed most effective, then share these instructional adjustments with district colleagues so others could benefit from their findings.[5]

Just as the public and education professionals fail to perceive the true nature of grant programs like RTTT and i3, however, they also misunderstand the actual nature of charter schools' innovations. RTTT and i3 do not offer a way to finally fund all the creative initiatives schools have long wished for, and the charter movement is nowhere near the instructional laboratory Shanker envisioned and the public still believes it to be.

The charter movement has gathered considerable momentum in its twenty or so years of existence. But it would be a real stretch to say these schools have delivered on the "laboratory" or the "innovation" parts of their original promise. School-governance structures and internal operations certainly look different in charter schools than they do in traditional public schools, but little proof exists that instructional innovation is much of a priority, let alone a mission accomplished.[6]

To date, student-achievement results from charters as a whole are too mixed and too contradictory to tell us whether the innovations they contributed are worth pursuing.[7] Though charters haven't failed outright, there isn't much proof they have found any particular methods for reducing longstanding achievement gaps.

Within charters that do record encouraging results, it is critical to note that the types of innovations in play are decidedly those of a right-side-up funnel. Schools in the Knowledge Is Power Program (KIPP) network, for example, regularly attract attention for their ability to succeed with historically underserved populations.[8] Referenced multiple times in this book, these schools are built on unquestionably right-side-up principles, including a strong academic curriculum, explicit instruction of institutionally preferred habits and behaviors, and high expectations of practitioners—particularly regarding availability to students.

Though these are not the types of innovations educators typically choose to implement in an effort to better serve the neediest students, the lessons of KIPPs and like-minded charters are worth enterprise-wide attention. This will likely be a struggle, however. As we saw in chapter 4, the successes earned by KIPP and similar "no excuses" schools are some of the most dismissed, derided, and downright excoriated of the entire charter movement.

One innovation charters are delivering is right in line with federal grant programs—the ability to attract and involve the private sector in public education. As Diane Ravitch notes in *Reign of Error: The Hoax of the Privatization Movement and the Danger to America's Public Schools*, the expansion of charter schools made many financiers see "public education as a potentially lucrative opportunity. They looked at the hundreds of billions of taxpayer dollars spent each year on schools and saw a market waiting to be exploited. Their interest was not philanthropy but making money on real estate deals and educational services, taking advantage of federal tax credits and a steady flow of no-risk public funding."[9]

It bears repeating that, though this may indeed help reformers meet their apparent goal of getting the private sector more authentically involved in education to improve efficiency and lower costs, the improvements to date have been minimal, for schools at least. Private-sector companies, on the other hand, are no doubt extremely satisfied with reformers' persistence in expanding charter schools, offering up a captive customer base that has been remarkably lucrative to exploit.[10]

COOL PRACTICES

At the programming and classroom levels, more genuinely innovative adjustments are being made—not simply Trojan horses filled with slick sales representatives and accountability-obsessed reformers.[11] New technologies, curricular materials, and comprehensive teaching approaches are innovations in the truest sense: brand-new tools teachers can use to enhance the power and quality of instruction.

Though these tools may be more literally innovative, however, they are not a panacea for the problems plaguing American students' readiness for post-K–12 institutions.

One reason most practice-level innovations should not be viewed in this way is because their rate of success is too uncertain to justify huge investments of time and money. An innovation growing in popularity right now, 1:1 iPad or digital tablet initiatives (in which all enrolled students at schools—entire districts, even—receive tablet devices to supplement learning activities and/or supplant textbooks), provides an interesting case in point.

Launching a 1:1 tablet program incurs costs and considerations far beyond the immediate expense of purchasing the hardware. Money and time must be allocated for maintenance, repair, and replacement, as well as software upgrades and installation, for locating and learning how to use effective instructional materials, for coordination of device check-in and check-out, for training of staff in optimal and continually evolving device applications, and for design and enforcement of acceptable-use policies and accountabilities. To handle all these considerations, schools often need additional or reassigned full-time staff.

Rather obviously, many U.S. schools are finding this trade-off worthwhile, and the logic is plain: if these devices can substantially improve academic performance and/or increase students' readiness for the future, then the high financial and infrastructural costs are worth it.

The problem with this mindset, however, is that no one can say for sure whether these devices will actually drive such improvements. The capacity of tablets to improve teaching and learning has essentially never been tested in the classroom. It was almost as if schools saw the ads for these devices, became instantly convinced their students needed them, and started ordering them by the truckload, no questions asked. Though the literature on similar recent digital initiatives shows very little conclusive evidence of positive effects on student achievement,[12] the apparent hope is that tablets will be somehow different or better (to be fair, however, they do run Angry Birds much better than a regular textbook).

The considerable dollars thrown into digital tablets, then, as well as the software required to make the devices classroom-ready and the personnel assigned to maintain them and the additional network bandwidth needed to make them run properly, and on and on, are all being invested, essentially, on a hunch. Even worse, it's a hunch that nobody wants to claim, a hunch most educators can't trace back to a definite origin.[13]

For the sake of argument, let's check the ROI (return on investment) to see how Operation iPad is transforming student achievement. In the early going, a few points seem clear: widespread use across education (Apple reports sales of ten million iPads to schools since 2010[14]) has not generated notable spikes in standardized test scores or reductions of demographic achievement gaps. (If this has indeed happened, successful schools and Apple are being awfully quiet about it—a near-impossibility in the Accountability Era.)

Of the limited research available about the instructional value of this technology, both the teachers (many of whom still aren't really sure where or how the new devices are supposed to fit into their instruction) and students (the assumed "digital natives" who will obviously appreciate and thrive under this shift) don't seem overly thrilled with the effect tablets have on their learning experiences.[15]

Nevertheless, companies like Apple, future-focused organizations like the Partnership for 21st Century Skills (P21), and "disruptively innovative" business and education thinkers like Harvard's Clayton Christensen[16] and Tony Wagner[17] all tell the educational enterprise not to worry. Students undoubtedly need these experiences to succeed in the global marketplace, they say, so an innovation like an iPad in every student's hands is absolutely worth every dollar and person-hour this decision may rack up.

(Keep in mind that these organizations and individuals stand to make handsome profits if more districts and schools first buy this argument and then buy their products, a coincidence that has not gone unnoticed[18] but does not seem to dissuade educators from hearing them out—or from ordering more iPads after they've heard them out.)

The tablet dynamic is by no means a unique example of the way "innovations" are not held accountable by accountability reformers. American education tends to give new programs and methods the benefit of the doubt; they sound so good they just had to be given a whirl, even without much proof of effectiveness. This has always been the case, even before the explosion of the ed-tech industry and the relentless emphasis on innovation by private-sector-inspired reformers. Indeed, American education has long favored *cool* practices over verified *best* practices.

It's a quality that seems somewhat unique to American education, a point raised repeatedly in works like Amanda Ripley's *The Smartest Kids in the World: And How They Got That Way*. Whether visiting a school in Poland, South Korea, or Finland, Ripley points out often how classrooms in other countries seem comparatively devoid of technological frills. But the difference really hits home when she surveys students.

In her survey of exchange students, including U.S. students studying abroad and students from fifteen other countries studying in America, students "overwhelmingly agreed that they saw more technology in U.S. schools," Ripley writes.

> Even students from high-performing countries said they saw more technology in their U.S. classrooms than back home. Seven out of ten American teenagers who had been abroad agreed. Americans had tricked-out classrooms with interactive white boards, high-tech projectors, and towers of iPads. However, there was little evidence that these purchases had paid off for anyone other than the technology vendors themselves.[19]

How does this make American schools different from these nations in terms of academic rigor? We've all seen the international scores of academic performance, of course. Putting those aside for a moment, does America's obvious technological predilection provide students with more authentic, challenging, and engaging learning experiences?

Not exactly. Not even a little bit, actually—at least according to Elina, a Finnish interview subject of Ripley's who studied as an exchange student in Colon, Michigan: "'Not much is demanded of U.S. students. . . . It was like elementary school in Finland,' she said."[20]

THE UPSIDE-DOWN NATURE OF ACADEMIC-*LIKE* ACTIVITY

The comparisons Ripley's interview subjects make between American and international classrooms are important. They converge with points made throughout this book to illustrate the final reason why so many instructional innovations, technological or otherwise, have done (and will do) so little to improve student achievement and ultimately wind up discarded, one after the next, like so many fad diets.

From a practical point of view, far too many of the innovations implemented in America's schools are designed around the (you guessed it) upside-down funnel. A quick tour of a few "cool practices" that ultimately fell short and were immediately forgotten (or discredited) demonstrates this quite starkly.

From "whole-language" reading instruction to "inquiry-based learning" to "computer-aided instruction" to interactive whiteboards to learning-styles-based theories, and on and on, all of these high-profile—and high-cost—attempts to improve instruction are usually based on two major principles of the upside-down funnel:

1. Engaging students with showy, more "authentic," or more personally relevant learning activities at the expense of genuine content mastery.
2. Skipping to higher-order, critical thinking tasks without proper regard for essential intellectual building blocks such as knowledge and comprehension.

In the end, *the type* of instructional innovation doesn't matter all that much. What does matter is the innovation'*s role in instruction*. If engaging innovations are employed but are not accompanied by expectations that students genuinely master standards-articulated content and skills, the innovative practice itself is little more than academic-*like* activity. (We could also note the lack of attendant plans to build, assess, and assist students toward content masteries in the typical academic-ish scenario.)

Here is an illustration and some reflection questions based on a (not fully fictional) sixth-grade science lesson, in which the teacher used hands-on kits (provided by the district's STEM grant) to model riverbed formations and flooding:

- Using sand, students built models of rivers and simulated flood conditions by pouring in buckets of water at various rates.
- Students observed the simulated rivers and recorded observations about erosion, bank formation and transformation, and overflow, then wrote paragraphs describing the observed phenomena.
- When the lesson was complete and the teacher reflected upon the class session, she reported that the kids liked the activity and completed it enthusiastically.
- For the first time all year, 100 percent of students completed the assigned journal paragraph summarizing the activity.
- On a standards-based benchmark test to monitor students' progress toward mastery of state science content standards, 30 percent of the class successfully demonstrated (answering correctly on at least 75 percent of terms) proficiency with the benchmark's flood-related vocabulary. Also, 25 percent of the class's students could correctly notate a graph of various flood stages.

Based on the above data, would the hands-on river-modeling activity be considered a successful lesson? In total, could it be classified as an academic activity or an academic-*like* activity?

If students can't apply standards-specified topographic or hydrologic concepts somehow (e.g., use flood-related vocabulary terms in sentences without hints or prompts, or accurately interpret a graph of river stages and identify when the river went from action stage to flood stage), the activity cannot be considered successful when we think about academic mastery in a world where the funnel is right-side-up. As it turned out here, the "innovative" instructional approach actually took class time away from moving kids academically.

"Students engaged and occupied" is great. "Students being happy" is also great. "Students learning something specific and useful, and the teacher is certain about it," however, trumps them both. It's what schooling should aim to do, after all, far before the first two.

Every innovative instructional approach or activity, from increased use of digital devices to full curricular programs to entire school models, should be judged according to whether it can help students learn specific, practical content. If it cannot, it should be considered upside-down, because it is only going to "work" for that narrow stream of students who would have succeeded anyway—who would succeed under pretty much any conditions. And it is going to disadvantage the students who stand to benefit most from genuine, straightforward content mastery.

This does not mean, however, that such activities are utterly worthless and should be removed from all schools' programming. On the contrary, activities and approaches like this can work wonderfully to *supplement* more rigorous content, either as extension or intervention learning, or simply as something fun to do on a snowy Friday when recess gets canceled.

Without a proper balance of rigorous and specific expectations articulated in state-, school-, or college-ready standards, such activities are, again, only academic-*like*. They are a facsimile. When teachers substitute academic-like work for academically rigorous work in an effort to make kids pay attention and participate, and then rate its effectiveness according to how much students liked it, they are privileging those students who regularly experience academically rigorous activity and disadvantaging those who do not.

Considering how experiences with academic content build in sequential complexity and ultimately help students acquire critical institutional virtues (remember the "school-as-resistance-medium" idea from chapter 6), it's a choice American education must stop making—no matter how cool the practice might seem.

In effect, many practical innovations only repackage upside-down ideals and recycle them into American classrooms on an endless loop. The effects on student achievement—and, crucially, *which* students are achieving the desired outcomes—won't change until American education *reverses* these ideals and chooses practical innovations that are right-side-up. As we have seen, entire countries understand this very well. So, too, do many American schools—even if, as with KIPP charters, families have to go outside traditional public schools to find them.

Remember the opening words of Naveen Jain: Coming up with a more innovative strategy is not the core issue; if American education does not adjust at a more fundamental level—if it does not turn its funnel right-side-up—no amount of creativity or innovation in strategy, planning, or practice will help the enterprise achieve the results it desires. This is not a playbook issue. It's a blocking-and-tackling issue, plain and simple.

A stronger sense of mission, combined with effective practice, provides a strong foundation from which to make more productive decisions about instructional programming and innovation. Right-side-up principles are not frequently consulted in the decision-making process, likely because practitioners see them as too traditional and quickly shut them down.

In light of the high costs upside-down innovations incur, however, and the low returns that eventually make them expendable, shouldn't we stop trying every new cool thing under the sun, technology based or otherwise, in the hope that a magic solution will materialize?

Even more certainly, despite the pressure coming from private-sector reformers to "innovate or die," despite the faulty assumptions these reformers make about what students need and which tools work best, American education must carefully measure which innovations are worth our time and energy, and which ones we need to refuse.

Few in the private sector, after all, would make huge capital investments in innovations with no established ROI model. If you're an executive, that's a decision that gets you fired. And that's *without* millions of children's futures hanging in the balance. Just as the private sector performs rigorous analyses to measure the risks and rewards of new ideas before they commit to the outlay, so must American education. Does it work? Can we prove it? Is it worth it? These are the questions we can't stop asking.

Conducting more effective studies will not be difficult; we are fortunate that considerable research and data is widely available. The hard part will be honesty. American education must be honest with itself about what works and why, what does not work and why, and what works for whom and why, and *then* choose instructional innovations based on strong evidence and the kids in front of them—not a TED Talk or a sales pitch or some other appeal to emotion. As cognitive scientist Daniel Willingham put it so well in his 2012 book *When Can You Trust the Experts? How to Tell Good Science from Bad in Education*,

> [U]nfounded beliefs related to schooling are of greater concern. The costs in time and money can be substantial; worse, faulty beliefs about learning can potentially cost kids their education. Scientific tools can be a real help in

sorting out which methods and materials truly help students learn and which do not. We cannot afford to let educational practice be guided by hunch or hope if better information is available. But even though scientific tools are routinely applied, the product is often ignored, or else it's twisted by people with dollars on their minds.[21]

NOTES

1. On a different level of the innovation-in-education conversation, but relevant here: U.S. educators are being urged to design learning experiences that will better meet students' "twenty-first century" ways of learning (built on the apparent assumption that modern conditions have so sped human evolution that young people's brains have become wired differently in the last two decades) and to ultimately produce innovative, creative *students*. The messages usually come from outside education—most times from experts in economic development forecasting areas of potential in the global marketplace—and moves educators toward the largely unproductive distinction discussed in chapters 4 and 5: focusing less on lower-order-skills-based outcomes and instructional methods and more on constructivist, inquiry-based, higher-order-skills-prioritizing student outcomes and instructional methods. Though it is not an innovation in practice or management, per se, the message's impacts, from institutional-preparatory and best-practical standpoints, make it an important consideration within education's innovation culture.

2. To review the Department of Education's leading message upon the official rollout of the Race to the Top grant program, see "Archived: The Race to the Top Begins—Remarks by Secretary Arne Duncan," U.S. Department of Education, July 24, 2009, https://www2.ed.gov/news/speeches/2009/07/07242009.html. Note in particular the speech's emphases on avoiding status quos and the Department of Education's relinquishment of its role as an overseer of compliance, and so forth.

3. "Race to the Top Program Executive Summary," U.S. Department of Education, 2009, http://www2.ed.gov/programs/racetothetop/executive-summary.pdf. See also "Investing in Innovation Fund (i3)," U.S. Department of Education—Office of Innovation and Improvement, December 20, 2013, http://www2.ed.gov/programs/innovation/index.html.

4. For a fine account of the connections between RTTT and the growing private-sector influence in American education, see Diane Ravitch, *Reign of Error: The Hoax of the Privatization Movement and the Danger to America's Public Schools* (New York: Alfred A. Knopf, 2013), 10–18.

5. Ibid., 156–57.

6. Robin J. Lake, "In the Eye of the Beholder: Charter Schools and Innovation," *Journal of School Choice* 2, no. 2 (2008): 115–27, http://www.crpe.org/sites/default/files/jrn_ncsrp_innovrsrch_apr08_0.pdf.

7. Matthew Di Carlo, "The Evidence on Charter Schools and Test Scores," Albert Shanker Institute, December 2011, http://shankerblog.org/wp-content/uploads/2011/12/CharterReview.pdf.

8. Joy Resmovits, "Mathematica 2013 Study: KIPP Charter School Students Outperform Public School Peers," *Huffington Post*, February 27, 2013, http://www.huffingtonpost.com/2013/02/27/mathematica-2013-study-kipp_n_2768476.html?utm_hp_ref=@education123. See also Mary Ann Zehr, "KIPP Middle Schools Found to Spur Learning Gains," *Education Week*, June 22, 2010, http://www.kipp.org/files/dmfile/EdWeek_6_22_10_PDF.pdf.

9. Ravitch, *Reign of Error*, 160–61.

10. Ibid., 167–74.

11. In order to actually reach the classroom and be included in practice, however, substantial amounts of business must take place between vendors and school districts. Indeed, a huge share of innovative methods/technologies/materials in use in classrooms are there not so much because practitioners sought them, but rather because the schools/districts/states they teach in adopted, purchased, and hence mandated their use widely.

12. For a short, well-summarized list of studies showing failures of various digital initiatives since 2000, see Mark Bauerlein, *The Dumbest Generation: How the Digital Age Stupifies Young Americans and Jeopardizes Our Future, Or, Don't Trust Anyone under 30* (New York: Jeremy P. Tarcher/Penguin, 2008), 119–24. For effect sizes on student achievement gathered from meta-analytic studies of computer-assisted instruction and web-based learning, see John Hattie, *Visible Learning: A Synthesis of Over 800 Meta-Analyses Relating to Achievement* (London: Routledge, 2009), 220–28.

13. In a commentary for *Teachers College Record* in January 2014, M. O. Thirunarayanan, associate professor of learning technologies in the College of Education at Florida International University, questioned the ethics of technology implementation without upfront research or testing, likening it to physicians treating patients with drugs whose effects have not been studied. See M. O. Thirunarayanan, "Is the Use of Untested Technologies in Classrooms Unethical?" *Teachers College Record*, January 24, 2014, http://www.tcrecord.org/Content.asp?ContentID=17393.

14. Devin Leonard, "The iPad Goes to School," *Bloomberg Business Week*, October 24, 2013, http://www.businessweek.com/articles/2013-10-24/the-ipad-goes-to-school-the-rise-of-educational-tablets#p1.

15. Ibid. For a more in-depth literature review and survey results from thousands of students and hundreds of teachers—though in Canada, not the United States—that echo several of the anecdotal pieces reported by Leonard, see Thierry Karsenti and Aurelien Fievez, *The iPad in Education: Uses, Benefits, and Challenges—A Survey of 6,057 Students and 302 Teachers in Quebec (Canada)* (Montreal, QC: CRIFPE, 2013), http://www.academia.edu/5364660/The_iPad_in_Education_uses_benefits_and_challenges._A_survey_of_6057_students_and_302_teachers_in_Quebec_Canada.

16. Clayton Christensen is coauthor, along with Michael B. Horn and Curtis W. Johnson, of the business-community-decorated *Disrupting Class: How Disruptive Innovation Will Change the Way the World Learns* (New York: McGraw-Hill, 2011), a book that essentially announced to the private sector that education's beaches were now perfect for storming, replete with all the twenty-first-century learning lingo one would need to know to resonate with "educational natives."

17. Tony Wagner is author of education-related titles like *Making the Grade: Reinventing America's Schools* (New York: RoutledgeFalmer, 2002), *The Global Achievement Gap: Why Even Our Best Schools Don't Teach the New Survival Skills Our Children Need—and What We Can Do about It* (New York: Basic Books, 2008), and *Creating Innovators: The Making of Young People Who Will Change the World* (New York: Scribner, 2012), which all center on common Progressive Education themes (e.g., subject-matter knowledge not as important as applied knowledge and critical thinking, a new type of learner is emerging, the world is changing in ways that demand a new set of skills, etc.) updated for the twenty-first century.

18. Stephen Sawchuk, "Motives of 21st-Century-Skills Group Questioned," *Education Week*, December 4, 2009, http://www.edweek.org/ew/articles/2009/12/09/14partnership_ep.h29.html?tkn=LOLFOt7k4DAGb2J88qtnXPi3D6weTWzi%2FXiL.

19. Amanda Ripley, *The Smartest Kids in the World: And How They Got That Way* (New York: Simon & Schuster, 2013), 64.

20. Ibid., 100.

21. Daniel T. Willingham, *When Can You Trust the Experts? How to Tell Good Science from Bad in Education* (San Francisco: Jossey-Bass, 2012), 12.

Chapter Nine

Too Scattered to Matter

Things which matter most must never be at the mercy of things which matter least.

—Johann Wolfgang von Goethe (1749–1832), German writer and politician

No matter how effectively refined or executed, education reforms inspired by the private-sector mindset stand very little chance of creating the system-wide corrections all American families and mainstream institutions desire, depend on, and deserve. Until reformers turn their attention to correcting the enterprise's upside-down mission and practice—in other words, insisting on a mission that serves the public good and using proven practices to fulfill it—their faulty assumptions–based reforms will only succeed in moving the fundamentally flawed system toward either a full seize-up or a pronounced deepening of its flaws.

Without this basic corrective action, private-sector-inspired reforms, such as tightening measurement and accountability, will at best correct inefficiencies that are certainly a source of pain but are nowhere near our most crucial or most critical problem. In fact, this approach guarantees that the largest source of inefficiency will continue undisturbed. It's like caulking the windows in a cold house instead of attending to the broken furnace.

At worst, reforms that apply innovative approaches to upside-down pedagogical principles merely make already-flawed practices even worse. This effect is compounded by lasting financial complications. Sticking with the home-heating analogy for a moment, this is like replacing the old broken furnace with a new defective furnace: it's a bad decision that not only doesn't solve the problem but also affects your ability to pay for a solution that will work.

As resentful as many educators may be about current reforms, we need to admit that we had it coming. Which is to say, education had *something* coming, anyway, thanks to a century or so of unfocused and misaligned practices based on Progressive principles. The cycle of poor results followed by requests for more money had to end somewhere. If anything, it should be a surprise that the public and policymakers took so long to act. The performance of American education has been widely considered unsatisfactory for fifty years or more, especially in terms of its demographically unbalanced success rates and graduates' lack of post-secondary readiness.

Many presidentially appointed commissions for improving education have been established during this period and have issued findings in reports like the historic *A Nation at Risk* from 1983. Produced by the Reagan administration's National Commission on Excellence in Education, this report officially put educators on notice, laying out recommendations for getting education right once and for all.[1] Many of its recommendations were summarily ignored,[2] and the cycle of disappointing results, not surprisingly, continued.

But it had to stop somewhere. It was only a matter of time before the right groups acquired the political capital necessary to make it happen.

Unfortunately for all of us involved in education, the groups who now hold the reins are headed in a (different) wrong direction. They blame weak outcomes on the wrong hypotheses (teachers are lazy bums, innovation will save the day), and they recommend wrong corrective actions (ramped-up accountability, more private-sector involvement) to match.

Contrast the current moment with Finland's "No Child Left Behind moment" in the 1970s, when students' academic expectations and teachers' qualifying standards were both raised dramatically and teacher colleges were rebooted accordingly.[3] Looking at this very different outcome from a similar national impulse, we can see how reform can (and should) be done differently. In two decades or so, Finland has created a model the rest of the world openly envies. Spurred by the same desire, the United States looks like it will have to let the current crop of misguided reforms die out before it can get down to the real work of righting the funnel.

For now, we simply have to make the best of a bad situation— namely, reforms that have been deemed "The Answers" by accountability-driven, market-admiring officials. Once again, these reforms will not change desired outcomes in any meaningful way. Yet they come at such an incredibly high cost—in terms of raw dollars, infrastructure, and declining morale—they are likely to go down in history as tragically wasteful.

In fact, we haven't even discussed all of the negative impacts of these reforms. One of the most devastating is the exacerbation of one of our deepest issues: a doomed mission.

Since the time of the progressives, the implicit mission of education—*schools exist to provide the whole development of each individual child*—has complicated operations past the point of effectiveness. Accountability reformers could very well worsen the situation, scattering the mission in ways that will seriously compromise performance and make the broken pieces nearly impossible to put back together.

Let's take a moment to remember what the funnel analogy represents—the foundational mission of American education. The current mission, based on Progressive beliefs, is this: *schools exist to provide the whole development of each individual child.* This mission is upside-down for two reasons. First, its top is too narrow; it works for the few instead of the many. Second, its bottom is too wide, preparing students as individually as possible for everything at once, and yet failing to prepare them for success in mainstream institutions. Of course, an upside-down mission is impossible to achieve. That's the bad news.

The even worse news is that the funnel's wide mouth is stretched further every day as various stakeholder groups try to make room for their own pet priorities. What makes the whole enterprise vulnerable to this? It all comes back to the weakness of schooling's implicit Progressive mission. If we examine this mission in detail, it quickly becomes clear that current attempts to reform American education threaten to widen the mission even further, delaying meaningful results and threatening deep, long-lasting damage.

The implicit, Progressive objective to educate the whole child insists that the child must lead the way; educators simply follow the child's particular strengths and interests. This approach stands directly opposed to a more general attempt to instill specific habits, knowledge, and skills in *all* children, even if these qualities would serve them well throughout their lives. Not surprisingly, trying to follow the leads of millions of different children has not brought a great deal of focus to education. On the contrary, it has tempted even more interest groups to pull and stretch the mission in even more distracting directions. (Remember what happens when you try to please everyone?)

American education has trained, organized, and presented itself more as a commune of endless possibility than an order-governing institution. As such, it has created a disturbing loophole, one that finds schools encouraging—and even enforcing—values and behaviors that are, flatly, outside its practical purview.

Because the mission is so open-ended, anyone can shove their way into it. Parents, community interest groups, high-level policymakers, and industry leaders alike have come to view public schools as the ideal place to train young Americans in a whole host of emerging societal issues. These issues are then pushed down into schools, where teachers—who may or may not understand these issues in depth, and may also have a whole spectrum of opinions about them—are responsible for shoe-horning these issues into the bigger educational picture.

Lacking the unimaginably huge amount of funding necessary to genuinely enable these efforts, schools find themselves stretched far past the point of effective instruction—unable both to execute on their own fractured, scattered objectives and to consistently prepare students for the expectations of post-K–12 institutions.

This is not a new situation, unfortunately. In *Left Back: A Century of Battles over School Reform*, educational historian Diane Ravitch notes how American education has struggled with this problem for a century or so.

Before the Progressive takeover, academics ruled. The academic curriculum, she asserts, provided American schooling with magnetic north, until it was shoved aside in a Progressive fervor in the early twentieth century, creating a void where there was once a clear purpose. This void has never stopped haunting the enterprise. In the decades since it came to be, Ravitch writes,

> reform movements would come and go with surprising rapidity, almost randomly, each leaving its mark behind in the schools. Over time, as this happened, educators forgot how to say "no," even to the loopier notions of what schools were for. Every perceived need, interest, concern, problem, or issue found a place in the curriculum or provided a rationale for adding new specialists to the school's staff. Once the hierarchy of educational values was shattered, once schools lost their compass, hawkers of new wares could market their stock to the schools. Every purveyor of social reform could find a willing customer in the schools because all needs were presumed equal in importance, and there was no longer any general consensus on the central purpose of schooling.[4]

Though *Left Back* was assessing American education over a century-long view, Ravitch's assertions describe the current climate so accurately that they seem downright eerie. Looking across American education for evidence of Ravitch's assessment today, the examples are overwhelming. At this time of writing—more than a dozen years after the publication of *Left Back*—schools are integrating programming to explicitly teach everything from bullying prevention to multicultural understanding to social media safety to responsible chemical use to acceptable sexual behavior to building persistence to selecting and paying for college to improving financial literacy. This list, quite literally, goes on. For *days*.

These current priorities will almost certainly change within two or three years to accommodate new stakeholder demands. (Early candidates include instruction to curb texting and driving, building students' community-service portfolios toward beefed-up college application packages, and expanding students' opportunities to write computer code.) Some will disappear entirely, leaving space for others to fill. Others will live on in individual schools' programming because the teachers and leaders there believe they are too developmentally important to discard.

Either way, schools must continue to accommodate all of this programming in addition to everything else they are trying to do. Because instructional hours are a scarce and finite resource, schools end up taking time away from academic subjects or asking teachers to superimpose in-the-moment content onto regular academic content where the two may, however remotely, be connected.

Carrying all of this societal baggage is particularly difficult in the current reform atmosphere because practitioners are subject to even more intense accountability while revised academic standards are raising expectations for reading and math and, in doing so, affecting programs of neighboring disciplines.

This is how institutions become more scattered, confused, and disorganized. And putting the student at the center is how we got here.

Again, we had it coming. (Again, we had *something* coming.) We brought this on ourselves. What came, however, is far from a real solution.

As we have seen, private-sector-inspired reforms purport to bring the vaunted "laser focus" of successful businesses into schools to help address these diffuse priorities. By redefining the relationship between schools and students (and their families) as one of vendor and consumer, however, they are actually making schools even more scattered.

Stanford University education professor and historian David Labaree describes this shift well in his 2010 *Someone Has to Fail: The Zero-Sum Game of Public Schooling*, noting that the Accountability Era kicked off by NCLB essentially transformed "education from a public good to a private good, and from a source of political community to a source of individual opportunity. . . . Gone is the notion that schools exist to promote civic virtue for the preservation of republican community; in its place is the notion that schools exist to give all consumers access to a valuable form of educational property."[5]

Behind this shift is the mindset that says increasing transparency and giving more control to "consumers" are common-sense ways to fix the marketplace of American education. And seen through a free-market lens—casting the American public as shareholders and the educational enterprise as a corporation—this is a sound conclusion.

What private-sector reformers seem unaware of, unfortunately, is that American education has had little independent control of its operations and programming since the early 1900s. Which is another way of saying the lack of institutional focus these reformers are hoping to fix is not the fault of schools alone. Rather, at least half of the scatter effect can be attributed to how little say the institution itself actually has in choosing its priorities.

Indeed, for all of the areas that need improvement, "terminal inflexibility" is not one of them. The educational institution, after all, does not exactly draw a line in the sand in the face of outside pressure. Even the most absolute positions, like zero-tolerance weapons and violence policies—designed to err on the side of student safety in the wake of Columbine—are bound to be questioned, overrun, and, ultimately, reversed.[6]

If that seems farfetched, ask anyone who's ever worked in education about what happens to a school's most deeply held and ironclad policies if a student or parent so much as mentions litigation. And they'll tell you that schools very rarely stand their ground, even if it costs them what they know to be the soundest, safest learning environments. Lacking the funding to cover legal battles and generally unwilling to endure very public losses of face, schools are far more likely to capitulate than stand and fight. Again, the confusion reformers see is real, but schools are not solely responsible for it.

A more effective way to improve schools' focus may actually be one that's pretty much the opposite of the "shareholder" model. Rather, reformers could help schools focus by ensuring they have sufficient legal, practical, and financial resources to defend themselves *against* the outside influences that seek to add more items to the list and remove the ones that really count.

Another reality that private-sector-inspired reformers disregard as they seek greater stakeholder control is one we touched on earlier: that students are not consumers. They are not paying for a service. They are the product, they are the outcome, and they are a particularly important part of the process. They are deeply responsible for their own transformation, and that takes work on their part. Work they may not readily commit to because . . . well, because it can be hard. As with any self-improving venture, it's supposed to be hard.[7] That's the whole point.

Done right, the product education creates is students who are stronger in academics and in institutional virtues, able to independently make sound, informed choices for their own good and the greater good. To build these strengths, schools have to use an appropriate resistance medium,[8] and the point of resistance medium is to resist; in this case, what it resists is students' innate preferences. (These include sloth, gluttony, pride, and a few others.) This process is not always pleasant for the student in question.

But the mission is not one of rest and relaxation. For the sake of the student, schools must occasionally deny preferred choices and replace them with institutionally virtuous decisions. For clients who have the most difficulty demonstrating these institutional virtues, it is the school's *duty* to guide students toward the understanding that this is what will be expected of them later in life, no matter what they decide to do. It is the school's duty to do this, even if it feels uncomfortable. Doing anything else is cheating the student out of future success.

All of this, of course, is very different from a typical vendor-consumer contract, in which consumers wield greater control. A consumer who is continually satisfied with a vendor is more likely to continue patronizing this vendor. Conversely, a consumer whose personal preferences are not honored by a vendor can take her business elsewhere, leaving the spurned vendor with a choice: learn from it to prevent future losses, ignore the lesson and risk future losses, or, accepting that no business can be everything to everyone, stop selling to the consumer's particular demographic group.

These two contracts—school-student and vendor-consumer—clearly rest on very different premises. Even so, private-sector reformers believe that "creating more competition in the marketplace" is the surest way to improve all schools' performance. Expansion of school choices, publicizing teachers' evaluation results and test scores, and requiring schools to involve site councils consisting of parents and community members are all ways that reformers seek to give consumers (and their parents) greater power and influence.

But the school-student contract is already heavily tilted toward the student thanks to the Progressive influence. The student is the center, leader, oracle, and sage. Which is why giving students an even louder voice will absolutely not improve outcomes. More voices only add to the general din, scattering priorities and policies further, making it even more difficult for schools to deliver the results mainstream institutions expect and many individuals desperately need.

Specifically, giving students and families the option to withdraw enrollments from a school because the classes are too demanding, or because the teachers expect perfect behavior, or because the student would rather work at his own pace online does not pressure the school to improve. If anything, it may persuade the school to do precisely what no school should ever do: lower expectations to stop the flow of withdrawals.

And sadly, offering "competition" to spur positive change may actually give students an escape hatch directly into environments that will not, frankly, help them handle the world that awaits them beyond their K–12 years.

To stop this from happening, schools must make this decision for the people they serve—namely, by refusing to cater to every community whim and refusing to treat citizens like mindless consumers. Consumer satisfaction should not be our guiding mission. We are not selling athletic shoes, laundry detergent, or four-door hatchbacks. We are undertaking something far more important. We are transforming students for smooth entry into mainstream institutions, the institutions we all depend on to maintain a stable and self-sustaining society.

It may be helpful to view the current free-for-all in education—influenced as it is by numerous external forces and increasingly pressured to treat kids like consumers—in light of another publicly funded, order-governing institution.

Imagine that, following a series of house fires in your town, a group of concerned citizens assembles to campaign against the local fire department. This group wants the department to stop breaking the windows and doors of burning houses to rescue the residents trapped inside.

As much as they appreciate the results the firefighters achieve by doing so—rescuing family members and pets—the citizens strongly prefer that firefighters perform this work without destroying the property. You see, some of these broken windows and smashed-in doors were not in the parts of the houses that were actually on fire, and the replacement costs were simply too high.

In this scenario, how should the fire department respond? Here are your choices:

1. Radically revise practices exactly as requested. Avoid any property damage at all—ever—in executing the primary mission. Ban the use of axes or Halligan tools. Redirect budget dollars to innovative technology—with no regard for its lack of verified reliability or its high cost—that enables urgent entry without breaking windows and doors.
2. Take the citizens' feedback into account and promise to fulfill the request whenever possible. Explicitly reserve the right, however, to use professional discretion and expertise to decide when fulfilling the request is simply impossible. Assert that there is simply no other way to do the job—that sacrifices must be made and, well, broken doors and windows seem like a small price to pay when lives and property can be saved.

Across U.S. education, the response is most often a version of number 1. They do this consistently for nearly every vocal interest group. Very rarely will a school hold fast to its guiding principles and simply respond, "Sometimes, when we are preparing your child for what comes after schooling, we have to use the practices we know are successful."

Without a clearly directed mission or well-defined ideas of how to execute this mission, American education has, as Diane Ravitch asserted in *Left Back*, little idea of how to say no, let alone which stakeholders to refuse. Over time, this uncertainty has produced a general lack of institutional will, which only exacerbates the situation.

American education has made everything a priority, which, as the saying goes, ultimately makes nothing a priority.

If reformers hope to reverse this, the first steps should not be those of the Accountability Era—"giv[ing] all consumers access to a valuable form of educational property," as David Labaree put it earlier—as this will only scatter things further.

Rather, reformers should help educators resist these multiple, contradictory influences, either by holding the line against them or by being more deliberate in determining which influences align with the mission and which do not. As much as stakeholders deserve to contribute input, schools must be able to "break the occasional window" in order to best prepare stakeholders'—not *share*holders'—children for the rest of their lives.

Of course, you can't defend a mission if it doesn't exist. Placing every single child at the center leads to nowhere in particular, as we've seen time and again. A very important first step toward righting the funnel is redefining our mission. An assertive and focused statement—like *American Education exists to prepare young citizens for meaningful participation in America's mainstream institutions*—shows great potential as a foundational platform.

NOTES

1. For a good recap of *A Nation at Risk*'s recommendations and themes, as well as how they contrast with the mandates and themes of No Child Left Behind, see Diane Ravitch, *The Death and Life of the Great American School System: How Testing and Choice Are Undermining Education* (New York: Basic Books, 2010), 22–30.
2. E. D. Hirsch, "An Epoch-Making Report, But What about the Early Grades?" *Education Week*, April 23, 2008, http://www.edweek.org/ew/articles/2008/04/23/34hirsch_ep.h27.html.
3. Amanda Ripley, *The Smartest Kids in the World: And How They Got That Way* (New York: Simon & Schuster, 2013), 88–90.
4. Diane Ravitch, *Left Back: A Century of Battles over School Reform* (New York: Touchstone, 2000), 16–17.
5. David F. Labaree, *Someone Has to Fail: The Zero-Sum Game of Public Schooling* (Cambridge, MA: Harvard University Press, 2010), 40–41.
6. Wesley Lowery, "Zero Tolerance Policies," *Public Broadcasting Service*, March 20, 2013, http://www.pbs.org/wnet/tavissmiley/tsr/education-under-arrest/zero-tolerance-policies-are-these-post-columbine-measures-putting-minority-students-on-the-fast-track-to-the-prison-system/.
7. For an expanded version of this argument, see the health club/exercise-to-schooling analogy in chapter 7.
8. For an expanded version of this argument, see the swimming-pool-to-schooling analogy in chapter 6.

Chapter Ten

Righting the Funnel: Issues to Solve, Actions to Take

> The school has again but one way, and that is, first and last, to teach [young people] to read, write, and count. And if the school fails to do that, and tries beyond that to do something for which school is not adapted, it not only fails in its own function, but fails in all other attempted functions. Because no school as such can organise industry, or settle the matter of wage and income, can found homes or furnish parents, can establish justice or make a civilised world.
>
> —W. E. B. Du Bois (1868–1963), American civil rights activist, to a Georgia convention of black school teachers in 1935, about schooling's role in improving American society

So who is wrong? Practitioners? Reformers? Policymakers? Parents?

The answer is all of the above.

To some extent, we're *all* wrong. Despite our passions for certain pedagogical practices or aspirations, continuing to use them may interfere with students' readiness for America's post-K–12 institutions. At the same time, the educational enterprise's shortcomings can't be blamed only on lazy-bum practitioners. And, unfortunately, the private sector's preferred methods of improvement may actually be an incredibly poor fit for the realities of modern education.

What this means is that American education is fundamentally upside-down, and none of the current reforms is going to correct this. Until our mission, practices, and organizational emphases are turned right-side-up, we should all expect to see more results like the ones that mobilized the current reformers in the first place. Even if we only look at results since the Accountability Era began, there is little reason to think we are on the right path. Think about the barely changed student results, the increasing institutional mission- and practice-scatter, and the continually rising frustration on all sides.

The funnel won't be easy to flip, especially with so many other reform efforts underway at the same time. In light of those two realities, here are some big questions we need to answer:

- How can we turn the funnel back over? Which parts of the system would need to be built, which parts could be revised, and which should be abolished?
- If upside-down ideals and practices are trained into (and accepted by) the practitioner workforce, how can we approach retraining?
- If this retraining is possible, how would the U.S. public react to the revised mission and its higher expectations of students? How should the revised mission and expectations be communicated, promoted, and reinforced?
- If the enterprise focuses on flipping the funnel, what happens to current reforms based upon measuring performance via standardized assessments, improving education's professionals, and providing greater school choice?
- What roles should government and advocacy groups play in the future maintenance and support of a right-side-up system?

In this chapter and the next, we will examine these questions closely in three ways:

- *Toward Right-Side-Up: Three Key Issues to Solve*: A general outline of major issues to improve or reverse; areas where reformers' energies and strategies could be spent more productively.
- *A Too Audacious Model of Right-Side-Up*: An ideal framework of K–12 education for wide U.S. adoption, engineered to address the three key issues.
- *Checking for Inversion*: Realistic and practical steps that practitioners, schools, and districts can take to make real progress on the three key issues.

TOWARD RIGHT-SIDE-UP: THREE KEY ISSUES TO SOLVE

There are three key issues that American education must solve, both systemically and locally, to create enough resistance to build up students' academic capacity and institutional virtues. In other words, addressing these issues will help flip the funnel. And while it's true that some schools and districts are working on these issues already, they are not doing so with any success precisely because they are approaching each one from a traditional upside-down perspective.

Just as schools can't teach everyone everything, reformers of any stripe can't take on every issue in education at the same time. This is part of the problem, of course. Because there are so many things in education that need fixing, approaching any one problem in a practical way will be difficult. What follows here are three big, bold priorities. Though many, many smaller things need attention, concentrating our efforts on these three issues will have a hugely positive initial impact and spark further change.

1. Review and Redesign Educators' Professional Preparation

Founded upon Progressive ideals a century ago and dominated by "Progressive-inspired" thought leaders since that time,[1] preparation and licensure programs for teachers are the biggest force keeping the funnel upside-down. By inculcating wave after wave of practitioners, schools of education present upside-down practices as unquestioned gospel truth, while right-side-up practices—even those that have been statistically verified to work—are cast as anathema.

The disconnect between what students need to succeed and what ed schools tell their teachers-in-training to do is a huge chasm. It is so pronounced that academics at Columbia University long ago—and not-so-jokingly—labeled the road separating Teachers College from the rest of campus as "the widest street in the world."[2] The criticism doesn't end with this quip, by a long shot: ed schools have been called out for their poor product, openly and by all kinds of critics, for decades.[3] As research about teacher quality has become more focused in the past decade, ideas that were once expressed only as opinions and anecdotes about the failings of ed schools have gathered objective momentum.[4]

Regardless of this pervasive lack of faith, however, ed schools remain undeterred. For a century they have remained baldly certain that Progressive, child-centered, constructivist methods are the best ways to teach and for all kids to learn. They have produced several generations of ground-level professionals trained in this manner, along with several generations of student-inequitable, institution-weakening results.

When questioned about these results, American ed schools react so defensively as to arouse suspicion. In 2013, when the National Council on Teacher Quality (NCTQ) attempted to more quantifiably assess teacher preparation across the United States, for example, university ed schools mobilized quickly to erect bureaucratic barriers.[5] Objecting to NCTQ's methods and sponsorship, most of these institutions refused to participate in the study.[6]

Dismissing outside review cannot be tolerated as we move toward meaningful systemic improvement. The entire system is already too closed off to fundamental operational reform. As most of its eventual leaders (e.g., administrators, thought-leading commentators, university scholars, etc.) emerge from the pool of ground-level practitioners, the ideals of the ed school have over time become so hardened into the arteries of the educational organism that they block any and all contrary practical ideals from passing through.

Though these obstructive ideals originate in ed schools, reforms designed to improve teacher quality rarely address preparatory requirements and principles. While the issue of teacher quality caught fire in the United States (an intense one, its flames fanned higher by deep-pocketed and highly visible supporters like Bill Gates[7]), the attendant reforms almost solely concentrate on processes within the teaching environment: performance feedback cycles, teacher-evaluation, and professional accountability, for example. Nobody is concerned with where the quality originates.

Though it is certainly appropriate for schools to shoulder the burden of defining better standards of practice and strengthening professional development programs, the choice to ignore teacher-preparatory institutions, where the standards of practice are established in the first place, seems curious. After all, this pre-professional training is what nearly all educational professionals have in common.

Which is why the time is right to closely examine—with an eye toward redesigning—teacher-preparatory institutions from the ground up.

Consider Finland, which recorded a benchmark-setting improvement of its schools over a period of less than three decades. The country's turnaround began in precisely this way. Realizing that able teachers would be required to usher students toward academic standards that had been raised across the board, Finland rebooted its ed schools by dramatically revising pre-professional curricula and significantly raising the bar for program entry requirements.[8]

Back in America, redesigning teacher preparation must begin by tempering Progressive ideals and practices with a strong dose of reality.

Specifically, traditional ideals and practices must be more tightly aligned with the institutional virtues that mainstream institutions demand, as well as the learning theories confirmed by three decades of cognitive-scientific and applied research. Ed schools can no longer dismiss on principle the evidence that has repeatedly shown how poorly actual students fare when all learning activities are designed around foundational Progressive slogans, including "students learn best by doing," "teach the whole child," "appeal to intrinsic motivation," and "move students to be critical thinkers."

Today, with the benefit of substantial evidence about the complex mechanisms of human learning—which the founding Progressives did not have, admittedly—education professionals-in-training must learn why it is crucial to test slogan-based practices within the crucible of research and hard proof. They must learn how to create learning environments that operate according to a more balanced approach, one that draws equally from constructivist ideals, cognitive reality, societal awareness, and post-K–12 institutional expectations. They must learn how best to assess which students have which needs, as well as how best to move forward with each student to ensure that each earns the skills, knowledge, and institutional virtues necessary for future success. As we've seen, when there is no balance, the results are all too familiar: watching movies instead of reading complex literary works, hands-on science activities that produce little content understanding, constructivist math instruction that is not concerned with answers. Without that balance, far too many students' ultimate academic and post-K–12 institutional readiness is being sacrificed.

The question of who should handle such ed school review and revision, however, is much more difficult to answer. The United States does not have a sound process for validating these schools' requirements or final products. Though each state has licensing requirements and articulated standards teachers are expected to follow, teacher-preparatory institutions themselves are not held to any kind of uniform national standards. Quality reviews are sometimes attempted by independent groups like the aforementioned NCTQ (which, given its right-wing political roots, is greeted with great suspicion by educators[9]), but ed schools can easily dismiss these attempts because they lack official clout. (Again, we see the peril of withholding consequences for poor performance.)

In many other professional fields that serve the general public, high-stakes finishing exams ensure alignment between training programs and expectations of the actual work environment. Medicine, law, and law enforcement—even the U.S. Postal Service—all have exams hopeful professionals must pass, and these exams help normalize the training of best practices in pre-professional programs. (Schools whose graduates fail to pass board exams aren't exactly tuition magnets.)

Graduates of American ed schools, however, rarely face a similar test. Though standardized tests are required of teachers applying for licensure in many states, these tests typically cover only basic content proficiencies and candidates' ability to regurgitate—you guessed it—Progressive pedagogical gospel, effectively neutralizing any potential screening power. Plus, unlike the U.S. Medical Licensing Exam or the bar exam, these tests typically do not have much effect on licensure, even if applicants fail; the results are only indirect in that they can either hurt or help a newly licensed teacher's employment opportunities.

Public education is just as important as our health care and our legal system. America must exert greater official power over teachers' preparatory cycle to determine what ed schools teach their teachers-in-training. Like medical schools and law schools or any pre-professional training program, ed schools must be guided by evidence, precedent, and a nationally set standard—not simply humanist philosophy or desired social outcomes. Accordingly, ed schools' operations and training programs must be regulated and monitored more thoroughly by entities of professional oversight, preferably originating from the federal government, to create greater nationwide agreement and consistency of effective practice.

(Of course, this assumes a right-side-up mindset at the federal level. As we have seen, the 2014 Department of Education should not in any way be considered the best authority on right-side-up educational principles; they're far too concerned with measuring education, holding it more accountable, making it more efficient and innovative, and all the rest. Given greater control over ed schools' operations and programming at this point, they would likely reduce all pre-professional training to courses in statistics, Microsoft Excel, and education technology. One can only hope that the department's April 2014 announcement that it is issuing new regulations about how it oversees, regulates, and funds teacher-education programs will make more sense than so many of its other reforms have.[10])

Taking a page from the institutions that train physicians and attorneys, ed schools' methods and programming would, in an ideal world, be driven by practical standards set from *within the teaching profession* itself. Physicians and attorneys establish national professional standards for their fields, granting accreditation to training institutions accordingly.

Most professional organizations for teachers, meanwhile, like the National Education Association (NEA), are really just unions that exist to protect teachers' rights, not raise professional standards. Though a National Board for Professional Teaching Standards exists in the United States, earning certification is a voluntary, additional process for interested teachers.

As much as raising professional standards—and demanding them from within—could do for America's kids, it could also significantly boost the public standing of teachers and help put an end to the lazy bum hypothesis. (That, of course, would be the start of a whole other book.)

Given this tangle of circumstances, it's tempting to think that changing the way ed schools operate has never been done before. But it has, many times. We only need to look outside our borders to see how educationally high-performing nations rebooted their ed schools. Finland, for example, began its dramatic education turnaround by raising academic standards and then matching those standards in its federal teacher-preparatory requirements. It's a great starting point for our own situation.

Now about those raised standards. . . .

2. Create and Implement Curriculum Based on Liberal Arts and Cognitive Science[11]

Regardless of when its preparatory structures are shored up, American education must rebuild itself on a foundational curriculum aligned to a controlled, deliberate set of desired academic outcomes that prepare all students to succeed in mainstream institutions.

This is not necessarily a call for a completely standardized national curriculum, of course, lest the anti–Common Core culture warriors be unleashed with great vengeance and furious anger. Rather, it is a call for a strong foundation of K–12 education based on a reasonable, manageable number of universally required specific content cornerstones and an accompanying programmatic guideline.

Basically, this foundation should outline what is necessary to create enough academic rigor (or resistance) to build the knowledge, skills, and institutional virtues students need to find institutional success. It should be crafted by a federally appointed panel of institutional leaders and researchers representing K–12 education, higher education, cognitive science, industry, and civic interests. In total, the foundation curriculum would specify the non-negotiable cornerstones of right-side-up instructional sequencing and methodology, giving states, districts, and schools a great deal of latitude to make the detail-level considerations.[12]

American education has made decent headway in this direction recently, thanks to the construction and implementation of the Common Core State Standards (CCSS) in literacy and mathematics. As we saw in chapter 6, the CCSS and their assessments are a major step forward for academic rigor. But these standards are just that: standards. They aren't curriculum in that, while they do provide some guidance about effective course sequencing, they do not specify the content to be covered.[13] Two other notable shortcomings of the CCSS are that they do not explicitly describe expectations for all subjects[14] (a necessity for right-side-up curriculum that works toward a clear goal) and state-by-state adoption is optional.[15]

As pretty well every expert in education would agree (aside from those selling curriculum, naturally), there is no "silver bullet" curriculum; no single curriculum can ever be considered a guaranteed fix. There is no particular sequence of content experiences, tasks, or courses that will act as a "learning whisperer" and make all students more college ready or get all students to engage more deeply in their schooling. A national foundation curriculum, then, should not be seen as anything like a panacea.

What a foundation curriculum *can* do, however, is stabilize all the disparate components of the education system, providing a common point of connection and alignment. A foundational curriculum makes it easier to train teachers effectively, for example, because teachers-in-training can become experts in a few critical content areas instead of barely familiar with an overwhelming catalog of possibilities.

Even rudimentary and general adjustments—like prescribing an emphasis on American literature during junior year English or setting the national graduation requirement in science at one full year each of biology, chemistry, and physics—could help ed schools better focus their efforts. Knowing what all U.S. students will be expected to master, ed schools could dedicate time to building specific content capacity and methodological skill in trainees.

A foundation curriculum provides a firmer platform on which to build national and/or statewide assessments, limiting them to well-defined areas of learning. This kind of control and definition would also benefit practitioners' ability to prioritize and design support for students who fall off track. Where students identified as struggling by current assessments are often assigned to periods of general "intervention time" in reading or math, more defined, subject-specific assessments would help practitioners pinpoint the nature of students' struggles—and assign additional learning activities and practice—with greater precision, and to greater effect.

Nations that consistently outperform the United States in international assessments of student progress figured this out long ago. Many feature standardized foundational curricula.[16] Several states in the United States, too, have long believed in the organizing power of a more centralized, specified curriculum.

Massachusetts, for instance, long known for its high-quality statewide curricular guidelines, is regularly touted as having the best education system in the country, recording results to rival entire nations that regularly outshine the United States on the whole.[17] Put the Massachusetts state English-Language Arts standards against those from Georgia, for example, and you'll get an idea of just how much standards can differ and why clear curricular cornerstones are so important to an education system's ultimate success.

For example, to demonstrate the types of texts students should be able to process successfully, Massachusetts's standards provide multiple specific exemplars of text complexity by grade level. They also provide groups of example texts, both to maintain topic consistency across grade levels and to promote and provide models of cross-disciplinary reading (without in any way specifying a day-by-day statewide instructional guide, it must be added).[18] Georgia, however, provides a rubric—and a pretty subjective one, at that—to help its teachers determine whether texts are sufficiently challenging or complex, and then encourages teachers to send in the names of the texts they choose and their accompanying completed rubrics so they can be added to the state's public resource library.[19]

The difference in outcomes is stark: state standards in Massachusetts are regularly cited at the top of many observers' lists. In 2008, Georgia's state tests declared 88 percent of its eighth graders proficient in reading; that same year, just 26 percent of the same eighth graders scored at or above the proficiency level on the National Assessment of Educational Progress (NAEP).[20]

The arguments for national curricular guidelines, of course, are all well and good. But the political volatility of the concept presents a colossal obstacle. In America, after all, any centralized curriculum is seen as a threat to the autonomy of local schools, if not a sure sign of big government brainwashing. Even the most cursory glance at how the Common Core is treated on social media and letters to the editor—a mix of tired complaints about new math and political bias mixed with more sinister theories about iris scans and testing students' DNA—shows just how wacky this conversation can turn.[21]

One compromise that could make national guidelines more politically palatable, of course, is that the foundation curriculum acts as an *instructional center* and not a comprehensive curriculum. This important distinction would allow states/districts/schools to maintain their autonomy and build on the foundation as they see fit. The foundation would specify pillars of essential content and skills for each grade and subject. In all, the mandated portion might represent 40–60 percent of all standards, leaving individual states, districts, and schools to figure out how best to apportion the rest.[22] Think of it as an actual foundation; you can build the house to look any way you want as long as it has three bedrooms, two bathrooms, and a kitchen.

In order to restore a more workable and student-beneficial balance of subjects and background knowledge, the pillars of the foundation curriculum would include specifications promoting broad, genuine liberal arts study. Assessments would be aligned to these subject-specific pillars, but would include cross-disciplinary exercises increasing in number and academic intensity with each succeeding grade.

This upward ramp would encourage natural cross-disciplinary relationships—such as writing position essays on historical events for a social studies assessment, or using algebra to solve complex problems in physics—and help measure students' progress toward standards more accurately by exposing the true reasons for assessment-expressed misconceptions. An incorrect answer on a physics problem, after all, may have as much or more to do with a student's algebra fluency as with her understanding of the physics concepts. Effective assessments would allow us to tell the difference and give us a sound basis to work from with each student.

Although the process of establishing a foundation curriculum is necessarily a collaborative one, here is one way it might look:

- To create and maintain a strong liberal arts basis, all uniformly specified content and coursework are built around five subject pillars: English/Language Arts, Mathematics, History/Social Studies, Science, and Fine Arts.
- Within each pillar, essential content and skills—as well as their sequence and guidelines for effective assessment—are determined by subject-specific subcommittees of education experts. In these subcommittees, a high premium would be placed on reasonable, escalating rigor to keep students

growing toward post-K–12 academic capacity and attendant institutional virtues. (Recall the pool and the marathon.) The Common Core State Standards already provide a good big-picture model of how to do this.

- Subject-specific subcommittees include K–12 and higher ed professionals, industry leaders, cognitive scientists, workforce analysts, and others, selected through an application process to the Department of Education–sponsored Foundation Curriculum group (see above for how this group could be constituted and appointed), working on exclusive, full-time, one-year contracts.
- Having established essential content, skills, and sequences within each subject pillar, the subcommittees then create specific curriculum, assessments, and teaching aids—even effective-instruction guidelines to foster subsequent teacher collaboration and supervisors' teacher evaluation—for guiding students to mastery. These resource warehouses are freely available to all U.S. schools online.
- Satellite committees work with the specified curriculum and assessments to anticipate student misconceptions and stumbling blocks, and then assemble intervention resources to aid schools with student support. Again, these resources are fully paid for and distributed to all U.S. schools online.
- Rollout does not happen immediately. After the construction year, states and districts have a full year to absorb the content and augment it to reflect local priorities. This portion could be as large as requiring a full year of math instruction in addition to what the foundation requires, or as small as including a social studies unit to cover a prominent local industry.
- In the first year of implementation, the federal government declares a moratorium on standardized nationwide and statewide assessment of foundation curricula with local customization. This period allows educators to learn the tools, and integrate them into practice and existing programming for optimum effectiveness before rolling out the accompanying assessment mechanisms.

Obviously, determining exactly what a foundation curriculum would look like is a discussion that could (and should) go on for days. Crucial as it is that it *should* be done, however, the scenario presented here is simply intended to show how it *could* be done.

However the pillars of a foundation curriculum might ultimately be positioned, the final, vetted version must be non-negotiable. It must be mandatory for all U.S. schools to follow, and comprehensively reviewed every five years for possible adjustments. Although the adoption of national standards could be made more politically appealing if it were optional for states, it has to be an all-or-nothing choice: either the entire foundation is adopted and implemented nationwide or it is not. Choosing the required content and performance standards for each discipline in a state-by-state, district-by-district, à la carte way, after all, is how we got here in the first place.

For example, consider the patently obtuse but far too common view that history and social studies could not be easily connected to other subjects deemed more important to students' future success. This initiated a cycle[23] resulting in structural damage far beyond the woeful results students achieve on civics assessments.[24] These are exactly the kinds of mistakes the educational enterprise must stop making.

If so many of the countries that consistently outrank us in terms of educational quality can overcome political differences and insecurities to improve the future of their children, their national economy, and their national heritages, there is no reason the United States cannot as well.

3. Narrow the Engagement Gap by Rewriting the Expectation Contract

In line with its scattered institutional mission, American education excels in mixed messages. It presents its students—and its professionals—with contradictory and confusing messages about what outcomes it expects and what virtues it truly values. A few examples:

- School attendance is required by law. Earning a diploma is not.
- Even though attendance is mandatory, students who do little or no classwork and earn failing grades are unlikely to face administrative consequences. (Their self-inflicted failure, however, does result in consequences for teachers.)
- Graduation requirements typically specify minimum sets of knowledge and or skills. But students can earn required credits with a D-minus, a grade that can usually be earned without demonstrating crucial competencies.
- Students must take standardized state tests, as dictated by NCLB. But their performance on these tests typically has no bearing on report cards, grade point averages, promotion, graduation, or post-secondary placement.
- Comprehensive standardized exams like ACT and SAT are routinely required by post-secondary institutions for consideration of admission. But poor scores are rarely a deal-breaker, and taking these exams is not mandatory for all students.
- The general public judges schools according to students' academic success. But students spend huge amounts of the school day on activities that have absolutely nothing to do with academics.

Contradictory messages make it difficult for students to know what to do and how to invest their time and energy. Mixed messages obscure the connection between their current experience and their possible futures, which is why so many fail to see school as a privilege (that should be) designed to enhance their future life. Worse, many of these messages omit or minimize students' individual responsibility for their own education.

Caught in the middle, students regularly wonder what schools expect them to do. Is it enough to just attend? Or should they actually apply themselves in classrooms? Should they make a genuine effort to learn specific content/skills, however challenging it may be? Or does it make more sense to simply do enough to pass? Should they actively build a résumé for their post-K–12 experience, or follow the path of least resistance? In what they say and do, schools do little to clearly explain to students what this whole schooling thing is even *for*.

The ever-expanding student-centered mission has created and sustained this dilemma for decades, and the Accountability Era has only intensified the situation. As responsibility for engaging students and helping them succeed has almost completely been shifted to teachers, any personal stakes students may have had in their own education have dwindled down to nothing.

What masks the true scale of the problem, however, is that the situation works just fine for many students—namely, those with strong academic backgrounds guided by sound virtues that already align with the expectations of mainstream institutions. These students are continually reminded by virtually every important adult in their lives that school is vital to their future success, and so they are expected to persist and give their best effort, even when their interest in a subject is low or its value is not immediately apparent.

Students without the same background, however, only have the contradictory guideposts to follow. As a result, they are much less likely to have a clear picture of what schooling can do for them. And when they choose the path of least resistance, nobody explains the impact their current decision will have on their future. Nobody redirects them. If they decide that it is far less trouble to disengage and offer only the barest minimum of attendance or effort, chances are good that no one will call them out or demand a better attitude.

Though a national push to narrow this engagement gap is underway, efforts to engage students often do so by sacrificing genuinely rigorous experiences with content. It's a transaction that is likely to increase attendance, but it does not help the students beyond entertaining them during what would otherwise be a pretty dull school day. This is a hallmark of upside-down thinking: increasing participation by suspending the rules of the game, effectively rendering its outcome meaningless. While other inventive strategies that do not sacrifice the academic resistance medium are being attempted (cash-for-grades arrangements, for example[25]), they are rarely sustainable, feasible for administration, or suitable for wide implementation.

Worst of all, many engagement strategies merely treat the symptoms of disengagement and not the root causes. Using non-academic motivators (like cash rewards or iPods or whatever else) to coax students into playing along with weak, contradictory expectations and consequences does not, after all, change the fact that schooling's expectations and consequences are weak and contradictory. Again, while these rewards may be a great way to get more students to complete tasks they see as soul-sucking but that the educational institution knows are good for them, the institution must make adjustments that are more foundational and permanent.

To address the foundational root cause, American education must rewrite its social contract with students and the general public. After uniformly raising levels of academic rigor (see number 2, previously), the enterprise must raise its expectations of students, demand a stronger commitment to meeting the standards, and do away with all the flaccid, contradictory messages that really tell students "We don't know what we're doing."

The enterprise must be more explicit about the reciprocal involvement necessary to fully transform every student into a person ready to join post-K–12 institutions. It must declare that this involvement is a basic expectation in all schools, and it must create policies and systems to support this expectation.

One important kind of support would be, of course, better education. Specifically, more deliberate and aggressive education to help all students understand how their schooling affects their futures. These kinds of instructional systems (typically called advisory programs) already exist, but they are currently too unreliable to fulfill this function effectively within an environment with elevated expectations. Many U.S. schools don't have well-defined advisory programs, for example, while others don't have advisories at all. At the very least, these programs can provide—even in their current state—the structural skeleton and programming space necessary to explicitly and meaningfully connect students' current schooling experiences to the rest of their lives.

Alongside these programming support systems, policies must be established to describe and enforce higher expectations for student engagement. Our students must no longer be legally required to attend school and yet systemically not required to get anything out of it. For the educational enterprise to serve as an effective funnel into mainstream institutions, one side of this equation must change.

Here are two solutions: After implementing a foundation curriculum to uniformly raise academic standards, the enterprise could become better at explaining that students get out of school what they put in, as well as expecting students to put in something more than an appearance, and finally holding students genuinely accountable. Schools also could allow students to bow out of schooling altogether and earlier, providing instead transitional supports to post-K–12 settings.

Several models exist to help American education figure out just how to do this. Some are in other countries, and some are right here at home. They include ramping up all students' education toward comprehensive exit exams that directly affect one's next steps in life[26]; signing "Commitment to Excellence" contracts that bind students, parents, and teachers to minimum levels of effort and specific behaviors[27]; and adjusting durations of compulsory education,[28] to name only a few. Many schools—entire national school systems, even—have found a way to redefine what they expect from themselves and students. Their funnels are right-side-up, and many are achieving the kinds of results we'd like to see.

It's one thing to itemize the issues and draw a map toward success. Actually following it in the real world is quite another. Next, we will finish up by describing the specific system-wide infrastructural adjustments American education needs to make in order for a widespread transformation to take place—one that rights the funnel once and for all.

NOTES

1. Remember here Stanford education professor David Labaree, from chapter 3: "Not for nothing has [Progressive Education thought leader John] Dewey's picture been found on the wall in so many ed school offices for so many years." From David F. Labaree, *The Trouble with Ed Schools* (New Haven, CT: Yale University Press, 2004), 157.

2. "Education: Change on 120th Street," *Time*, May 3, 1954, http://content.time.com/time/magazine/article/0,9171,890921,00.html.

3. For a quick tour of such critiques, see Labaree, *The Trouble with Ed Schools*, 4–8. See also Jeffrey Mirel, "Bridging the 'Widest Street in the World': Reflections on the History of Teacher Education," *American Educator* (Summer 2011), http://www.aft.org/pdfs/americaneducator/summer2011/Mirel.pdf.

4. One such example would be the unreliable correlation between teachers' possession of advanced education degree credentials and their students' ultimate results. See Dan Goldhaber and Joe Walch, "Gains In Teacher Quality," *Education Next*, October 30, 2013, http://educationnext.org/gains-in-teacher-quality/.

5. "Attempted" is the most apt term here, as not even 1 percent of the United States' ed schools fully agreed to cooperate in the study. Then, within months of the NCTQ report—which, for all its debatable qualities, roundly gave legitimate reasons to be concerned about teachers' preprofessional preparation in the United States—the American Association of Colleges for Teacher Education activated a page on its website ready with anti-NCTQ talking points and responses written by everyone from university presidents to education commentators to national education-advocacy groups. See "Responses to 2013 NCTQ-*U.S. News & World Report* Review | NCTQ/USNWR Review of Education Schools," American Association of Colleges for Teacher Education, January 10, 2014, http://aacte.org/resources/nctq-usnwr-review/responses-to-2013-nctq-us-news-a-world-report-review.html.

6. For a discussion of NCTQ's methods and aims from NCTQ President Kate Walsh, see her response to commentator Jay P. Greene's sweeping critique: Kate Walsh, "A Response to Jay Greene," *Education Next*, July 10, 2013, http://educationnext.org/a-response-to-jay-greene.

(For Greene's original piece, see Jay P. Greene, "NCTQ Doesn't Know What Works," *Education Next*, July 10, 2013, http://educationnext.org/nctq-doesn't-know-what-works/.)

7. Victoria Barret, "Bill Gates: It's the Teacher, Stupid," *Forbes*, January 26, 2009, http://www.forbes.com/2009/01/26/bill-gates-letter-tech-enter-cz_vb_0126billgates.html.

8. Amanda Ripley, *The Smartest Kids in the World: And How They Got That Way* (New York: Simon & Schuster, 2013), 84–94.

9. Diane Ravitch, "Ravitch: What Is NCTQ? (and Why You Should Know)," *The Answer Sheet* (blog), *Washington Post*, May 24, 2012, www.washingtonpost.com/blogs/answer-sheet/post/ravitch-what-is-nctq-and-why-you-should-know/2012/05/23/gJQAg7CrlU_blog.html.

10. Motoko Rich, "Obama Administration Plans New Rules to Grade Teacher Training Program," *New York Times*, April 25, 2014, http://www.nytimes.com/2014/04/26/us/obama-administration-plan-seeks-to-rate-teacher-training-programs.html?_r=0.

11. This is less a number 2 priority and more of a number 1A, as it should work in full concert with number 1, above. In fact, the principles outlined here should inform the ultimate oversight of ed school programming and methods.

12. For a great description of the curriculum as guiding force and for more reasons why improving the national curriculum should be considered a central improvement peg, see Diane Ravitch, *The Death and Life of the Great American School System: How Testing and Choice Are Undermining Education* (New York: Basic Books, 2010), 231–38.

13. While not specifying or prescribing certain content, CCSS appendices do provide exemplars to serve as models of intended rigor (in literacy/ELA) and models of course design to meet requisite standards in effective sequences (in mathematics). See Common Core State Standards Initiative, "Common Core State Standards for English Language Arts & Literacy in History/Social Studies, Science, and Technical Subjects: Appendix B: Text Exemplars and Sample Performance Tasks," Common Core State Standards Initiative, accessed March 23, 2013, http://www.corestandards.org/assets/Appendix_B.pdf, and Common Core State Standards Initiative, "Common Core State Standards for English Language Arts & Literacy in History/Social Studies, Science, and Technical Subjects: Appendix A: Research Supporting Key Elements of the Standards/Glossary of Key Terms," Common Core State Standards Initiative, accessed March 23, 2013, at http://www.corestandards.org/assets/CCSSI_Mathematics_Appendix_A.pdf.

14. The CCSS in literacy do help considerably toward raising rigor and text experiences in all content areas, however, by outlining the various types of nonfiction texts students should be able to comprehend and work with by grade level (see Literacy Appendix B, from note 13) and weaving such comprehension exercise into students' ultimate assessment. Though such could ultimately serve as a referendum on how comprehensively schools are teaching all subject areas, the CCSS's choice to bury these expectations within the literacy standards is thus far causing little radiation outward into the subject areas. And until schools more regularly internalize and operate around the idea that deep reading should take place in all subject areas to properly prepare students for the post-K–12 world, the emphasis on meeting the CCSS will likely all remain on the typical English class. "What gets tested gets taught," indeed—only perhaps more like "What *subject* gets tested gets *regular reading assignments*."

15. Through March 2014, forty-five U.S. states had fully adopted the CCSS in literacy and mathematics, with one state, Minnesota, adopting literacy, but not mathematics.

16. Common Core, *Why We're Behind: What Top Nations Teach Their Students but We Don't* (Washington, DC: Common Core, 2009), http://commoncore.org/maps/documents/reports/CCreport_whybehind.pdf.

17. For an interactive and customizable, state-by-state study of overall education outcomes in the United States, see "Quality Counts: District Disruption and Revival—School Systems Reshape to Compete—and Improve, State Report Cards," *Education Week*, January 3, 2014, http://www.edweek.org/ew/qc/2014/state_report_cards.html. For Massachusetts's ability to compete internationally, see Massachusetts Department of Elementary and Secondary Education, "TIMSS Results Place Massachusetts among World Leaders in Math and Science," Massachusetts Department of Education, December 9, 2008, http://www.doe.mass.edu/news/news.aspx?id=4457.

18. "Massachusetts Curriculum Framework for English Language Arts and Literacy," Massachusetts Department of Elementary and Secondary Education, March 2011, http://www.doe.mass.edu/frameworks/ela/0311.pdf.

19. "Common Core Georgia Performance Standards, English Language Arts—Text Complexity Rubrics," Georgia Department of Education, 2013, https://www.georgiastandards.org/Common-Core/Pages/TextComplexityRubrics.aspx.

20. Paul E. Peterson and Frederick Hess, "Few States Set World-Class Standards," *Education Next* 8, no. 3 (Summer 2008), http://educationnext.org/few-states-set-worldclass-standards/.

21. "Common Core Posts Archive," *Right Wing Watch*, March 12, 2014, http://www.rightwingwatch.org/category/topics/common-core.

22. States adopting CCSS follow a similar process. Percentages of state-determined standards are smaller—85 percent CCSS/up to 15 percent state-determined—than proposed here.

23. The cycle in question looks something like this:

1. History/social studies not tested.
2. History/social studies time in curricular programs reduced/de-emphasized accordingly.
3. Crucial content knowledge about the world, U.S. democracy, and so forth—and essential to effective reading comprehension—never gained by many students.
4. Reading test scores stay low.
5. *More* time and dollar resources given to reading and taken away from history/social studies and other nontested subjects.
6. Return to step 3; repeat.

24. NAEP, "Civics 2010: The Nation's Report Card," National Center for Education Statistics, 2010, http://nationsreportcard.gov/civics_2010/.

25. Some U.S. districts have gone so far as procuring private funds to *pay* students for earning certain grades or for enrolling in certain classes. See Mary E. Flannery, "Cash for Grades?" *NEA Today*, January 2011, http://www.nea.org/home/42011.htm.

26. Ripley, *The Smartest Kids in the World*, 191–94.

27. Jay Mathews, *Work Hard. Be Nice: How Two Inspired Teachers Created the Most Promising Schools in America* (Chapel Hill, NC: Algonquin, 2009), 88–91.

28. "Duration of Compulsory Education around the World," ChartsBin, 2011, http://chartsbin.com/view/xo6.

Chapter Eleven

Funnel of the Future

An Audacious Ideal Model and What to Do Locally, Starting Today

A rising tide doesn't raise people who don't have a boat. We have to build the boat for them. We have to give them the basic infrastructure to rise with the tide.

—Rahul Gandhi, vice president of Indian National Congress party, to the 2013 Confederation of Indian Industry conference

A TOO AUDACIOUS IDEAL MODEL OF RIGHT-SIDE-UP SCHOOLING

If we commit to implementing all of the right-side-up initiatives we just discussed, we have to start with the most basic of basics: infrastructure. American education's underlying infrastructure—daily and annual schedules, physical facilities, credit systems, information technology, and all the rest—needs serious changes in order to accommodate right-side-up initiatives and ensure the quality of delivery.

This infrastructure was built for upside-down schooling. Trying to realize right-side-up practices in this world is like driving a Humvee in rush hour traffic. You can do it, but you're not going to enjoy it. It's going to be frustrating and difficult, because the Humvee is meant for much different terrain, and city streets aren't designed for four-wheeling adventure.

Right-side-up approaches to teacher development, common foundation curriculum, student expectations, and engagement gaps would be the Humvee inching along the cramped side streets. Though each recommendation is inspired by schooling models that generate the results we all want to see, these models also require much different infrastructural support to work as they do.

Putting these initiatives to work within existing infrastructure *can* help create some positive change. Grafting them directly onto American education with no corresponding infrastructural changes would almost certainly have at least as large an impact as a decade of NCLB. These initiatives, however, can have even greater impact working within an infrastructure that is designed to suit them.

While the details may differ depending on the state or district, there are a number of system-wide infrastructural adjustments that will optimize delivery of right-side-up principles and practices. This is an audacious proposal, to be sure. The financial, logistical, and emotional toll of replacing long-standing systems and processes is always significant, and even more so when done to make room for a completely new operational concept.

So, however unlikely it is that these changes would be universally implemented across the entire enterprise, it's important to see what that would look like. What we will see is that a right-side-up infrastructure would accomplish three critical goals:

1. Provide the basic space, sequence, and student expectation contract necessary to execute right-side-up instructional actions successfully, without needing to completely replace the current practitioner base.
2. Increase teacher quality and satisfaction by offering a range of practical environments, each with focused, definite objectives regarding student outcomes.
3. Honor the desire of students and families to choose the most appropriate and beneficial school setting.

Once we consider what these infrastructural adjustments might look like, we can describe the actions educators can take today to see if their local funnel is upside-down and work toward right-side-up principles and practices in local districts, schools, and classrooms.

RIGHT-SIDE-UP INFRASTRUCTURE: SYSTEMIC CONSIDERATIONS

More Time

To provide sufficient time for teaching and studying the expanded content of the common foundation curriculum, and to minimize learning opportunities lost to extended school breaks, operating expenditures must be increased and professional contracts adjusted to extend the length of the school day and the school year. While these requirements are currently left up to individual states and tend to hover around 180 days per year, new guidelines should mandate a minimum of 220 school days per calendar year across all K–12 grades.[1] That's an increase of 22 percent.

Different Charters

To combine enterprise resources more effectively and tightly focus the institutional mission, charter schools must play a different role. A new wave of charters would provide outlets for students who transition out of education earlier (more on this in a bit) or return to seek formal secondary degrees much later. Standards would be revised for the authorization and approval of new charter schools. Curricular and student-expectation standards at current charters would be monitored more closely, and conditions would be established in order to dissolve these schools if they fail to improve students' academic achievement significantly. Finally, processes and accountabilities would be tightened to regulate administrative matters that affect other schools, such as financial management and student transfers.

Better Instructional Design

To supply practitioners with high-quality learning materials and professional development that are better aligned with a national foundation curriculum, attuned to the realities of locally enrolled students, and organized according to right-side-up principles of practice, states and districts would actively build internal capacity for content and instructional design. What we now call "departments of curriculum and instruction" or "departments of teaching and learning" would move beyond this charge to identify curricular needs, engage with third-party vendors, and supply materials. These offices would provide targeted solutions based on careful population research, instructional product vetting, research and testing, and continual product performance monitoring. Ideally, instructional designers would work toward constructing these teaching tools internally to minimize cost and remove vendor-specific conditions.

Optional Attendance

To enable right-side-up principles and practices, compulsory education laws would be reconsidered and rewritten. One possibility is to lower the minimum age at which students can opt out to fifteen. Another, more preferable option would be to set minimum competency descriptions for dropping out: to "satisfactory completion of middle-grades competencies," for example, or to "satisfactory completion of, at minimum, one-year secondary transition program" (more detail on these conditions to follow).

RIGHT-SIDE-UP INFRASTRUCTURE: GRADES K–4

Build the Foundation

In this model, grades K–4 become the wide mouth of the funnel, delivering right-side-up sequenced, broad liberal arts–based, and state/district-augmented foundation curriculum. This stage is crucial to all others because its purpose would be to ensure that essential knowledge, skills, and institutional virtues are instilled to prepare these students for the increasing academic rigor of the middle and high-school grades.

Test Smarter

To gauge student progress and monitor school-site effectiveness in terms of student and professional support, students in grades 3 and 4 would take one mid-year and one end-of-year exam annually, with no other standardized tests widely administered. Each test would contain sections assessing student understanding in five core areas: English/Language Arts, Mathematics, History/Social Studies, Science, and Fine Arts. The U.S. Department of Education, working with the states, would supply test items aligned to the common foundation curriculum, testing templates (into which states could add locally determined minimum standards), and all exam processing and report-generation services. Results would be made public, but the ultimate purpose of these tests would be to inform subsequent instructional decisions (e.g., identify students who need support and evaluate programmatic strengths and weaknesses), not to drive accountability.

RIGHT-SIDE-UP INFRASTRUCTURE: GRADES 5–8

Envision the Future

Grades 5–8 would begin funneling students more deliberately toward post-K–12 decisions. In these middle grades, explicit instructional time would be dedicated to building students' commitments to—and understandings of—their schooling. Students would not advance to the next grade simply because a year has elapsed; minimum levels of academic competency across the curriculum would be required for promotion.

Set the Stage

In addition to the foundation curriculum's five core areas, all students in grade 5 would begin explicit advisory coursework at least twice per week. The grades 5–8 advisory sequence would focus chiefly on building students' understanding of their education and education's relationship to their futures: types of careers, required education and skills for these careers, connection between secondary schooling and post-secondary placement, long-term benefits of various degree-completion, course-selection ramifications, possible pathways for high school, current academic progress, and more. While grades 5 and 6 would take a more generalized approach, grades 7 and 8 would use this course space directly toward crafting decisions for grades 9–12.

Make Failure Acceptable; Encourage Mastery

In a major departure from most current middle-grades models, middle grades in the right-side-up model would be built upon minimum competency demonstration, not grade completion and promotion. All students' course requirements would begin in a similar way. For example, "To meet Middle Grade competency requirement in Mathematics, earn passing grades in Arithmetic–Math I–Math II–Math III courses." Each course would correspond to the most common grade level (i.e., Arithmetic = Grade 5, Math I = Grade 6, etc.), but registration for courses would be fluid across grades and depend on students' demonstrations of minimum content competency. Standards would be determined locally, but mandated system-wide at no lower than 70 percent. Students who do not reach required levels of competency would be required to repeat sequence courses or demonstrate minimum mastery via exit exams (see below).

Provide Better Help

To aid students in remaining on track toward mastery in light of significantly raised expectations, academic intervention and support structures would be built into each school day. These would ease students' access to support and allow teachers to design and oversee competency-specific practice.

Limit Testing

As in grades 3 and 4, grades 5–8 would take one mid-year test and one end-of-year test (based on the five core subjects) to monitor progress and design students' and teachers' subsequent action. While "grade" is a much more relative term in a competency-based school, students would take exams corresponding with their entering class year. Scores on year-end tests for each "grade" would be built into students' final report-card marks. End-of-year tests would be used to make decisions about students' eligibility for promotion and could, in certain situations, accelerate students into more challenging coursework.

Ramp Up Advisory

End-of-year exams would tie directly into advisory programs. Results from grade 8's mid-year test would work in concert with each student's grade 5–8 transcript to inform the advisory for the year's second half: choosing the best high school option, declaring the selected option, and preparing for the selected option.

RIGHT-SIDE-UP INFRASTRUCTURE: GRADES 9–12

Add Pathways

Grades 9–12 form the neck of the funnel, leading students directly into post-K–12 institutions. To streamline this process, students earning passage through the K–8 sequence by demonstrating required minimum competencies in the middle grades would be able to choose from four secondary schooling options: (1) a four-year college preparatory program, (2) a four-year exploration program, (3) a two-year pre-career training program, or (4) a one-year transition program.

The two four-year choices—college-preparatory and exploration—would closely resemble current U.S. high schools. The main difference would be the expectation contract all students sign.

Within the college-preparatory option—which would be noted on student transcripts and viewed preferentially by post-secondary admissions officials—students would be taught according to a high-rigor academic curriculum that is directly aligned to collegiate expectations and replete with commensurate expectations of academic commitment, assigned homework, and standards of academic honesty. Students would be expected to meet targeted standards of advanced high school coursework (e.g., "earned credit in Math IV/Pre-Calculus or higher," "at least three passing scores on AP exams," "credit earned in at least four International Baccalaureate HL courses," "earned credit in Spanish IV or higher," etc.), and placement in the program could be revoked—and the student placed into the exploration program (see below)—if they fall too far off track.

The four-year exploration program would prepare students for post-secondary study, but would do so according to a regimen more like today's average American high school. A basic core of coursework would be prescribed, but with fewer minimum performance standards. Practitioners would have greater latitude to design learning activities: higher-engagement exercises that are not purely academically focused could be employed, and more elective courses would be offered. Not explicitly geared for post-secondary study, the exploration program would not confer automatic preference by post-secondary admissions officials.

The two-year pre-career training program and one-year transition program represent the most severe departures from current upside-down practice. They openly allow students to end their formal education sooner than they can today. But remember, though these programs would give students greater flexibility with respect to ending their required educations, this flexibility would only be offered after students built certifiably stronger academic foundations through the right-side-up, liberal arts–based course of study in grades K–8. Prepared in this way, facing this decision, and counseled intensively about their choices in the eighth-grade year, students would not choose these options as readily as they might within the current system. (To boot, consider all the great conversations in U.S. homes when students reach this point of their educations. How would *you* react if your son told you he was planning to take the two-year option?)

The two-year pre-career training program would, in collaboration with cooperating industries, guide students through early occupational experiences and move them toward financial independence. Several such programs, like the Alamo Area Academies in San Antonio, Texas, are already assisting students with productive transitions into local workforces and are largely viewed as win-win-win arrangements for students, businesses, and communities.[2] And just as in the Alamo Area Academies, the bulk of students' school weeks during these programs would be spent on job sites, interning to gain real-world skills, contacts, work habits, and experience. Back at school, students' program teachers would act chiefly as new-employment counselors, augmenting students' work experiences with courses in financial management, civic involvement, and personal fulfillment.

The one-year transitional option would be designed for students who are not interested in continuing their formal education. The one year of schooling after students' successful completion of middle-grades competencies would be much like that of the career-preparation program's participants: building awareness of financial management, civic participation, and so on. Plus, educators in a program like this would help students prepare job-application skills and materials.

ARE LOCAL FUNNELS RIGHT-SIDE-UP? HOW TO CHECK FOR INVERSION

Considering how much legislative jousting, school restructuring, and paradigm-shifting would be required to rewrite compulsory education laws or extend the school year, we shouldn't hold our breath waiting for these sweeping infrastructural adjustments to happen. But we have to start somewhere. So think of these recommendations as a modest proposal for changing our collective mindset and building momentum from within. Think of these audacious ideas as offered out of "no other motive than the public good of my country." (Hat tip: Jonathan Swift, *A Modest Proposal*, 1729—minus, of course, the extremist satire.)

Just because something is difficult, however, does not mean it should be abandoned. In fact, if you're reading this book as a teacher, administrator, parent, or even a student, and you recognize your own school's challenges, you can get to work right away. There are many steps individuals can take locally, right now, to start building an educational enterprise that is more right-side-up than upside-down.

The first thing you can do is check your funnel. What follows is a brief checklist to help you do that, as well as some key criteria for helping schools start implementing right-side-up instructional practices, policies, and procedures—all without the need for new legislation or thousands of dollars in grants. These questions should fit easily within existing processes for teacher observation, collaborative planning, and professional development, as well as data study and self-evaluation by school leadership.

1. Consequences

One critical way we prepare students for the expectations of post-K–12 institutions, obviously, is helping them understand the consequences of behaviors. Schooling offers many decision points for students to choose between behaviors that mainstream institutions demand and ones they reject. Do students complete the work according to the teacher's guidelines? Is the quality of the work up to the teacher's standards? Did the student make a reasonable effort to succeed? Is the student behaving disruptively in class? As a result, the educational enterprise has an important opportunity—and obligation—to give students a sense of how mainstream institutions will respond to their choices. Clear consequences are fundamental to right-side-up schooling, but in upside-down schools consequences are often diluted or dismissed.

To check these for right-side-up practices, consider the following questions:

- Do the consequences students experience reflect consequences they will face later in life for similar behaviors? Are students actually learning how certain actions will trigger certain reactions?
- Are consequences reinforced consistently? Do your school's behavior policies reflect the importance of consistency and repetition, and the need to reflect mainstream institutional expectations? How about your school's grading policies?
- For students who repeatedly experience negative consequences—especially those who repeat particular unacceptable behaviors—what additional steps are taken to change the behavior? Are these methods effective? How

do they compare to the consequences the student will face in the world beyond schooling?

- Observe how positive consequences and rewards are assigned in your school, both for behaviors and academic accomplishments. Are students regularly rewarded for baseline, reasonably expected behaviors and work, or for somehow going above and beyond? Again, how do these consequences compare to how positive consequences are earned in the world beyond schooling?

2. Student Engagement

Observations of practice—administrator-teacher, peer-to-peer, PLC-based practice shares, learning walks, and so on—are ideal forums to look for a right-side-up mindset.

Recall that in right-side-up learning environments, activities designed to build student engagement are *not discouraged*. What should be discouraged, however, are attempts to engage students that compromise—or sacrifice entirely—the academic rigor that prepares students for success in post-K–12 institutions.

To ensure that rigor is preserved, consider the following questions or embed them into practice observation:

- Are teachers lowering expectations and removing the rigor that will prepare students for future success in an effort to engage them?
- Are learning activities aligned to standards? Does the activity include an effective way to gauge whether students have achieved the standard? Can the teacher explain how this activity allows them to assess students with respect to the target standard?
- Is it clear how learning activities will benefit students later in life? Can you name a place or situation where this type of activity will directly benefit them or be of academic or practical use?

3. Awareness of Life after Schooling

Right-side-up schooling inspires students to build lasting institutional virtues: grit, persistence, delay of gratification, effective goal-setting, and what old-schoolers might call "stick-to-itiveness." For academic study to simulate the real world, it is crucial for students to be aware of how schooling will benefit them later in life. That connection simply has to be made. Students who approach schooling with this awareness are engaged in ways that empower them to overcome even the most challenging circumstances. As such, check your school's operations and learning opportunities in the following ways:

- Do students understand all of their options with respect to future mainstream institutions? Have they considered all the possible paths?
- Do students know where they're going after K–12? Do they know how to get there? If not, do they know how school can help them with this quest?
- Are teachers and others making students aware of how their choices today will affect their options tomorrow? Do they know what will be asked of them in the world after their K–12 experience?
- What structures are currently in place at your school to approach these issues with students in a consistent, systematic way?

4. Curriculum

Recall Bloom's Taxonomy and the ways that upside-down schooling frequently misapplies it. As you think about your school's curricular programming with respect to your enrolled population and various achievement data, be on the lookout for these upside-down applications.

Begin by building staff understanding of effective learning sequences and balances, checking closely against articulated standards like the Common Core State Standards (CCSS) or accepted state standards. Observe and reflect on why students struggle with exercises assigned via programming. Review exam strand data as available to assist with this reflection. In conducting such review/reflection, consider questions like these:

- What types of tasks/skills/exam strands are students struggling with? How well are these kinds of tasks/skills/strands covered by current curriculum and learning exercises?
- If current curriculum is not covering these tasks/skills/strands, what types of extra practice do struggling students receive to eventually master them? Do systems exist for getting these students the additional practice they need? Or are groups of struggling students large enough that larger programmatic changes must be made?
- Does curriculum sufficiently follow sequences that are proven effective to spur intellectual growth? In light of student assessments, are students sufficiently prepared with requisite background knowledge, comprehension ability, and so forth to move productively into Bloom's Taxonomy's upper levels?

5. Students "Furthest Away"

For students who are very far from attaining proficiency, it is critical to determine what they need most—both in terms of foundational skills/abilities and the resources to make this happen—*as soon as possible*. Schooling is the one great common mechanism for ushering all Americans toward future opportunities. If schooling doesn't do all it can—as quickly as it can and as early in their educations as possible—to help struggling kids realize these opportunities, their struggles will only get worse. To check how your school is doing with respect to the "furthest away" students, consider the following:

- What types of academic interventions are the "furthest away" students receiving? Are the interventions targeted specifically to the areas that cause the most difficulty? What types of screening mechanisms are in place to assess why students struggle?
- How do settings affect these "furthest away" students' ability to succeed? Are they placed with the best teacher for their particular challenges? Are they placed with the best classmates? Can systems be adjusted to work with these students more effectively?

NOTES

1. For a study of typical school days per year in the United States versus other nations and its relative effects on student learning, see Karl L. Alexander, Doris R. Entwisle, and Linda S. Olson, "Schools, Achievement, and Inequality: A Seasonal Perspective," *Education Evaluation and Policy Analysis* 23, no. 2 (Summer 2001): 171–91.

2. For a government report, with student case studies, see Texas Workforce Investment Council, "Alamo Area Academies," *Profiles in Success* 3 (2009), http://governor.state.tx.us/files/twic/Profile_Alamo_Academies.pdf. See also Sophie Quinton, "San Antonio's Ingenious Plan to Get Kids Good Jobs out of High School," *The Atlantic—Cities*, March 6, 2013, http://www.theatlanticcities.com/jobs-and-economy/2013/03/san-antonios-ingenius-plan-get-kids-good-jobs-out-high-school/4890/.

Chapter Twelve

An Awesome Responsibility

> However much we might pretend otherwise, we humans are not complete enough to complete ourselves. We are not rich enough that we can do without institutional attachments and intergenerational kisses. We simply do not have the fullness of resources that would be required. If nothing is important but self-fulfillment, there is nothing of substance available to help us do the filling.
>
> —Hugh Heclo, American political scientist, in *On Thinking Institutionally*

So here we are at the end. We've laid the problems bare. We've discussed some practical solutions. We've seen how it all might come together in an ideal world. We've talked and thought more about funnels than you probably thought was possible. But let's remember that public education is a hugely complex and hugely important issue. Its problems stretch back for more than a century. But the solutions aren't nearly that far away. To see why that's true, let's recap:

1. PUBLIC EDUCATION IS A FUNNEL

From government to medicine to mass media to the military, mainstream institutions turn chaos into order. From anarchy, government organizes society. From sickness, medical practitioners bring about health. From many views, journalists find the story. From conflict, the military realizes peace. Public education is just such an institution.

And like many of these world-ordering institutions, education works like a *funnel*. It moves material from its original state into a more ordered, useful state. It is designed to move as much of that material as possible, as efficiently as possible, with as little waste as possible. Specifically, education should move as many young American citizens as possible from their original, unschooled state toward one important goal: meaningful, successful, and personally fulfilling participation within all the other institutions that make up our public sphere. (Or, as some people call it, "having a life.")

2. THE FUNNEL IS UPSIDE-DOWN

The wide mouth at the top was originally intended to gather as many children as possible, from as many different backgrounds and abilities and untapped potentials as possible. Today, the narrow stem is facing up, and it collects very few kids—the ones closest to the middle, so to speak, who tend to have stronger preparation and ongoing support, the ones who would succeed no matter what.

In the same way, the original narrow focus of public education was to give students baselines of general knowledge and strength of character to continue driving the U.S. democracy and to be further teachable whether they chose to attend college, enter public service, join the military, pursue an art, or open a business.

Today, the wide mouth is facing down, representing an attempt to teach everyone everything, using methods that honor students fully as they are, not where they must be for success within mainstream institutions. Schools are trying to impart general academic knowledge and skills alongside social mores, foreign languages, technology, health and safety, finance, emotional intelligence, Advanced Placement courses, web design, relationship skills, self-esteem, and on and on, and they're trying to do it as interestingly as possible for each individual.

3. PROGRESSIVE PHILOSOPHY PUT IT THAT WAY

The funnel has been upside-down since the late nineteenth and early twentieth centuries, when the Progressive Education movement, inspired by the European Romantics, challenged the original notions of what schooling should accomplish and how it should be done. This challenge redefined the enterprise's mission and practical ideals, focusing them around the notion of schools existing to provide the whole development of each individual child. At that moment, when the preferences of the individual became more important than the collective well-being of everyone in society, the funnel flipped.

There is very little proof that these Progressive ideas actually work. Nevertheless, they dictate instructional methods and operations, and they have done so with little opposition for nearly a century. Contrary to their purported ability to catalyze equitable educational outcomes for all system participants, upside-down ideals and practices only work well for children entering school already aligned to the expectations of mainstream institutions. Everybody else spills down the sides.

4. REFORMERS ARE WORKING ON THE WRONG PROBLEM

After decades of spillage—unsatisfactory results followed by unheeded recommendations followed by collective frustration among parents and policymakers alike—American education was seized by government-based, grassroots-organized, and billionaire-backed reformers in the early twenty-first century, kicking off education's Accountability Era.

This movement is currently reshaping many of the enterprise's core operations. Without regard for how little education resembles the private sector, or how the current mission and practice remain upside-down, reformers are attempting to retrofit public schools with private-sector ideas about organizational improvement: tighter measurement of bottom-line results, more stringent accountabilities and consequences, a greater emphasis on innovation, a more diversified marketplace of educational options, and a full transformation of students into consumers.

Based on hypotheses that, at best, only partially address education's deepest issues, these reforms have failed—and will continue to fail—to improve the consistency or reliability of students' readiness for post-K–12 life. Worse, these reforms are threatening to fracture the system in ways that will be difficult and expensive to repair. Worst of all, the funnel is still upside-down, continuing to produce prodigious puddles of squandered potential.

5. REFORM NEEDS TO BE REFRAMED

No question, education in the United States needs reforming. Getting it right is too important to allow matters to continue as they have, especially for demographic groups that education perpetually leaves below the line. And especially to stanch the flow of billions spent trying—and failing, and trying again, and failing again—to find just the right reform formula. This is critical in today's global marketplace, where our kids' competencies are compared very directly to those of kids from countries with better preparatory machinery.

To end our cycle of frustration and prepare all students in ways that make good on our nation's foundational opportunity and means, we'll have to turn the institutional funnel right-side-up. One hundred years of trying upside-down practices has resulted in too much spillage. As this funnel is remarkably heavy, we'll need to make strategically big changes at some of education's most fundamental levels to turn it over and earn the buy-in of the American people. Remember, few in the American public have experienced a right-side-up education that explicitly seeks to build students' academic competencies and institutional virtues in a mutually reinforcing fashion toward the greater national good.

6. THREE PRIORITIES LOOM LARGE

Specifically, three key areas require immediate, systematic review and revision: America's teacher-education programs, national curricular guidelines, and the student-schooling expectation contract. Revising all of these areas can cut down the number of contradictory messages and impossible expectations built in to education, bringing its mission and methods into clearer focus.

As reforms in the Accountability Era have shown, simply writing policy and coming down harder on teachers will not create the results we seek for our kids. To truly enable the top three priorities, substantial adjustment must be made to the infrastructure of American education. These changes will require substantial cost and time to implement.

In the meantime, there are a number of things schools can do right now to correct their local funnels if they are indeed upside-down. In fact, teachers, administrators, and others can look at five factors and start making changes today. These factors are: consistency of consequences, methods of student engagement, students' awareness of life after schooling, balance of curriculum, and means of dealing with students who are "furthest away" from the center of the funnel. The details will be different for every school, but the principles should fit easily into existing structures of practical evaluation, teacher evaluation, and data review.

7. THE NEW MISSION MATTERS MOST

Education transforms people: from stagnant to spirited, from apathetic to sympathetic, from reactionary to rational. Though transformation comes in many shapes and sizes, the fact remains: designers and providers of education transform people as a matter of course.

Because of this, public schools have an awesome responsibility. They must provide education that transforms students properly. In other words, they must move students toward acquiring the knowledge and virtues they need to find fulfillment in—and contribute to the improvement of—the world outside of school.

This is our mission: to prepare young citizens for meaningful participation in mainstream institutions.

Doing so will require an institutional funnel that is right-side-up, not upside-down as it has been for more than a hundred years. It won't always be fun, and lots of people are likely to yell at us for doing so. But we must stick with it. The well-being of our society depends on it.

Bibliography

ACT, Inc. *The Condition of College & Career Readiness: Low Income Students* (Iowa City: ACT, Inc., 2012). http://www.act.org/newsroom/data/2012/states/pdf/LowIncomeStudents.pdf.

ACT, Inc. *Ready for College and Ready for Work: Same or Different?* (Iowa City: ACT, Inc., 2006). http://www.act.org/research/policymakers/pdf/ReadinessBrief.pdf.

Adelman, Clifford. *Answers in the Tool Box: Academic Intensity, Attendance Patterns, and Bachelor's Degree Attainment*. Washington, DC: U.S. Department of Education, 1999.

Adelman, Clifford. *The Toolbox Revisited: Paths to Degree Completion from High School through College*. Washington, DC: U.S. Department of Education, 2006.

Alexander, Karl L., Doris R. Entwisle, and Linda S. Olson. "Schools, Achievement, and Inequality: A Seasonal Perspective." *Education Evaluation and Policy Analysis* 23, no. 2 (Summer 2001): 171–91.

Alliance for Excellent Education. "A Time for Deeper Learning: Preparing Students for a Changing World." *Alliance for Excellent Education*, May 26, 2011. http://www.all4ed.org/files/DeeperLearning.pdf.

American Statistical Association. "ASA Statement on Using Value-Added Models for Educational Assessment." American Statistical Association, April 8, 2014. http://www.amstat.org/policy/pdfs/ASA_VAM_Statement.pdf.

Anderson, J. R., L. M. Reder, and H. A. Simon. "Applications and Misapplications of Cognitive Psychology to Mathematics Education." *Texas Educational Review* (Summer 2000). http://memory.psy.cmu.edu/downloadPaper.php?name=Applic.MisApp.

"Archived: The Race to the Top Begins—Remarks by Secretary Arne Duncan." U.S. Department of Education, July 24, 2009. https://www2.ed.gov/news/speeches/2009/07/07242009.html.

Ball, Deborah Loewenberg, Heather C. Hill, and Hyman Bass. "Knowing Mathematics for Teaching." *American Educator* 29, no. 3 (Fall 2005): 14–17, 20–22, 43–46.

Barret, Victoria. "Bill Gates: It's the Teacher, Stupid." *Forbes*, January 26, 2009. http://www.forbes.com/2009/01/26/bill-gates-letter-tech-enter-cz_vb_0126billgates.html.

Bauerlein, Mark. *The Dumbest Generation: How the Digital Age Stupefies Young Americans and Jeopardizes Our Future, *Or, Don't Trust Anyone under 30*. New York: Jeremy P. Tarcher/Penguin, 2008.

Bauerlein, Mark. "The Paradox of Classroom Boredom." *Education Week*, August 6, 2013. http://www.edweek.org/ew/articles/2013/08/07/37bauerlein.h32.html.

Beckett, Lois. "America's Most Outrageous Teacher Cheating Scandals." *Propublica.org*, April 1, 2013. www.propublica.org/article/americas-most-outrageous-teacher-cheating-scandals.

Bernstein, D. A., L. A. Penner, A. Clarke-Stewart, E. J. Roy, and C. D. Wickens. *Psychology*. 6th ed. Boston, MA: Houghton Mifflin, 2003.

Bidwell, Allie. "Education Department Loosens NCLB Requirements." *U.S. News & World Report*, November 14, 2013. http://www.usnews.com/news/articles/2013/11/14/education-department-loosens-nclb-waiver-requirements.

Bransford, John D., Ann L. Brown, and Rodney R. Cocking, eds. *How People Learn: Brain, Mind, Experience, and School*. Washington, DC: National Academy Press, 2000.

Cantrell, Steven, and Thomas J. Kane. *Ensuring Fair and Reliable Measures of Effective Teaching: Culminating Findings from the MET Project's Three-Year Study*. MET Project/Bill & Melinda Gates Foundation, January 2013. http://www.metproject.org/downloads/MET_Ensuring_Fair_and_Reliable_Measures_Practitioner_Brief.pdf.

Carlozo, Lou. "Why College Students Stop Short of a Degree." *Reuters*, March 27, 2012. http://www.reuters.com/article/2012/03/27/us-attn-andrea-education-dropouts-idUSBRE82Q0Y120120327.

Carnine, Douglas. *Why Education Experts Resist Effective Practices (And What It Would Take to Make Education More Like Medicine)*. Washington, DC: Thomas B. Fordham Institute, 2000. http://www.edexcellence.net/sites/default/files/publication/pdfs/carnine_9.pdf.

Center for Public Education. "Trends in Teacher Evaluation: How States Are Measuring Teacher Performance." 2013. www.centerforpubliceducation.org/Main-Menu/Evaluating-performance/Trends-in-Teacher-Evaluation-At-A-Glance/Trends-in-Teacher-Evaluation-Full-Report-PDF.pdf.

Chenoweth, Karin. *How It's Being Done: Urgent Lessons from Unexpected Schools*. Cambridge, MA: Harvard Educational Publishing Group, 2009.

Chenoweth, Karin. *It's Being Done: Academic Success in Unexpected Schools*. Cambridge, MA: Harvard Educational Publishing Group, 2007.

Christensen, Clayton, Michael B. Horn, and Curtis W. Johnson. *Disrupting Class: How Disruptive Innovation Will Change the Way the World Learns*. New York: McGraw Hill, 2011.

Clark, D. R. "Bloom's Taxonomy of Learning Domains." Performance Juxtaposition, 1999. http://nwlink.com/~donclark/hrd/bloom.html.

Collins, Jim. *Good to Great: Why Some Companies Make the Leap . . . and Others Don't*. New York: HarperCollins, 2001.

Common Core. *Why We're Behind: What Top Nations Teach Their Students but We Don't*. Washington, DC: Common Core, 2009. http://commoncore.org/maps/documents/reports/CCreport_whybehind.pdf.

"Common Core Georgia Performance Standards, English Language Arts—Text Complexity Rubrics." Georgia Department of Education, 2013. https://www.georgiastandards.org/Common-Core/Pages/TextComplexityRubrics.aspx.

"Common Core Posts Archive." *Right Wing Watch*, March 12, 2014. http://www.rightwingwatch.org/category/topics/common-core.

Common Core State Standards Initiative. "Common Core State Standards for English Language Arts & Literacy in History/Social Studies, Science, and Technical Subjects: Appendix A: Research Supporting Key Elements of the Standards/Glossary of Key Terms." Common Core State Standards Initiative. Accessed March 23, 2013. http://www.corestandards.org/assets/Appendix_A.pdf.

Common Core State Standards Initiative. "Common Core State Standards for English Language Arts & Literacy in History/Social Studies, Science, and Technical Subjects: Appendix B: Text Exemplars and Sample Performance Tasks." Common Core State Standards Initiative. Accessed March 23, 2013. http://www.corestandards.org/assets/Appendix_B.pdf.

Cremin, Lawrence A. *American Education: The Colonial Experience, 1607–1783*. New York: Harper and Row, 1970.

Cremin, Lawrence A. *The Tranformation of the School: Progressivism in American Education 1876–1957*. New York: Random House, 1961.

Danielson, Charlotte. "2013 Framework for Teaching Evaluation Instrument." The Danielson Group, 2013. http://www.danielsongroup.org/userfiles/files/downloads/2013EvaluationInstrument.pdf.

Darling-Hammond, Linda. *The Flat World and Education: How America's Commitment to Equity Will Determine Our Future*. New York: Teachers College, Columbia University, 2010.

Davis, Michelle R. "Ed. Companies Exert Public-Policy Influence: Some Observers Are Alarmed at What They See as Increasingly Aggressive Moves by Companies." *Education Week*, April 24, 2013. http://www.edweek.org/ew/articles/2013/04/24/29ii-politicalpower.h32.html?tkn=SMZFnrqOI%2BEeHnBpv0iXitdqj8R7P1Y%2B1c7w&cmp=SOC-EDIT-LI&intc=EW-II413-LI.

Dewey, John. *Dewey on Education: Selections*. Edited by Lawrence A. Cremin. New York: Bureau of Publications, Teachers College, Columbia University, 1959.

Di Carlo, Matthew. "The Evidence on Charter Schools and Test Scores." Albert Shanker Institute, December 2011. http://shankerblog.org/wp-content/uploads/2011/12/CharterReview.pdf.

Dillon, Sam. "In PISA Test, Top Scores from Shanghai Stun Educators." *New York Times*, December 7, 2010. http://www.nytimes.com/2010/12/07/education/07education.html.

"Duration of Compulsory Education around the World." ChartsBin, 2011. http://chartsbin.com/view/xo6.

"Education: Change on 120th Street." *Time*, May 3, 1954. http://content.time.com/time/magazine/article/0,9171,890921,00.html.

Egan, Kieran. *Getting It Wrong from the Beginning: Our Progressive Inheritance from Herbert Spencer, John Dewey, and Jean Piaget.* New Haven, CT: Yale University Press, 2002.

"Facts about TFA." Teach For America. Accessed February 8, 2014. http://www.teachforamerica.org/our-organization/faq.

"Fast Facts." National Center for Education Statistics. U.S. Department of Education. Accessed February 8, 2014. http://nces.ed.gov/fastfacts/display.asp?id=28.

Flannery, Mary E. "Cash for Grades?" *NEA Today*, January 2011. http://www.nea.org/home/42011.htm.

"Four Leading Education Organizations Join Partnership for 21st Century Skills." *Reuters/PR Newswire*, July 12, 2011. http://www.reuters.com/article/2011/07/12/idUS151518+12-Jul-2011+PRN20110712.

Gardner, Howard. *Frames of Mind: The Theory of Multiple Intelligences*. 3rd ed. New York: Basic Books, 2011.

Gewertz, Catherine. "Common-Standards Rumblings in Utah and South Carolina." *Curriculum Matters* (blog), *Education Week*, March 1, 2012. http://blogs.edweek.org/edweek/curriculum/2012/03/cato_on_south_carolina_fair.html.

Gewertz, Catherine. "Final Version of Common Standards Unveiled." *Education Week*, June 2, 2010. http://www.edweek.org/ew/articles/2010/06/02/33common.h29.html.

Goldhaber, Dan, and Joe Walch. "Gains in Teacher Quality." *Education Next*, October 30, 2013. http://educationnext.org/gains-in-teacher-quality/.

Goodnough, Abby. "Mayor Tries to Reassure Providence Teachers as Furor Grows over Firing Notices." *New York Times*, February 25, 2011. http://www.nytimes.com/2011/02/26/us/26providence.html.

Grasgreen, Allie. "ACT Scores Fall to Lowest Level in Five Years." *Inside Higher Ed*, August 21, 2013. http://www.insidehighered.com/news/2013/08/21/act-scores-fall-lowest-level-five-years.

Gray, Lawrence. "Public Statement on Math Reform." Speech to Minnesota State Higher Education and Public Policy Joint Committee, February 18, 2013. http://www.math.umn.edu/~gray/testimony.html.

Greene, Jay P. "NCTQ Doesn't Know What Works." *Education Next*, July 10, 2013. http://educationnext.org/nctq-doesn't-know-what-works/.

Grossen, Bonnie. "The Story behind Project Follow Through." *Effective School Practices* 15, no. 1 (Winter 1995–1996). http://pages.uoregon.edu/adiep/ft/grossen.htm.

Hattie, John. *Visible Learning: A Synthesis of Over 800 Meta-Analyses Relating to Achievement.* London: Routledge, 2009.

Heclo, Hugh. *On Thinking Institutionally.* Boulder, CO: Paradigm, 2008.

Hedges, Chris. *Empire of Illusion: The End of Literacy and the Triumph of Spectacle*. New York: Nation Books, 2009.

Hirsch, E. D. "An Epoch-Making Report, but What about the Early Grades?" *Education Week*. April 23, 2008. http://www.edweek.org/ew/articles/2008/04/23/34hirsch_ep.h27.html.

Hirsch, E. D. *Cultural Literacy: What Every American Needs to Know*, Rev. ed. New York: Random House, 1987.

Hirsch, E. D. *The Knowledge Deficit: Closing the Shocking Education Gap for American Children*. Boston, MA: Houghton Mifflin, 2006.

Hirsch, E. D. *The Making of Americans: Democracy and Our Schools*. New Haven, CT: Yale University Press, 2009.

Hirsch, E. D. *The Schools We Need: And Why We Don't Have Them*. New York: Doubleday, 2006.

Hobbs, Tawnell D. "'Exemplary' Dallas ISD School Skipped Science, Social Studies for 3rd-Graders." *Dallas Morning News*, November 18, 2011. http://www.dallasnews.com/news/education/headlines/20111118-exemplary-dallas-isd-school-skipped-science-social-studies-for-3rd-graders.ece.

Hsu, Duncan. "U.S. College Graduation Rates by Race by State." *EdPond—Education Pondered*, April 23, 2012. http://edpond.blogspot.com/2012/04/us-college-graduation-rates-by-race-by.html.

Hull, Jim. "Trends in Teacher Evaluation: How States Are Measuring Teacher Performance." Alexandria, VA: Center for Public Education, 2013.

"Investing in Innovation Fund (i3)." U.S. Department of Education—Office of Innovation and Improvement, December 20, 2013. http://www2.ed.gov/programs/innovation/index.html.

Jacoby, Susan. *The Age of American Unreason*. New York: Pantheon, 2008.

Karsenti, Thierry, and Aurelien Fievez. *The iPad in Education: Uses, Benefits, and Challenges—A Survey of 6,057 Students and 302 Teachers in Quebec (Canada)*. Montreal, QC: CRIFPE, 2013. http://www.academia.edu/5364660/The_iPad_in_Education_uses_benefits_and_challenges._A_survey_of_6057_students_and_302_teachers_in_Quebec_Canada.

Kilpatrick, William H. "The Project Method: The Use of the Purposeful Act in the Educative Process." *Teachers College Record* 19 (September 1918). http://historymatters.gmu.edu/d/4954/.

Kirschner, Paul A., John Sweller, and Richard E. Clark. "Why Minimal Guidance during Instruction Does Not Work: An Analysis of the Failure of Constructivist, Discovery, Problem-Based, Experiential, and Inquiry-Based Teaching." *Educational Psychologist* 41, no. 2 (2006): 75–86.

Klein, David. "Math Problems: Why the U.S. Department of Education's Recommended Math Programs Don't Add Up." *American School Board Journal* 187, no. 4 (April 2000): 52–57.

Kliebard, Herbert M. *The Struggle for the American Curriculum, 1893–1958*, 3rd ed. New York: RoutledgeFalmer, 2004.

Kolker, Robert. "A Is for Apple, B Is for Brawl: Why New York's Reading Wars Are So Contentious." *New York Magazine*, May 1, 2006. http://nymag.com/news/features/16775/.

Labaree, David F. *The Trouble with Ed Schools*. New Haven, CT: Yale University Press, 2004.

Labaree, David F. *Someone Has to Fail: The Zero-Sum Game of Public Schooling*. Cambridge, MA: Harvard University Press, 2010.

Lake, Robin J. "In the Eye of the Beholder: Charter Schools and Innovation." *Journal of School Choice* 2, no. 2 (2008): 115–27. http://www.crpe.org/sites/default/files/jrn_ncsrp_innovrsrch_apr08_0.pdf.

Leonard, Devin. "The iPad Goes to School." *Bloomberg Business Week*, October 24, 2013. http://www.businessweek.com/articles/2013-10-24/the-ipad-goes-to-school-the-rise-of-educational-tablets#p1.

Lowery, Wesley. "Zero Tolerance Policies." *Public Broadcasting Service*, March 20, 2013. http://www.pbs.org/wnet/tavissmiley/tsr/education-under-arrest/zero-tolerance-policies-are-these-post-columbine-measures-putting-minority-students-on-the-fast-track-to-the-prison-system/.

Luh, Tami. "Income Gap Continues to Affect College Graduation Rates." *CNNMoney*, November 21, 2011. http://money.cnn.com/2011/11/21/news/economy/income_college.

"Massachusetts Curriculum Framework for English Language Arts and Literacy." Massachusetts Department of Elementary and Secondary Education, March 2011. http://www.doe.mass.edu/frameworks/ela/0311.pdf.

Massachusetts Department of Elementary and Secondary Education. "TIMSS Results Place Massachusetts among World Leaders in Math and Science." Massachusetts Department of Education, December 9, 2008. http://www.doe.mass.edu/news/news.aspx?id=4457.

Mathematica Policy Research, Inc., and SRI International. *Effectiveness of Reading and Mathematics Software Products: Findings from the First Student Cohort.* Washington, DC: National Center for Education Evaluation and Regional Assistance, March 2007. Rep. ERIC document reproduction service no. ED496015. http://www.eric.ed.gov/PDFS/ED496015.pdf.

Mathews, Jay. "Why Common Core Standards Will Fail." *Class Struggle* (blog), *Washington Post*, February 23, 2012. http://www.washingtonpost.com/blogs/class-struggle/post/why-common-core-standards-will-fail/2012/02/23/gIQATLgbUR_blog.html.

Mathews, Jay. *Work Hard. Be Nice.: How Two Inspired Teachers Created the Most Promising Schools in America*. Chapel Hill, NC: Algonquin, 2009.

Mirel, Jeffrey. "Bridging the 'Widest Street in the World': Reflections on the History of Teacher Education." *American Educator* (Summer 2011). http://www.aft.org/pdfs/americaneducator/summer2011/Mirel.pdf.

NAEP. "2013 Mathematics and Reading." National Center for Education Statistics, November 7, 2013. http://nationsreportcard.gov/reading_math_2013/#/.

NAEP. "Civics 2010: The Nation's Report Card." National Center for Education Statistics, 2010. http://nationsreportcard.gov/civics_2010/.

Nathan, Joe. "Did Different Standards Help Increase Minnesota's High School Graduation Rate?" *Hometown Source* (ECM Publishers), February 20, 2014. http://hometownsource.com/2014/02/20/joe-nathan-column-did-different-standards-help-increase-minnesotas-high-school-graduation-rate.

National Council of Teachers of Mathematics. "Welcome to the Curriculum Focal Points" (2006). Accessed March 2, 2013. http://www.nctm.org/standards/content.aspx?id=270.

National Reading Panel. *Teaching Children to Read: An Evidence-Based Assessment of the Scientific Research Literature on Reading and Its Implications for Reading Instruction.* Washington, DC: National Institute of Child Health and Human Development, April 2000. http://www.nichd.nih.gov/publications/pubs/nrp/Documents/report.pdf.

Nielsen, Lisa. "Is the Common Core an Attack on Progressive Education?" *Huffington Post*, March 3, 2013. http://www.huffingtonpost.com/lisa-nielsen/common-core-cirriculum_b_2802147.html.

Null, J. Wesley, and Diane Ravitch, eds. *Forgotten Heroes of American Education: The Great Tradition of Teaching Teachers*. Greenwich, CT: Information Age Publishing, 2006.

Pashler, Harold, Mark McDaniel, Doug Rohrer, and Robert Bjork. "Learning Styles: Concepts and Evidence." *Psychological Science in the Public Interest* 9, no. 3 (2008): 105–19.

Paulos, John Allen. *Innumeracy: Mathematical Illiteracy and Its Consequences*. Rev. ed. New York: Hill and Wang, 2001.

Payne, Charles M. *So Much Reform, So Little Change: The Persistence of Failure in Urban Schools*. Cambridge, MA: Harvard Education Press, 2008.

Pelto, Jonathan. "Child Abuse in the Form of the 'No Excuses' Education Model." *Wait What* (blog), October 4, 2013. http://jonathanpelto.com/2013/10/04/child-abuse-form-excuses-education-model.

Peterson, Paul E., and Frederick Hess. "Few States Set World-Class Standards." *Education Next* 8, no. 3 (Summer 2008). http://educationnext.org/few-states-set-worldclass-standards/.

Pew Research Center. "Americans' Reading Habits over Time." *Pew Research Center RSS*, June 25, 2013. http://www.pewresearch.org/2013/06/25/library-readers-book-type/.

Phillips, Anna M. "Nonfiction Curriculum Enhanced Reading Skills, Study Finds." *New York Times*, March 11, 2012. www.nytimes.com/2012/03/12/nyregion/nonfiction-curriculum-enhanced-reading-skills-in-new-york-city-schools.html?_r=1&emc=tnt&tntemail1=y.

Pierce, Charles P. *Idiot America: How Stupidity Became a Virtue in the Land of the Free*. New York: Doubleday, 2009.

Plumer, Brad. "These Ten Charts Show the Black-White Economic Gap Hasn't Budged in 50 Years." *Wonkblog* (blog), *Washington Post*, August 28, 2013. http://www.washingtonpost.com/blogs/wonkblog/wp/2013/08/28/these-seven-charts-show-the-black-white-economic-gap-hasnt-budged-in-50-years.

Pondiscio, Robert. "The 57 Most Important Words in Education Reform. Ever." *Core Knowledge Blog*, Core Knowledge Foundation, September 20, 2012. http://blog.coreknowledge.org/2012/09/20/the-57-most-important-words-in-education-reform-ever/.

Porter, Eduardo. "Stubborn Skills Gap in America's Work Force." *New York Times*, October 8, 2013. www.nytimes.com/2013/10/09/business/economy/stubborn-skills-gap-in-americas-work-force.html?_r=0.

"Quality Counts: District Disruption and Revival—School Systems Reshape to Compete—and Improve, State Report Cards." *Education Week*, January 3, 2014. http://www.edweek.org/ew/qc/2014/state_report_cards.html.

Quinton, Sophie. "San Antonio's Ingenious Plan to Get Kids Good Jobs out of High School." *The Atlantic—Cities*, March 6, 2013. http://www.theatlanticcities.com/jobs-and-economy/2013/03/san-antonios-ingenius-plan-get-kids-good-jobs-out-high-school/4890/.

Quirk, William G. "The NCTM Calls It 'Learning Math.'" *Understanding the Original NCTM Standards.* Accessed February 24, 2013. http://wgquirk.com/chap4.html.

"Race to the Top Program Executive Summary." U.S. Department of Education, 2009. http://www2.ed.gov/programs/racetothetop/executive-summary.pdf.

Ravitch, Diane. *The Death and Life of the Great American School System: How Testing and Choice Are Undermining Education*. New York: Basic Books, 2010.

Ravitch, Diane. *Left Back: A Century of Battles over School Reform*. New York: Touchstone, 2000.

Ravitch, Diane. "Ravitch: What Is NCTQ? (and Why You Should Know)." *The Answer Sheet* (blog), *Washington Post*, May 24, 2012. http://www.washingtonpost.com/blogs/answer-sheet/post/ravitch-what-is-nctq-and-why-you-should-know/2012/05/23/gJQAg7CrlU_blog.html.

Ravitch, Diane. *Reign of Error: The Hoax of the Privatization Movement and the Danger to America's Public Schools*. New York: Alfred A. Knopf, 2013.

Ravitch, Diane. *The Troubled Crusade: American Education 1945–1980*. New York: Basic Books, 1985.

Ravitch, Diane. "The Vergara Trial Teachers Were Not 'Grossly Ineffective.'" *Diane Ravitch's Blog*, June 11, 2014. http://dianeravitch.net/2014/06/11/were-the-vergara-trial-teachers-grossly-ineffective-no.

Ravitch, Diane. "Why I Cannot Support the Common Core Standards." *Diane Ravitch's Blog*, February 26, 2013. http://dianeravitch.net/2013/02/26/why-i-cannot-support-the-common-core-standards.

Recht, Donna R., and Lauren Leslie. "Effect of Prior Knowledge on Good and Poor Readers' Memory of Text." *Journal of Educational Psychology* 80, no. 1 (March 1988): 16–20.

Reese, William J. *America's Public Schools: From the Common School to "No Child Left Behind."* Baltimore, MD: Johns Hopkins University Press, 2005.

Resmovits, Joy. "College Dropout Crisis Revealed in 'American Dream 2.0' Report." *Huffington Post*, January 24, 2013. http://www.huffingtonpost.com/2013/01/24/college-dropout-crisis-american-dream-20_n_2538311.html.

Resmovits, Joy. "Common Core Stakes Moratorium Proposed by Unions as National Standards Face Backlash." *Huffington Post*, April 30, 2013. http://www.huffingtonpost.com/2013/04/30/common-core-moratorium-teacher-evaluations_n_3187419.html.

Resmovits, Joy. "Mathematica 2013 Study: KIPP Charter School Students Outperform Public School Peers." *Huffington Post*, February 27, 2013. http://www.huffingtonpost.com/2013/02/27/mathematica-2013-study-kipp_n_2768476.html?utm_hp_ref=@education123.

"Responses to 2013 NCTQ-*U.S. News & World Report* Review | NCTQ/USNWR Review of Education Schools." American Association of Colleges for Teacher Education, January 10, 2014, http://aacte.org/resources/nctq-usnwr-review/responses-to-2013-nctq-us-news-a-world-report-review.html.

Rich, Motoko. "Obama Administration Plans New Rules to Grade Teacher Training Programs." *New York Times*, April 25, 2014. http://www.nytimes.com/2014/04/26/us/obama-administration-plan-seeks-to-rate-teacher-training-programs.html?_r=0.

Ripley, Amanda. *The Smartest Kids in the World: And How They Got That Way*. New York: Simon & Schuster, 2013.

Rowe, Ken. "Effective Teaching Practices for Students with and without Learning Difficulties: Issues and Implications Surrounding Key Findings and Recommendations from the National Inquiry into the Teaching of Literacy." *Australian Journal of Learning Disabilities* 11, no. 3 (2006): 99–115.

Ryan, Julia. "This Year's SAT Scores Are Out, and They're Grim." *The Atlantic*, September 26, 2013. http://www.theatlantic.com/education/archive/2013/09/this-years-sat-scores-are-out-and-theyre-grim/279999/.

SABIS Educational Systems. *Closing the Achievement Gap—2013*. Eden Prairie, MN: SABIS Educational Systems, 2013. http://www.sabis.net/downloads/systems-brochures/closing-the-achievement-gap-2013-the-sabis-experience.pdf.

Santos, Fernanda. "City Teacher Data Reports Are Released." WNYC, February 24, 2012. http://www.wnyc.org/story/301783-teacher-data-reports-are-released.

Sawchuk, Stephen. "Motives of 21st-Century-Skills Group Questioned." *Education Week*, December 4, 2009. http://www.edweek.org/ew/articles/2009/12/09/14partnership_ep.h29.html?tkn=LOLFOt7k4DAGb2J88qtnXPi3D6weTWzi%2FXiL.

Schneider, Wolfgang, and Joachim Körkel. "The Knowledge Base and Text Recall: Evidence from a Short-Term Longitudinal Study." *Contemporary Educational Psychology* 14 (1989): 382–93.

Shenkman, Rick. *Just How Stupid Are We? Facing the Truth about the American Voter*. New York: Basic Books, 2009.

Shulman, Lee. "Those Who Understand: Knowledge Growth in Teaching." *Educational Researcher* 15, no. 2 (February 1986): 4–14.

Simon, Stephanie. "Advanced Placement Classes Failing Students." *Politico*, August 21, 2013. http://www.politico.com/story/2013/08/education-advanced-placement-classes-tests-95723.html.

Slavin, Robert E., Alan Cheung, Cynthia Groff, and Cynthia Lake. "Effective Reading Programs for Middle and High Schools: A Best-Evidence Synthesis." *Reading Research Quarterly* 43, no. 3 (2008). Accessed at Best Evidence Encyclopedia. http://www.bestevidence.org/word/mhs_read_Jul_2008_RRQ.pdf.

Smarick, Andy. "10 Things to Know about the Vergara Decision." *Flypaper* (blog), Thomas B. Fordham Institute, June 10, 2014. http://edexcellence.net/articles/10-things-to-know-about-the-vergara-decision.

Spencer, Herbert. *Essays on Education, etc.* Introduction by Charles W. Eliot, 1911. London: Dent, reprint 1928.

Staub, Fritz, and Elsbeth Stern. "The Nature of Teachers' Pedagogical Content Beliefs Matters for Students' Achievement Gains." *Journal of Educational Psychology* 94, no. 2 (2002): 344–55.

Stern, Sol. "A Brilliant Experiment in Reading: But Will New Schools Chancellor Fund Revolutionary Program?" *New York Daily News*, July 14, 2011. http://articles.nydailynews.com/2011-07-14/news/29788729_1_reading-test-reading-program-naep.

Sticht, Tom. "Confusing Ignorance with Illiteracy." *EducationNews.org*, February 20, 2011. http://www.educationnews.org/Commentaries/108159.html.

Strauss, Valerie. "Is This the Beginning of the End of Teacher Tenure?" *The Answer Sheet* (blog), *Washington Post*, June 11, 2014. http://www.washingtonpost.com/blogs/answer-sheet/wp/2014/06/11/is-this-the-beginning-of-the-end-of-teacher-tenure.

Strauss, Valerie. "Key PISA Test Results for U.S. Students." *The Answer Sheet* (blog), *Washington Post*, December 3, 2013. http://www.washingtonpost.com/blogs/answer-sheet/wp/2013/12/03/key-pisa-test-results-for-u-s-students.

Strauss, Valerie. "What Does Being 'College and Career Ready' Mean?" *The Answer Sheet* (blog), *Washington Post*, April 29, 2010. http://voices.washingtonpost.com/answer-sheet/no-child-left-behind/what-is-being-college-and-care.html.

Students First Illinois. "*Chicago Sun Times* Editorial: Fuzzy Teaching Ideas Never Added Up." Students First Illinois, September 13, 2006. http://www.studentsfirst.us/news/contentview.asp?c=184307.

Symonds, William C., Robert B. Schwartz, and Ronald Ferguson. *Pathways to Prosperity: Meeting the Challenge of Preparing Young Americans for the 21st Century*. Report issued by the Pathways to Prosperity Project, Harvard Graduate School of Education. February 2011.

Texas Workforce Investment Council. "Alamo Area Academies." *Profiles in Success* 3 (2009). http://governor.state.tx.us/files/twic/Profile_Alamo_Academies.pdf.

Thirunarayanan, M. O. "Is the Use of Untested Technologies in Classrooms Unethical?" *Teachers College Record*, January 24, 2014. http://www.tcrecord.org/Content.asp?ContentID=17393.

Thomas, P. L. "Education Reform in the New Jim Crow Era." *Truthout*, May 17, 2013. http://truth-out.org/opinion/item/16406-education-reform-in-the-new-jim-crow-era.

"TIMSS Results Place Massachusetts among World Leaders in Math and Science." Malden, MA: Massachusetts Department of Elementary & Secondary Education, December 9, 2008. http://www.doe.mass.edu/news/news.aspx?id=4457.

Tough, Paul. *How Children Succeed: Grit, Curiosity, and the Hidden Power of Character*. New York: Houghton Mifflin, 2012.

Trilling, Bernie, and Charles Fadel. *21st Century Skills: Learning for Life in Our Times*. San Francisco, CA: Jossey-Bass, 2009.

Twenge, Jean M. *Generation Me: Why Today's Young Americans Are More Confident, Assertive, Entitled—and More Miserable than Ever Before*. New York: Free Press, 2006.

Ujifusa, Andrew. "Scores Drop on Ky.'s Common Core-Aligned Tests." *Education Week*, November 2, 2012, accessed March 24, 2013. http://www.edweek.org/ew/articles/2012/11/02/11standards.h32.html?r=1746345602.

U.S. Department of Education. "National Mathematics Advisory Panel, Preliminary Report." U.S. Department of Education, January 2007. http://www2.ed.gov/about/bdscomm/list/mathpanel/pre-report.pdf.

U.S. Department of Education. "The Opportunity of ESEA Flexibility: Protecting Students and Supporting Local Education Solutions." Washington, DC: U.S. Department of Education, 2012. www2.ed.gov/policy/elsec/guid/esea-flexibility/resources/esea-flex-brochure.pdf.

Vollmer, Jamie R. "The Blueberry Story: A Business Leader Learns His Lesson." *Education Week*, March 6, 2002. http://www.edweek.org/ew/articles/2002/03/06/25vollmer.h21.html.

Wagner, Tony. *Creating Innovators: The Making of Young People Who Will Change the World*. New York: Scribner, 2012.

Wagner, Tony. *The Global Achievement Gap: Why Even Our Best Schools Don't Teach the New Survival Skills Our Children Need—and What We Can Do about It*. New York: Basic Books, 2008.

Wagner, Tony. *Making the Grade: Reinventing America's Schools*. New York: Routledge-Falmer, 2002.

Walsh, Kate. "A Response to Jay Greene." *Education Next*, July 10, 2013. http://educationnext.org/a-response-to-jay-greene/.

Walsh, Russ. "Colonialism in the Inner City: Charter School Discipline Practices." *Russonreading* (blog), October 6, 2013. http://russonreading.blogspot.com/2013/10/colonialism-in-inner-city-charter_6.html.

Webb, Beatrice. *My Apprenticeship*. Harmondsworth, UK: Penguin, reprint 1971.

Weddle, Eric. "How Common Core Disintegrated in Indiana." *Indianapolis Star*, March 29, 2014. www.indystar.com/story/news/education/2014/03/29/common-core-disintegrated-indiana/7051891/.

Will, George F. "Doubts over Common Core." *Washington Post*, January 15, 2014. http://www.washingtonpost.com/opinions/george-will-doubts-over-common-core-wont-be-easily-dismissed/2014/01/15/68cecb88-7df3-11e3-93c1-0e888170b723_story.html?hpid=z5.

Willingham, Daniel. "The Cognitive Science of Skills and Learning." Common Core. Accessed April 21, 2014. https://www.commoncore.org/maps/documents/reports/willingham.pdf.

Willingham, Daniel. "Hall of Shame: Willingham Uses Science to Blast 'EyeQ.'" *The Answer Sheet* (blog), *Washington Post*, November 10, 2009. http://voices.washingtonpost.com/answer-sheet/checking-it-out/hall-of-shame-willingham-uses.html?wprss=answer-sheet.

Willingham, Daniel. "How We Learn: Ask the Cognitive Scientist—Allocating Student Study Time: 'Massed' vs. 'Distributed' Practice." *American Educator*, Summer 2002. http://www.aft.org/newspubs/periodicals/ae/summer2002/willingham.cfm.

Willingham, Daniel. "Reading Is Not a Skill—And Why This Is a Problem for the Draft National Standards." *The Answer Sheet* (blog), *Washington Post*, September 28, 2009. http://voices.washingtonpost.com/answer-sheet/daniel-willingham/willingham-reading-is-not-a-sk.html.

Willingham, Daniel. "Teaching Content Is Teaching Reading." YouTube video, January 9, 2009. http://www.youtube.com/watch?v=RiP-ijdxqEc.

Willingham, Daniel. *When Can You Trust the Experts? How to Tell Good Science from Bad in Education*. San Francisco, CA: Jossey-Bass, 2012.

Willingham, Daniel. *Why Don't Students Like School? A Cognitive Scientist Answers Questions about How the Mind Works and What It Means for the Classroom*. San Francisco, CA: Jossey-Bass, 2009.

Wilson, Todd Alan. "Senate Supports Limiting Testing for 3rd Graders." *Daily Press* (Newport News, VA), January 24, 2012. http://articles.dailypress.com/2012-01-24/news/dp-nws-miller-sol-bill-20120124_1_science-and-history-tests-sols-graders.

Yatvin, Joanne. "A Flawed Approach to Reading in the Common-Core Standards." *Education Week*, February 27, 2012. http://www.edweek.org/ew/articles/2012/02/29/22yatvin.h31.html?tkn=PRWFzRBijMBBvGLwtLADnxtlOjLWbhDgIH%2FI&cmp=ENL-EU-VIEWS1.

Zehr, Mary Ann. "KIPP Middle Schools Found to Spur Learning Gains." *Education Week*, June 22, 2010. http://www.kipp.org/files/dmfile/EdWeek_6_22_10_PDF.pdf.

Zezima, Katie. "A Vote to Fire All Teachers at a Failing High School." *New York Times*, February 24, 2010. http://www.nytimes.com/2010/02/24/education/24teacher.html.

Zoch, Paul A. *Doomed to Fail: The Built-In Defects of American Education*. Chicago, IL: Ivan R. Dee, 2004.

About the Author

Eric Kalenze's fifteen-plus years in education have included posts in teaching, coaching, administration, and developing content and curriculum in the private sector. He lives in Minnesota's Twin Cities metro with his wife, two daughters, and one Puggle.